ESQUIRE'S WORLD OF JAZZ

Esquire's
World
of
Jazz

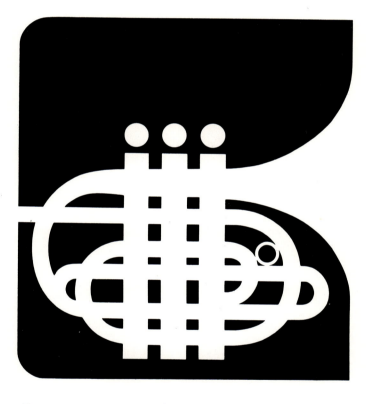

Commentary by **James Poling**

THOMAS Y. CROWELL COMPANY
Established 1834   New York

Library of Congress Cataloging in Publication Data

Esquire.
    Esquire's world of jazz.

    Discography: p.
    Includes index.
    1.   Jazz music.   2.   Jazz musicians.   I.   Title.
ML3561.J3E85   1975   781.5′7   75-12838
ISBN 0-690-00967-4

1 2 3 4 5 6 7 8 9 10

Editor-in-Chief	**Lewis W. Gillenson**
Art Director	**Ira Teichberg**
Associate Editor	**Philip Doyle**
Production Director	**Brendan Wood**
Assistant Editors	**John Lissner**
	Sally Weinstock
Revision Editor	**George T. Simon**

Introduction

When ESQUIRE'S WORLD OF JAZZ was originally published in the early sixties, those of us in the jazz fraternity immediately tabbed it *the class* jazz publication of all time. For, in addition to a batch of fine articles that had appeared in the magazine over a span of twenty-eight years (no other mass media publication could make such a claim!), it featured some fascinating paintings, drawings and photographs, all elegantly laid out on big, wide, handsome pages. There just had never been another jazz book like it.

Now, of course, there is one: the book you're holding in your hands, a revised, updated version that reflects some of the current changes in jazz and in the attitudes of those who play and listen to it. To achieve this, Lew Gillenson, who edited and produced the original, and who is now the President of Thomas Y. Crowell Company, has asked me to select additional jazz articles from more recent *Esquire* issues, and to do whatever else was necessary to bring the book into the mid-seventies.

Actually, WORLD OF JAZZ was so good in the first place that I couldn't see changing much. We did select three fairly recent and exceptionally attractive *Esquire* pieces: one by Duke Ellington (1973), another by Louis Armstrong (1971), and a third by Michael Zwerin (1968) that shows rather poignantly how jazz musicians must travel outside their own country to achieve recognition. We also invited Marian McPartland, an Englishwoman who found success in America, to write about the emerging role of women in jazz, and Dan Morgenstern, former editor of *Down Beat*, to bring us up to date on what

has been happening to jazz during the last twelve years, especially in relation to changes in popular music in general. Finally, we also asked John Lissner, who writes about jazz for *The New York Times* and other publications, to update (actually it turned out to be a completely new listing) the selective discography that he had prepared for the original edition.

Those of you who own that original edition will notice some other minor changes. To put all the pieces in their proper perspectives and tie all of them together, we have added to the running commentary the dates they originally appeared in *Esquire*. Also we have deleted some articles to make room for what we feel are more important and more interesting replacements.

Pictorially, we have retained most of the colorful paintings, sensitive drawings and often touching photographs that have made this such a standout among all jazz books. In addition, Lew Gillenson, who assembled all the art pieces, has added some immensely attractive new ones to illustrate the additional editorial material and to keep us *au courant* with the relationship between today's music and graphics.

It is our hope that you will find this new edition of *Esquire's World of Jazz* as fascinating, as informative, and as much fun as we found the original to be. We—and you, too—couldn't ask for very much more.

George T. Simon

Contents

Part One

The Nature of Jazz

Stop for a moment, and listen.... No matter where you are, chances are good that you'll hear music: a radio muffled through the walls, a jukebox, somebody whistling in the street. Listen a little closer, and the chances are about fifty-fifty that what you're hearing is American jazz.

If you've always thought of jazz as nothing but the uproar that results when five or more musical illiterates punish instruments they cannot master, perhaps your only reaction to this will be to wish that jazz would go back to the cellars from which it came. But if, like us, you *came down* with jazz sometime in adolescence and have never quite recovered from it; if you remember the time when the very word meant something you do with a girl; if you crept into music shops, very much like a convert to a small and unpopular religion, to spend your hoarded pennies on the latest 78 release; if, to the dismay of your parents, you searched the radio night and day for the barest snatch of Lester Young, and a passion for Bix developed over the years into a reverence for Bird; if, in short, you've spent more time and more money than you care to calculate on an obsession that occasionally seems to take on the proportions of a vice—then the very fact that jazz is there to be had at the flick of a wrist, or the investment of a dime, will seem amazing enough.

But if, also like us, your experience of jazz in the Dark Ages before LP's was mostly associated with vaguely disreputable clubs somewhere downtown, and straight shots of bourbon, and the night side of life, you're liable to be surprised when you study the concert schedules in your newspapers, the summer music-festival announcements, and even the curricula of perfectly respectable universities.

For, these days, you are just as likely to find jazz being discussed in the planning division of the State Department as in the columns of *Down Beat*. The Voice of America probably broadcasts even more jazz than that swinging little station down near the end of the dial. Your bookstore has a shelf of volumes covering everything from the autobiography of Louis to the birth of bop. And, if your record dealer has heard of Vivaldi, he's probably hip to Gillespie as well.

Something strange and wonderful has happened to jazz. Whether you know it or not, you are living in the most exciting, most creative, and perhaps most crucial age through which our native music has ever passed.

It is an age when Louis Armstrong makes an appearance at Lewisohn Stadium with members of the New York Philharmonic, and Friedrich Gulda does gigs at Birdland. It is an age when jazz theory, history, and playing are taught in schools and colleges. It is an age when clergymen discuss the religious significance of the blues, and psychiatrists find improvisation a symptom of the democratic urge. It is an age when Dizzy blows in Damascus, and Benny in Moscow; when that cello you hear is liable to be playing something by Mingus, rather than Mozart. At last jazz has been given full recognition as an art form.

Art form? There are still some who may pull up short at that. They will point out that thousands are alive today who were born before jazz first raised its unruly voice somewhere in the southern part of the United States (there are now disputes as to just *where* it happened) some sixty-odd years ago (there are also disputes as to just *when*). They will add that never in the

history of man's need to express himself in song has half a century sufficed to transform a folk music into an art music.

But one of the wonders of our time is that precisely this has happened in jazz. What began as the unpremeditated and artless music of a socially depressed people has, in less than seventy years, appropriated most of the techniques, and a large number of the forms, painstakingly developed by Western music over the five preceding centuries. It is a music that has so continually changed and expanded that it is only now, in a period of relative stability, that the direct link between, say, Jelly Roll Morton and Bud Powell can be recognized. More important, in this brief period jazz has succeeded in transcending the limitations of its original harmony and orchestration, and has matured to the point where it is now capable of communicating its exhilarating message in Lebanon as well as Los Angeles.

In short, we are living in the Golden Age of Jazz.

You can find diehards who would disagree with this January, 1959, paean by jazz critic John Clellon Holmes. They would argue that jazz has lost its golden, pristine warmth and vigor and declined into a "cool" senility. Others, equally biased, would argue that the Golden Age of Jazz still lies in the future, with the path to it only now being opened up by the controversial Pied Piper, Ornette Coleman. But implicit in Holmes's argument is one unassailable fact that no one can deny. Whatever else it may be called, this is unquestionably the Universal Age of Jazz. If any proof is needed, recall some jazz events of recent years.

In addition to his Russian triumph, Benny Goodman was mobbed in Malaya by fans who kept screaming for chorus after chorus of what they called "Sling, Sling, Sling," while in Bangkok, the jazz-loving King of Siam leaped onto Goodman's bandstand and blew with him in an unrehearsed soprano sax-clarinet gig that made front pages all over the world.

In Stockholm, Louis Armstrong shattered box-office records set by Sibelius. When he played Hamburg, fans rioted because the hall was sold out and police were forced to turn fire hoses on them. And on the African Gold Coast, Louis blew his horn to history's largest jazz-concert crowd, 100,000 people, some of whom had come 400 miles through the jungle to hear him.

In Berlin, trumpeter Rex Stewart played in a concert hall crowded with Russians who had crossed boundaries illegally to hear him.

In Japan, Gene Krupa received an ovation that he described as, "the most tremendous thing I've ever experienced; even greater than the big days with Goodman."

In the revered Concertgebouw in Amsterdam, Lionel Hampton had to be rescued by the militia from being trampled by his adoring fans.

All of which, of course, raises a question. Just what is there about this young music—once described as born in a whorehouse, nurtured in a speakeasy—that has enabled it to win respectability and worldwide acclaim in a matter of only a few decades? What, exactly, is jazz?

No one has ever come up with an exact definition of jazz. It's true that for the musically educated there are technical analyses of jazz couched in such terms as polyphony, blue triads, afterbeats, flatted fifths, etc. But when critics try to define jazz for the layman they usually give up in disgust, or end up with some meaningless phrase like, "Jazz is a man telling the truth about himself." Or, "Jazz is a fallen god remembering heaven." Of course, trying to define the elusive quality of any music in expository words is rather like trying to explain the magic of a Shakespeare sonnet by playing a clarinet solo. But if jazz can't be concisely defined, it is still possible to convey some understanding of its nature and its characteristics.

To understand jazz one has to know something of its background. In September, 1950, novelist Budd Schulberg wrote a case history of *Tiger Rag* that, in a broad sense, tells the whole story of the origins of jazz, with particular emphasis on its highly derivative nature.

Like a whole generation, I grew up tapping one foot to *Tiger Rag* without knowing who wrote it or how we came by it. It wasn't until I'd slipped into my middle thirties that I heard the *Saga of Mr. Jelly Lord,* the musical autobiography of Jelly Roll Morton, recorded on 116 sides for the Archives of the Library of Congress under the supervision of Allan Lomax.

What I heard was the inside story of New Orleans in the fabulous marching-band and barrel-house days of Buddy Bolden, King Oliver and Tony Jackson. For the first time, through Jelly Roll's words and piano, I heard the real story of the birth of jazz.

It was no wonder, we learn from Professor Jelly Roll, that jazz started in New Orleans. For here the Negroes brought to Congo Square their pulsing drumbeats, the profound emotion of the blues, and a therapeutic genius for breaking through melancholy to new levels of elation. But jazz obviously wasn't a one-race job. It took the French, with their Opera House and their quadrilles; it took the Italians with their operatic street music; the Creoles de Couleur with their blend of European refinements and Negro vitality and imagination; it took a city unhampered by Puritan influences, by Anglo-Saxon inhibitions, a city that was born in sophistication and didn't have to inherit or import it like our great metropolitan sponge, Manhattan.

Jelly Roll Morton, like his *Tiger Rag,* like New Orleans itself, was a product of miscegenation. "My folks were in the city of New Orleans long before the Louisiana Purchase," Jelly Roll tells us, in a spontaneous blend of narration and impressive chords. "All my folks came directly from the shores, not the shores, I mean from France, across on the other side of the world —in the other world. Long as I could remember these folks, they never could speak a word of American or English."

It may be difficult to reconcile the brassy, blaring, ripsnorting *Tiger Rag* as played by the average popular band with an elegant, traditional French quadrille. But you begin to bridge the gap as you hear Jelly Roll play the original quadrille as he played it in the ballrooms of the wealthy French and Creole families of New Orleans and in the social halls of the dance-mad city. "...THIS *Tiger Rag* happened to be transformed from an old quadrille that was in many different tempos," says Jelly Roll, "and I'll no doubt give you an idea how it went."

As he plays the sedate melody—unmistakably kin to our own *Tiger Rag*—you seem to see the swallow-tailed swains and their bustle-gowned ladies tracing the graceful dance patterns of a nineteenth century quadrille. Now the quadrille introduction flows into a waltz, and though *Tiger Rag* in waltz time may seem inappropriate, he demonstrates what a gracious waltz it was.

"Also they'd have another strain that belong—that comes right beside it," Morton explains. "The mazooka time." And, under his remembering fingers, the *Tiger Rag* becomes a stimulating mazurka. "And of course they had another strain. And, er, that was in a different tempo."

The different "tempo" sounds suspiciously like early ragtime. We begin to feel the beat. The melody comes through with fresh vitality: An irresistible force breaks through the sedate pattern of the traditional dance music.

"What time is that?" Lomax calls from somewhere back in the studio.

"That's a 2-4 time," Jelly Roll says. And then: "Of course they had another one."

Jelly Roll warms up, just as this old French quadrille warmed up and boiled over as hot jazz spirit into *Tiger Rag* half a century ago. Just by flipping a switch, we're sitting in on the birth of a great new music.

"Now I will show you how it was transformed," Jelly Roll is saying. "It happened to be transformed by your performer at this particular time. *Tiger Rag* for your approval—"

"Who named it *Tiger Rag?*" Lomax breaks in.

"I also named it. It came from the way I played it by making the tiger on my elbow. A person said once, 'It sounds like a tiger hollering.' I said, 'Fine.' To myself I said, 'That's the name.' So I'll play it for you."

Rising from the ashes of the prim nineteenth-century forms is our twentieth-century phoenix, red-hot, everlastingly fresh, *Tiger Rag*, with its tantalizing beat, exciting breaks, solid chords, brilliant runs, its now-familiar but never tiresome *roar* of the tone clusters, its dynamic riff, surprising finale—and yet, brilliantly preserved in spite of all this variation and invention, the simple theme we recognize from the old quadrille.

So *Tiger Rag* isn't pure French, or Negro, or Creole, or English, or Italian, Spanish, or Irish—it isn't quite pure anything except jazz and American which at their best have in common a unique vitality, a unique ability to assimilate the special gifts of myriad races. Maybe that's why *Tiger Rag* is so firmly established as a popular classic. It's our own exuberant music, from sound hybrid stock, as American as Joe Di Maggio, and Jelly Roll Morton."

Obviously, a new musical form can no more be produced by spontaneous generation than a living creature. And just as this country has been a racial melting pot, our native jazz has been a musical melting pot in which an immense variety of foreign sounds have been wedded. In it can be found accents, inflections and rhythms gathered from around the world; traces, for example, of ballads, hymns, folk music, spirituals and work chants, some of them native to Africa or the Caribbean, many to Western Europe, a few even to Elizabethan England. Jazz owes a debt, too, to Ravel, Milhaud, Stravinsky, Vivaldi, Debussy and many other classical performers. And in addition to quadrilles and mazurkas it has also drawn heavily on military marches, dirges and polkas. In fact, there is probably no strongly rhythmic musical form that jazz hasn't seized on and transmuted into its own idiom.

Here, in the words of jazz scholar B. S. Rogers, is how this unique idiom is coined. (You will notice that Mr. Rogers, writing in the April and May, 1939, issues of *Esquire*, used the words "jazz" and "swing" interchangeably, though many writers consider swing only one form of jazz.)

In building on the past, the jazz musician tries to develop tones that are completely different from those heard in classical and 'popular' performances. Such conductors as Toscanini or Guy Lombardo try, on the other hand, to make their tones as symphonic or as lyrical as possible. Hence, if you were to say that they achieve beautiful tones, you would merely be saying that they reproduce tones that you are used to and which you have always considered beautiful. If you find the tones used in swing music hard or shrill, it is because you are not used to them. They *are* unlike all traditional tones. But surely they may have a beauty of their own? Jazz musicians can, in fact, achieve tonal beauties. But the listener must do two things in order to learn to appreciate them: he must give up the idea that only the traditional, classical tones can be beautiful; and he must be willing to yield to the rather primitive moods and emotions of genuine swing.

Music, like oratory, is not only something said, but something said in a certain way; and since it appeals exclusively to the emotions, the manner of delivery is crucial. The manner of delivery in jazz has been given a descriptive label: 'the hot intonation.'

This way of playing has several remarkable features. To begin with, the way a note is attacked in jazz differs sharply from the way it is attacked in classical performance. In the latter the attack is gradual in volume but constant in pitch, and the change in volume is upward—from soft to loud. In jazz both volume and pitch change; the note is attacked full, then *diminished* in volume, while the pitch drops too. The second point is the technique of slurring, *i.e.*, sliding from one note to another without the slightest pause. In classical performance, on the other hand, each note is attacked individually and cleanly. What results from the jazz technique is the sounding of tones which are foreign to classical music. The smallest recognized interval in Western music is the semi-tone. But when you pass from one note to the next without pausing, as you do in jazz, you pass through the quarter-tone, eighth-tone, sixteenth, etc. Thirdly, there is the extremely important phenomenon of vibrato. In classical performance vibrato is permitted only to the string instruments. The brasses and reeds are strictly disciplined to play without benefit of the pulsating quality which gives a musical sound its tension—its *nerve*, so to speak.

To describe the effect of this way of playing music—to describe what the listener hears—is scarcely possible. Certain things we can indeed pick out: The introduction of fractional tones, especially quarters and eighths, is strange and distinctly stimulating; the vibrato of the wind instruments imparts a feeling of suppressed passion; the barely perceptible diminuendo which follows each note is subtly suggestive of melancholy. But the total effect is something that must be left to the individual.

Comin' Home and Hard Times
By Burt Goldblatt

But to describe what hot music is and how it got that way is something else again. That, I believe, can be done. In a phrase, it is the act of singing through an instrument—singing the way a Negro sings. This doesn't mean that the structure of the melodic line is vocal, for it is much too complicated for that. It means that the intonation is derived from a certain vocal tradition. The way the notes are attacked, the slurring of notes, the enjoyment of vibrato—all these things have their source in Negro singing. In fact, they are true of folk-singing generally. It is *natural* to vibrate the voice, to slur notes, and to attack the notes full and strongly. Listen to the singing of Scotch or Irish ballads, or even Russian. It is only in cultivated song, in the concert or opera, that vibrato is restrained, slurring discouraged, and the crescendo attack favored. The cultivated professional singer does not come by his attack naturally. He acquires it arduously and through discipline.

In the case of the Negro this *natural* employment of the voice was not corrupted by scholastic influences and was accentuated by his African heritage. Fractional tones are used—indeed they are constant—in African music. The Negro saw no reason to discard this usage merely because he had to learn to sing in

it is hardly necessary to point out that in Africa, music is rhythm rather than melody. The Negro added to his English song the intense rhythmic qualities he remembered from his native song. The Negro sang before he played, and when at last he began to play instruments like the trumpet, trombone, clarinet, and saxophone, he put into them the peculiar intonations of his singing. He sang through his instruments. He made hot music. He made jazz.

The perfect examples of Negro singing are the performances of Bessie Smith, a huge black woman who died in an automobile accident. She was far and away the greatest of them all, and her records, which are fortunately numerous, will never disappear from the musical library of jazz. It may legitimately be argued that her singing influenced the instrumental work of most of the early hot musicians. It is said that she influenced even the great Bix Beiderbecke, who often went to hear her. Be that as it may, one discovers in her singing all the characteristics of hot *playing:* slurring, vibrato, gradation of tone and pitch, and improvisation. Simply as a *voice*, moreover, she was wonderful: rich in timbre, primitive in feeling, passionate when she wanted to be, infinitely supple.

a new language and in new forms. Slurring is also characteristic of African (and Oriental) singing, and the Negro carried it over to the songs with English words, changing the emphases in these words and even dropping syllables from them wherever it was necessary to make them conform to his conception of correct inflection and rhythm. So far as rhythm is concerned

Altogether different but no less significant, no less germinal as an influence on jazz performance, and no less enjoyable is the astonishing voice of Louis Armstrong, perhaps the greatest trumpet player jazz has ever known. Thick, hoarse, rasping, even brutally rough, it is surcharged with passion. It quivers with feeling, it breaks with excitement when it has to, it sobs with sentiment when called upon.

Now, many critics have observed that his singing and trumpet playing have the same style, "Even when he sings he is really playing trumpet solos with his voice," wrote one critic. But I am convinced that the thing should be the other way around: When he plays trumpet solos, he is singing through the instrument. It does not matter that he didn't begin to sing for the public until long after he had established his trumpet style. The song was instinctive with him; he sang for himself long before he learned to play his instrument in masterly fashion; he acquired from his people the way of singing which determined his way of playing the horn.

When all of the foregoing is added up, it is easy to see not only why swing is exciting but why it has contributed much to the art of making music. The style and manner of hot performance have enabled the great jazz instrumentalists to develop techniques, to get sounds out of their instruments, which were never dreamed of by classical performers.

Now to get down to brass tacks. What, in simple terms, does the audience hear when it listens to these great instrumentalists?

strongly syncopated dance music which is not particularly good jazz. The question is what is happening on top of the syncopated 4/4 measure.

Above the base—the unchanging, ever-recurring meter with its strangely upsetting offbeats—which is maintained by the rhythm section of the band, the melodic section plays music which is rhythmically contrapuntal to it. This means simply that the wind and reed instruments (trumpet, trombone, clarinet, sax) are creating a rhythm which is startlingly different from the one laid down by the percussion group (drums, piano, guitar, string bass). The former are playing not just one but a whole sequence of different rhythms—an almost infinite variety of them in a single piece—which oppose or contrast with the base rhythm, yet correspond with it at certain definite points.

Now you should be aware of one of the most striking distinctions between jazz and the Guy Lombardo type of music. In Lombardo's band the melodic and rhythm sections usually play in exactly the same rhythm. Now, too, you should realize how jazz is distinguished from a piece of classical music which has contrapuntal rhythms. In jazz there is always an insistent rhythm, a rigid base, against which the varying rhythms are

The basis of swing is syncopated music in 4/4 time. In ordinary 4/4 time—that is, in folk and classical music—the accent is on the first and third of the four beats which make up the measure. In syncopation the accent is on the second and fourth beats (the offbeats).

But there is more to the story than that. It is possible to get

played. But when there are contrapuntal rhythms in classical music, *all* the rhythms are varying: none of them persists unchanged throughout the composition. (I know there are exceptions to this rule.)

Producing the insistent rhythm is not as simple as it may sound. Obviously, it depends upon the performers having a perfect time-sense and a keen feeling for syncopation. But a really first-rate rhythm section does more than beat out the base. It makes the base rich, full, and complex; it fills in the "breaks" in the melodic line with effects and passages that are interesting in their own right; it gives the performance color and arresting tone at appropriate moments.

So much for the playing of the instrumentalists who maintain the insistent rhythm. Their importance can't be over-emphasized, for, as I have suggested, the forceful syncopation on which swing music is founded comes to a large degree from them. But they alone, as I have also suggested, don't by any means make jazz. It is the work of the melodic section that really determines whether a band is swinging or not—in other words, whether it is playing hot music or mere ting-a-ling.

I spoke before of rhythms being *created* by the wind and reed

instruments. The word "created" is the clue. The men performing on the melodic instruments are improvising. They are inventing rhythms as they go along. Moreover, they are developing an original melodic tune. Each man in a small band—each group in a big one—is creating his own melodic line. But these melodic lines are not only rhythmically contrapuntal to the base rhythm; they often are contrapuntal, rhythmically and melodically, to each other. So now you know what a musician thinks of when he hears that phrase, "collective improvisation," which has been so glibly bandied about by people who haven't the slightest idea what it actually means.

Let's break it down. A six-piece band begins to play *Sweet Sue* or *Ida*. The rhythm section of three pieces (piano, drums, and string bass) does its definite, set job while the melodic section (trumpet, clarinet, and tenor sax) plays the tune as

written for one chorus, or maybe two. Then, with the rhythm instruments continuing as before, one of the melodists takes a solo chorus in which he improvises. That is to say, he changes the tune, re-phrases it, introduces new figures ("licks"), and injects ornamentation and pauses which were not there before, sometimes riding out into a melodic line which barely resembles the original tune. Then the second melodist and, after him, the third take their choruses in solo, each improvising a melodic line of his own—one which fits the character of his particular instrument—and at the same time changing the rhythms. Perhaps there is also a passage for piano. In the last chorus they swing together, each melodist improvising while the rhythm section beats it out with fury. The collective improvisation will be noise and confusion if the musicians are incompetent; if they are able and inspired, it will be a thrilling piece of business.

Think of what the improviser is doing. At the same time that he is creating an original melodic line, inventing or adapting hot licks to the mood and tempo of the piece he is playing, he must keep in mind the tune he started out with as a harmonic background, for his improvisation is within the outline of the piece as written. His chords are developments of the written chords. If they aren't, they don't belong; they are forced, artificial, corny. In *collective* improvisation—where there are several improvisers performing simultaneously (a jam session)—he is not only listening to the base rhythm and remembering the written chordal structure, but is also subconsciously listening to the improvisations of the performers beside him. There must, after all, be some relationship between the various melodic lines; there must be agreements as well as contrasts in rhythm and melody.

It is also worth noting at this point that a written score can direct and control improvisations. Indeed, the performance of a large band, containing something like three trumpets, two trombones, and three or four saxes is almost inconceivable without such a score. Thus an arranger like Fletcher Henderson or the Duke will not only indicate where a solo improvisation should occur and for how many bars, but will also write in the harmonic chords for the soloist's guidance. That is just to say, an outline is provided—a pattern which enables the soloist to improvise music which bears some sought-after relationship to the music being played by the others (both individuals and groups or sections). Without that notated chordal structure the performance would probably be a mess, for you can't expect eight or nine wind and reed instruments to wander around and still make sense. But this should not be misunderstood: arrangers or composers of hot music don't write melodic lines for their soloists, but merely the material from which the soloist can get off.

This brings up a question: why improvise? Most people who have only recently "discovered" swing put the question this way: why does a jazz musician take a popular song and make something so different out of it that you can't recognize the tune he started out with? Benny Goodman once answered it by saying that after a musician has played a tune over and over again what can he do but "kick it around"?

The real answer, of course, is that the performers are creative musicians. They want to speak out for themselves; to test, exploit, and develop the full potentialities of their talents and their instruments. Improvisation is their artistic breath of life.

Improvisation also is the soul of jazz. Without it there is a body but no personality. Listen to a performance which hasn't got it and you take nothing away: not emotion, no feeling of energy, no impression of character. It isn't necessary—in fact, it's impossible—for every man in a large band to improvise. Sometimes one man does it against the normal rhythmic background, while the other melodic instruments quietly support the rhythm section. Sometimes an entire group does it: the saxes, perhaps, while the brass ensembles provide a harmonic accompaniment. No matter how it's done, the music called jazz—its surprising, shocking rhythms, its colors and fascinating contrapuntal effects—is produced by improvisation. Without it the music is dull, flat, nerveless. It isn't jazz.

If improvisation is the soul of jazz, the blues are its impassioned heartbeat. For, structurally, most of the jazz we know is built on the 12-bar blues form. Harmonically and melodically, too, most of what you hear in the playing of the great jazz musicians is inspired by the blues. This was true when the first jazz note was blown and it's true today. But there was a period in the Fifties when many of the young jazzmen turned their backs on the blues. The results were disastrous. In attempting to intellectualize jazz, to make it academically respectable, they almost reduced it to limp sterility.

Fortunately, before the end of the decade there was a return to reason. It was due in part to the fact that the most influential of all modern jazzmen, Charles (The Bird) Parker, never forgot the wellsprings of the music he played so beautifully. In fact, the majority of his recordings, no matter how experimental in nature, are versions of the blues. And, just before his untimely death, he made the flat statement, "The blues—that's the basis of jazz. And it's a sad thing some of the young guys coming up don't remember it."

In time, the young guys did remember it—after it finally dawned on them that respectability is the kiss of death to a music that exists in part because it is a protest against artistic and social orthodoxy. They also had to learn the hard way that you can't successfully intellectualize a music that has for its primary purpose the expression of deep feeling and surging emotion. But they did learn, and today the blues have been "rediscovered" as a fount of strength.

If you go back far enough, you'll find the blues originated in the piercing cries of hurt and shame and fear that sprang from the holds of slave ships sailing the South Atlantic from South Africa and South America to our own South, as jazz critic Barry Ulanov puts it. But the blues is not only a music for melancholia. There is joy in the blues too, a great joy, as well as nostalgia, and lust, and greed, and romance, and, in fact, every human emotion. For the good people who sang those songs left them free to say anything they felt, open to the improvisation that makes yesterday's blues a kind of living history of the hinterlands of America, today's blues a lyric reflection of the world we've made for ourselves and must, willy-nilly, live in.

One who has gone back far enough to capture the true spirit of the blues is E. Simms Campbell, the popular black artist. In January, 1939, he wrote with deep feeling of what the blues have meant to his people, and to jazz.

The Blues are simple, elemental—they have the profound depths of feeling that is found in any race that has known slavery and the American Negro is no stranger to suffering. Out of the work songs and Spirituals that they sang sprang this melancholic note—rising in a higher key because of its very intensity and enveloping the Spirituals because of its very earthiness.

One cannot continually ride in chariots to God when the impact of slavery is so ever-present and real.

"Some day ah'm gonna lay down dis heavy load—gonna grab me a train, gonna Clam aboh'd—gonna go up No'th, gonna ease mah pain. Yessuh Lord, gonna catch dat train"—this isn't mystical. It was the cry of a human being under the lash of slavery—of doubts—of fears—the tearing apart of families— the caprices of plantation owners—these hardships of slavery all fusing themselves together to burn into the Negro this blue flame of misery.

And yet it was never a wail, but a steady throbbing under-tone of hope. "Times is bad but dey won't be bad always" is the lyric carried in a score of Blues songs—times are tough but somehow, somewhere, they'll get better.

"Gotta git better 'cause dey cain't git w'us"—Stevedores sweating on the levee, chain gangs in Georgia, cotton pickers in Tennessee, sugar cane workers in Louisiana, field hands in Texas, all bending beneath the heel of Southern white aristocracy, the beautiful "befo de wah" south of the crinoline days.

One might as well be realistic about slavery. The South was as cruel as any Caesar to its slaves—and many slaves were as vindictive as any Richelieu to their masters, but both sides have profited. Without pain and suffering there would have been no Blues and without an understanding white America there would have been no expression for them. And now—what are the Blues and into what category of music do they fit? They are not Spirituals and they are not Work songs nor do they fit into the pattern prescribed by many musical critics as folk music in a lighter vein.

Funeral March
By Bruce Mitchell

To me—they are filled with the deepest emotions of a race, they are songs of sorrow charged with satire, with that potent quality of ironic verse clothed in the raiment of the buffoon. They were more than releases, temporary releases from servitude. The Blues were the gateway to freedom for all American Negroes. In song, the Negro expressed his true feelings, his hopes, aspirations and ideals, and illiterate though many of them were, there was a spiritual and ennobling quality to all of the music. True, many of the Blues lyrics are downright vulgar and the suggestive quality has crept in with the passing years, understandable enough when you realize that many audiences, both white and colored, wished to find those meanings in them. As paid entertainers, Negroes were only catering to popular taste and the taste of the American public in the mauve decade was decidedly that of a slumming party toward any reception of Blues.

Basically, the Blues are similar to Spirituals and it is important to note that the musical bars are practically the same length. For those musically minded take the song *Minnie the Moocher* or *St. James Infirmary*. The Spiritual *Hold on—Keep Your Hands on the Plow* reminds me so much of them—and it was written more than forty years ago.

This background of the "why" of the Blues is essential to understand them properly and to get a fuller understanding of their true meaning. None of them was ever written to music before the 1890's because the majority of Negroes had had no musical education and the flood of ragtime pieces that immediately followed, in the early nineteen hundreds, were merely melodies that have followed the Blues pattern these many years. There is a definite pattern to the Blues, just as there is for poetry and other forms of creative expression that have survived the centuries. It is no hit or miss musical form.

In fact, the Blues pattern is as rigid in its way as the pattern of a sonnet. Briefly and non-technically, the Blues always consists of 12 bars divided into three equal parts, with a different chord for each 4-bar section. In a Blues composition the original theme is struck in the first four bars, the next four bars are relief, and in the last four bars the theme is restated with variations on the composition's major chords. Often one hears pieces termed Blues which are merely bastard products because some well-known orchestra has insisted on stepping up 12 bars to 24 or even 32. But as Clarence Williams told me, "The flavor and the color are taken from the Blues when one takes liberties with their original form."

I went to see Clarence Williams because he is possibly the greatest blues writer of them all. He wrote *Sister Kate*—remember the shimmy shi wabble? *Royal Garden Blues, Gulf Coast Blues, You Don't Know My Mind, West End Blues, Sugar Blues, Squeeze Me, I Ain't Gonna Give Nobody None of This Jellyroll*, one of the bluesiest-sounding and feeling of all songs, *Baby, Won't You Please Come Home*, as well as novelties like *I Can't Dance* and *I've Got Ants in my Pants*. The list is endless.

In talking to Clarence Williams I asked him why the blues, as we know them today, were always written about love, someone's baby leaving him, hard luck dogging one's trail and the "misery 'roun yo door." "It's the mood," he exclaimed. "That's the carry-over from slavery—nothing but trouble in sight for everyone—there was no need to hitch your wagon to a star because there weren't any stars, you got only what you fought for. Spirituals were the natural release—Times gonna git better in de promised lan'—but many a stevedore knew only too well that his fate was definitely tied up in his own hands. If he was clever and strong, and didn't mind dying, he came through—the weak ones always died. A Blue mood—since prayers often seemed futile, the words were made to fit present situations that were much more real and certainly more urgent. Ef ah kin jes grab me a handfulla freight train—ah'll be set—Always the urge to leave, to go to a distant town, a far city, to leave the prejudices and cruelty of the South. Superstition played its part too—a large part—black cats, black women, conjurers, charms, sudden death, working in steel mills, cotton fields, loving women, fighting over women, all of the most intimate and earthy pursuits."

I asked another question and that started a discussion that went on for hours. I asked—"Mr. Williams, if you were a white man, you'd probobaly be worth a million dollars today, wouldn't you—because the radio and motion picture rights as well as all mechanical rights to all of your songs would be copyrighted—think hard now—wouldn't you have rather been born a white man?"

He laughed out loud—uproariously, and replied, "Why I'd never have written Blues if I had been white—you don't study to write Blues, you *feel* them. It's the mood you're in—sometimes it's a rainy day—cloud mist—just like the time I lay for hours and hours in a swamp in Louisiana, Spanish moss dripping everywhere, but that's another story—it's a mood though—white men were looking for me with guns—I wasn't scared, just sorry I didn't have a gun. I began to hum a tune—a little sighing kinda tune—you know like this . . ."

Clarence Williams was seated at the piano and his large muscular fingers began to caress the keys—eerie chords rumbled along—he sang—"Jes as blue as a tree—an old willow tree—nobody 'roun here, jes nobody but me"—the melody trailed off. "Never wrote that down, never published it either, I don't know why I'm playing it now." I didn't intrude on his thoughts. "You never knew Tony Jackson did you—no, of course not, you were too young"—Williams was not conscious of my presence in the room. He talked and played. I listened.

Tony Jackson was probably the greatest Blues pianist that ever lived. He was great because he was original in all of his improvisations—a creator—a supreme stylist. This all happened thirty years ago when the wine rooms flourished.

These were nothing more or less than sedate saloons, with a family entrance for ladies and potted palms and the usual ornate bric-a-brac in every corner. There was the inevitable three or four piece orchestra with the diva belching out ballads, trailing her ostrich plumes as she coyly made her exit, and the mustached dons of the period keeping a sharp eye out for a well turned ankle. Informality was the keynote, and any of the patrons who wished could render a song, vocal or otherwise, provided of course, that they were not too terrible. Booing was much too mild for a poor performance in those days. Negroes had their wine rooms, patterned as nearly as possible after the white ones, but they were necessarily less pretentious in every way.

Often their wine rooms were combination billiard and pool parlors, saloon and clubroom for the tougher gentry. There were no paid entertainers, no orchestra, and the only music provided was that played and composed on the spot by these ragtime and Blues piano players.

New Orleans was the focal point for Negro musicians, all of them coming down from the various river towns but particularly from Memphis and St. Louis on the many boat excursions that would wind up in the delta. Blues was looked upon as "low music" forty years ago because its greatest exponents were hustlers and sports, itinerant musicians who played in river joints and dives because these were the only places sympathetic to their type of playing. Negroes have always loved the Blues but in attempting to imitate the white man, many of them were trying to stamp out of their consciousness this natural emotional tie because of its background of slavery.

Being ashamed of one's heritage is usually predominate in minority groups—and in imitation of the music of white America, many Negroes were contributing nothing worthwhile to American music. These Blues musicians were the pioneers, those who refused to compromise with their music—and they were creating and forming the basis for present-day American music. Gershwin's *American in Paris* as well as his *Rhapsody in Blue* are outstanding examples of Blues harmonies—you don't think he pulled them out of the air do you?

Cities and towns figure in the names of so many Blues because the writers of these pieces were definitely associated with the towns. In these early "jam sessions" many of them held in these wine rooms in New Orleans, individual musicians would compete with one another. They came from the length and breadth of the Mississippi and their styles of playing were as different as the sections of the country from which they came.

To the Southerner, St. Louis and Kansas City were looked upon as Northern cities and a great many Southerners, both black and white, settled there. The Negroes that came brought with them the Blues of the cotton fields and plantations of the deep South, not influenced in any fashion by the Spanish or French. That is why even today among musicians, the purest Blues and the real "low-down Blues" as they frequently call them, were born in these cities. New Orleans gave a lilt to the Blues, the other cities gave them their solidity. Being born in St. Louis and intensely interested in Blues, I was on many a boat excursion that carried these early Negro bands—and all of them never played any other type of music. Jelly Roll Morton from Kansas City had probably the greatest Blues band—there were Fletcher Henderson, Charlie Creath and Fate Marable, Benny Moten, I could go on by the hour. All of these men, however, were preceded by Tom Turpin, Scott Joplin and Louis Chauvin, a great natural piano player. In 1896 Tom Turpin—his full name was Tomas Million Turner, of St. Louis had published the *Harlem Rag*, the *Bowery Buck*, the *Buffalo*, and Scott Joplin had just written the *Mapleleaf Rag*. This was white America's first introduction to ragtime, which was patterned after the Blues. The Blues were so essentially a part of Negro life that many musical pioneers rightly felt that America would not accept them, thus this offshoot, ragtime, which did happen to strike the public's fancy. It was gayer and was more in keeping with the mood of the American white man. Blues were always played among Negroes, seldom among white audiences; when they were played—they were set apart—as the *pièce de résistance* of the evening.

"—And today," Clarence Williams concluded with a chuckle, "Lo and behold, the Blues are played in symphony halls, with lots of high hats and ermine wraps in attendance."

We had been exchanging experiences, talking nothing but the Blues for over five hours and the lights of Broadway were beginning to flash. I made a start to leave, although I really didn't want to leave—when the door was quietly opened and a straight, elderly copper-colored man walked in.

"Didn't knock Clarence—knew you'd be here—just dropped in for a chat," he said as he sat down in an overstuffed chair.

I got up and was about to make my departure when the amiable Williams stayed me. "I'd like you to know Reese D'Pree," he said. I shook hands with the man, and I could see a look of resignation in his face, he seemed very tired and worn. Williams went on—"Reese D'Pree wrote a number about forty-three years ago, wrote it in Georgia, Bibb County to be exact—will you tell Campbell about that piece, Reese?" In simple language he told me of the number he had written and sung—made money on a ship in 1905 wearing a chef's cap and apron and singing his song. He used to sing it at pound parties in the South—pound parties were community affairs given by Negroes at that time where one would bring a pound of "vittles" of anything edible, a pound of chitterlings, of pigs' feet, of hog maw, barbecue, butter—anything that contributed to the feast. It was a simple little piece but everywhere he went, they wanted him to sing it. At the present time he is having copyright trouble—D'Pree did not impress me as being a wealthy man but the song must have earned over a million dollars for someone. Possibly you've heard it too—it's called *Shortnin' Bread*. Reese D'Pree loves the Blues as much as Clarence Williams and as I left the office I will always remember what that man told me the Blues meant to him. "Son," he said—"the Blues regenerates a man."

It should be clear by now why jazz has never been successfully defined. For how can a definition encompass the lament of a Negro field hand, vibrato, eighth and sixteenth tones and flatted fifths, a French quadrille played with a new beat, improvisation, hot instrumental intonations, African rhythms, and all the other technics and influences that go to make up the music we call jazz? It is difficult enough even to hint at its complex nature. Yet jazz does have one characteristic that stands out above all its many other traits: No other musical form equals it as a music for self-expression. In an increasingly regimented world, where even entertainment is tailored on an assembly-line to the lowest common denominator of public taste, good jazz still swings with integrity and a free spirit. And it is still played by uncompromising individualists who say, "This is the way I feel. This is *me*. If you don't like what you hear, go away. Just go away and let me blow. Because I won't change."

The world's Big Brothers and blue-noses will always be suspicious of jazz. And with good reason. For it is music that nourishes the soul of everyone to whom meek conformity is anathema.

Part Two

The
Evolution
of
Jazz

New sounds from the Crib Houses

Oh say can you hear by the dawn's early light? That was the time of day when the ragtime was just getting good along San Francisco's Living Picture Alley back in the nineties . . . when you could hear those back-room professors playing for the New York swells in the Saratoga gambling houses . . . or for the Klondike gold dust millionaires in the Seattle honky-tonks.

In Topeka, Wichita, Dodge City—in the crib houses and in the mill-town saloons, America was changing its musical point of view. Frankie shot Johnny in St. Louis and the news travelled up and down the river, like any other commodity.

In Chicago, in 1897, a parade band marched up State Street. Suddenly it splashed into an impromptu version of an unwritten strain popular in Chicago cabarets. The soloists called the liberties they took with the melody "faking", instead of improvisation, and the bandmaster with the golden epaulettes was twenty-four-year-old W. C. Handy.

In Buffalo, in the disreputable Alamo, they were singing *Willie the Weeper*. On the banks of the Wabash far away, Paul Dresser felt the new mood and worked it into his songs. All along the Mississippi and all its tributaries the ragtime flowed, changing America's music.

In Henderson, Kentucky, the curbstone quartets improvised a song about a local scandal involving a prominent citizen. The roustabouts and musicians carried it to New Orleans. It became an American classic, *Careless Love*.

In Memphis, composer Bill Handy first wrote down the three-line stanza of complaint we call the blues, perhaps the first jazz manuscript to be accepted by the public. An old song says, "Take me to that land of jazz, I want to get the kind of blues that Memphis has." Handy called his composition the *Memphis Blues*.

And in New Orleans, on a drink-stained upright piano in the gold-plated surroundings of Madam Lulu White's famed pleas-

Lulu White, famed New Orleans madam, introduced jazz to her bordello patrons in the beginning 1900's.

ure pagoda, Mahogany Hall, Spencer Williams composed his classic *Basin Street Blues*. Basin Street . . . called Amorous Avenue . . . the dream thoroughfare where Buddy Bolden, Jelly Roll Morton, Porter King, and all the other great old-timers played. Basin Street in New Orleans—*Won't you come along with me, down the Mississippi, we'll take a boat to the land of dreams, steam down the river, down to New Orleans. . . .*

All across the land, in countless towns and cities, a new sound was beginning to be heard, a new music was slowly emerging. It was a seminal moment, a heady and exciting period of transition. Artist E. Simms Campbell had the good fortune to live through it and in January, 1938, described it as he saw it.

Somewhere near the turn of the century, in the era of tinsel and gilt, heavy furniture and mustache cups, jazz was born. Where it was born is not particularly important. Memphis, Kansas City, St. Louis and a host of Southern towns have claimed credit, and there's no doubt that they all played a part in helping bring jazz into the world. But the principal midwife was unquestionably New Orleans, if only because of the huge number of ragtime Negro musicians gathered there.

At this time New Orleans was steeped in wickedness, bawdy houses running full blast, faro games on most street corners and voluptuous creole beauties soliciting trade among the welter of gamblers, steamboat men and hustlers of every nationality. New Orleans was not unique in this respect, as most American cities had their proscribed redlight district, but New Orleans was more colorful.

Here in this port of all nationalities, this western hemisphere Marseilles, came a conglomerate group of itinerant musicians—Coon shouters, honky tonks, black butt players (Negro musicians who could not read music)—all of them seeking their pot of gold in this paradise of pleasure. Most of them had little or no training in their respective instruments but they had a rhythm and a timing that appealed to the catholic tastes of this segment of America. The sky was the limit in "hot" ballads and there was no such thing as controlled music. New York was too far away and New Orleans was the mecca of entertainment to these Southern minstrels, for New Orleans had gone on a bender. And when a man or a city goes pleasure-mad they want music with "umph"—something that's on the naughty side, that tickles the senses, that starts them bunnyhugging. Ragtime filled this bill perfectly.

Possibly the first ragtime number originated in a bagnio and I know of more than a score that were actually created in them, having traced them back to the musicians who wrote them, tracing others through musicians who had played in bands with the original composer. A few of the numbers I actually saw created, written all over the backs of envelopes and policy number slips in all-night joints in St. Louis (pardon my misspent youth) and I have heard these same numbers, years later, presented for the edification of jazz enthusiasts on the concert stage. Without mentioning names, many of our greatest jazz artists have played, at some time or another, in these dens of iniquity or halls of learning—according to your esthetic tastes.

Ta-Ra-Ra-Boom-Dee-A was written in the house of Babe Connors, one of the more colorful Negro madams, in 1894. It was essentially ragtime—in 4-4 time, the name rag being given because the playing was ragged—one played between the beats, not on them. If you have ever seen Negroes dancing, that is dancing two-steps and one-steps and waltzes, you will notice that they do not dance exactly in time with the music. They dance to the rhythm of the number and are usually in step. It's this "feel" of the dance that's important and once one has the rhythm, there is no need to wonder or worry if you are exactly in time to the music. It was as natural for Negroes to create ragtime as it was for the rest of America to fall in step with them.

But coming back to the madams, these house-mothers of wayward America, they were continually on the lookout for added attractions to their establishments. With the rise of vaudeville, they now hoped to please their patrons with special music as well as other forms of special entertainment.

Every house with any pretentions to class had a beautiful mahogany upright piano, strewn with the usual bric-a-brac, cupid, Daphne and Apollo and ornate throws and the ever-present mandolin attachment. It added tone.

These madams were ever on the hunt for good musicians, but particularly good piano players, as a piano could be toned down and the less noise in the wee hours of the morning, the better. Possibly a tired Romeo could be coaxed into spending just a little more if the music fitted in with his mood.

The usual procedure would be to invite the chosen entertainer to stay at the house while he was in the city—and musicians at that time were not getting any hundred a week for their playing—and his cakes and coffee were free, with of course all the liquor he wished to hold. He could play any way he wanted to as long as he was good, and he could improvise all he wanted—just so long as he didn't stop. No matter how often he played certain numbers, the audience was continually changing. Here, when liquor, used to fight off exhaustion, had befogged the brain, many of the discordant and eerie chords of jazz were born.

Negro musicians were paid next to nothing, the finer white dance halls barring them, and their greatest revenue came from playing "gigs" (outside jobs—special groups of three or four who were especially hired to play for wealthy white patrons at private house parties) and in playing in the finest sporting houses.

Many of them have played the Redlight Circuit from New Orleans to Seattle.

You must remember at that time that Negroes had no union of their own, were not admitted to white unions, and it was impossible for them to market their songs unless they sold them outright to white publishers—and the top price was fifteen dollars with ten being about the average.

This shunting aside naturally made the Negro draw into himself. With no outlet to exchange ideas on music other than with members of his own race, he became more and more essentially Negroid in musical feeling and in interpretation. Jam sessions are as old as the hills among them—it was their only medium of expressing themselves, of learning—and it was the

W. C. Handy in his 20's, at the turn of the century. The young cornetist was then the bandmaster of a minstrel company. Soon afterward he began his blues-writing career. The two famous songs below followed his first blues creation called *Mr. Crump*, in honor of Boss Crump of Memphis, Tennessee.

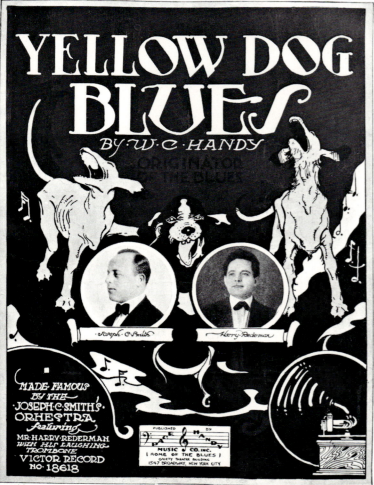

used by permission

used by permission

A typical early New Orleans marching band which played at parades, funerals, weddings, camp meetings and dances and almost always played jazz.

training school for the colored boy who hoped some day to become an accomplished musician. None of them had enough money to study their instruments, learning everything they knew from these early jam sessions, improvising and going ahead purely on natural ability. All of them patterned their playing after some musical giant who was the legendary John Henry of his day, some powerful cornetist or piano playing fool whose exploits on his chosen instrument were known throughout colored America. Camp meetings, funerals and lodge dances gave the embryo musician his first chance, and much later, about

1908 I believe, when the T. O. B. A. (Theatrical Owners Booking Agency) was formed, these musicians as well as entertainers had an opportunity to play before small theatres in the colored sections of various cities.

Before that time, minstrels and itinerant peddlers of tunes would go from town to town, but because of the precarious way in which they made a living, many towns never had an opportunity to hear them. Now this was all changed. Bessie Smith, Mamie Smith, Ma Rainey, Ida Cox, Clarence Williams, Butterbeans and Susie, all great names in the "blues" constellation to

Negroes throughout the United States, were swinging and playing the blues years before white America recognized them. Tom Turpin of St. Louis, Scott Joplin, Jelly Roll Morton were the early great jazz pianists, and by great I mean that their pieces were as intricate as Bach. They wrote trick arrangements, exciting tempos, difficult passages, and at this time the great Handy was writing. *Atlanta Blues, St. Louis Blues, New Orleans Blues, Memphis Blues, Beale Street Blues, Rampart Blues, Market Street Blues*—all these were written before 1912—just about the time Benny Goodman was six years old.

And later—the great flood of records, records that are now collector's items to the jazz enthusiast. A respectable family of the nineteen twenties would not be found dead with any of these abominable discs in their homes.

The old Decca records, Columbia, Okeh, but particularly the Paramount and Black Swan or Race records as they were called. This meant especially made for the Negro race as few white people would ever buy them. I quote from old catalogues of mine and the names are authentic. *Red Hot Mamma* and *Drunk Man's Strut, Lonnie Johnson's Blues, Salty Dog Blues* (which had particularly low-down lines), *Mr. Freddie's Blues, Barrelhouse Blues, Toad Frog Blues, Ride Jockey Ride, Death Letter Blues, Mean Man Blues, Lemon Jefferson's Blues, The Woman Ain't Born, Grave Yard Bound, Long Gone Blues, Black Hand Blues*— the list is endless. *Mecca Flat Blues*, named after a row of disorderly houses in Chicago and even *Tickler*, which is a standby today.

It has been given various names—*Squeeze Me—The Little Boy in the Boat* and *The Bulldagger's Dream* and at the present time it is called *Rolling* or *RollEm*. It was written by a Negro musician in Detroit many years ago—was never set to music until about 1920 and was later featured by both Bob Crosby and Benny Goodman.

All through the nineteen twenties, this endless stream of Blues records—and who bought them? White dealers did not and the chances are ten thousand to one that you haven't five of them in your collection. They were a solace to Negro domestics who after working for hours over laundry tubs, mopping floors and shining brass, would go to the dingy comfort of a one-room flat in the Negro tenements and there put these records on their victrolas. It was a release from things white —they could hum—pat their feet—and be all colored. "Blues blues—jes' as blue as ah can be—Nogood man done lef'—and lef' po' me."

Sporting houses were possibly the next best bets for these records and they bought them by the armful. The records sold for fifty cents with a top price of seventy-five and they were continually needing replacement as the patrons would play certain favorites over and over again until the grooves in the discs were worn down. Every joint from New Orleans all through the Delta up to St. Louis, Kansas City, Chicago, Detroit, on out to the coast had stacks of these records. Dim lights—and the blues—the lowdown gutbucket blues—heady music as intoxicating as any of the wares for sale.

During the summer, on Monday nights, the Negroes of St. Louis were privileged to use the older of two paddle-wheel steamers for their boat excursions. I remember the names of both of them—*The J. S.* and *The St. Paul*—*The St. Paul* was the one we used. Lodges and fraternal orders of all sorts would get together and have a benefit—to this day I have never found out what the benefits were for—but they always meant plenty of ice cream and cake for us, and above all—music, the blues. Music that was decidedly frowned upon by respectable Negro and white families, but we kids loved it. These boat rides usually ended up in fist fights, knife fights and bottle throwing contests. Drinking St. Louis corn, packed on the boat like cattle, bunny-hugging to the tunes of Jelly Roll Morton, some too ardent boy friend would cut in on another's girl—then fireworks! I can still see an excited crew, redfaced and panting among a sea of black faces, trying to restore order—and then the clear strains of Charlie Creath's trumpet drowning out the noise and the scuffling. Charlie Creath of the one lung (he had literally blown his other lung out in New Orleans proving his superiority over other trumpet players)—Charlie had cut loose on the *St. Louis Blues*.

Fights and even gun play meant nothing to these musicians who had seen it all too often—Charlie was playing a monu-

Gut-bucket trombonist. By Tomi Ungerer.

"The Boat" by Peter Blume. The Museum of Modern Art collection. Gift of Mrs. Sam A. Lewisohn.

The jazz sounds began far down south on the Mississippi and moved north along the river to St. Louis, Chicago and around the country.
Jelly Roll Morton, (below) one of the earliest of the great jazz pianists, with his famed *Red Hot Peppers* "dressed-up" band.

used by permission

used by permission

used by permission

mental solo—*Oh Play It, Mr. Charlie, Play It*—. The trumpet was in the clear now, it would not be denied—sweet and hot, the staccato notes splintered among the crowd and even the boy wielding the knife was transfixed. Someone bellowed out, "Oh play it Mr. Charlie, play that thing!" There was laughter and the tenseness disappeared—the trumpet was laughing now—"What's a few cuts—doctor below deck'll fix 'em up and BOY—does you realize we on'y got a half-hour t'dance?"

The crowd that had formed a semicircle to watch the men fight surged forward and blended together—they were one—Charlie had won another fight.

These early Negro geniuses like Charlie Creath were evolv-

Typical sheet music of the 20's. The word *jazz* was picked up by Tin Pan Alley and incorporated into pop tune titles of the day.

ing today's jazz. Many of the popular tunes of the day were written by whites as well as Negroes but there was this undercurrent of music—this music behind even the blues—this forbidden land as it were, that only a kid with all eyes and ears could catch. There were glimpses of it on these stolen boat rides when a lean black man would become intoxicated with the rhythm of his playing and break off into a magnificent solo—leaving the piece that the orchestra played entirely and swinging out into musical no-man's-land. He was swaying the crowd—he was "sending" them, and I was an apt disciple—I was willing to be "sent."

What this lean black man was doing, of course, was impro-

vising—giving a masterful exhibition on the spur of the moment of technical virtuosity fused with inspirational playing. And if that wasn't jazz—then there's no such animal."

Of course it was jazz, lowly of origin and still primitive, but jazz nonetheless, leaving the Deep South, moving northward upstream on the riverboats. It came up the long course of the Mississippi slowly at first, from New Orleans and Memphis and St. Louis to Chicago. Then, quickening its pace, it spread from coast to coast. Finally, the whole country rocked to an inescapable jazz beat.

But the road from Madam White's Mahogany Hall to New York's Carnegie Hall is strewn with evidence of the titanic

The Second Line
By Bruce Mitchell

Collection of Dr. James L. Harrison

struggle this new music had to put up to win even the smallest recognition. Pioneers like The Original Creoles, The Olympia Band, Scott Joplin, and Jelly Roll Morton were engaged in a continuous battle with obscurity. The world was occupied with other things, prior to 1917, and ragtime and jazz were considered insignificant accompaniments to war and vice. But jazz history was being made just the same. By 1915, Creamer and Layton had composed *Dear Old Southland*, Shelton Brooks had written *Some Of These Days*, and W. C. Handy had set down a host of Negro folk tunes.

Nevertheless, America remained indifferent to jazz. Abroad, conversely, Will Marion Cook's Orchestra was playing a highly successful engagement at no less a place than London's Philharmonic Hall, with Sidney Bechet as clarinet soloist. As early as 1919, the French classical conductor, Ernest Ansermet, who was a frequent listener, said: "The first thing that strikes one about the Southern Syncopated Orchestra is the astonishing perfection, the superb taste and the fervor of its playing."

And of Bechet's many brilliant performances, M. Ansermet wrote: "They gave the idea of a style, with a brusque and pitiless ending like that of Bach's second *Brandenburg Concerto*. What a moving thing it is to meet this very black, fat boy with white teeth, who is glad one likes what he does, but who can say nothing of his art save that he follows his 'own way.' One thinks that this 'own way' is perhaps the highway the whole world will sing along tomorrow."

A few years afterward, Igor Stravinsky composed his *Ragtime* suite, explaining later: "It's dimensions are modest, but it is indicative of the passion I felt at that time for jazz, which burst into life so suddenly when the war ended. At my request, a whole pile of this music was sent to me, enchanting me by its truly popular appeal, its freshness, and the novel rhythm which so distinctly revealed its Negro origin."

Once it developed that jazz might be assuming a position of importance and influence, the opposition began to muster its forces. The relaxation of morals and general licentiousness of the twenties had to be pigeonholed in the least embarrassing manner; consequently crime, a growing indifference to religion, and freedom of sex were all ascribed to the increasing prevalence of jazz, although, oddly enough, these same social cankers were also deemed curable by Prohibition. The literature of the day erupted with essays on the general depravity of the Jazz Age, even otherwise enlightened men like the late Dr. Frederick Stock being moved to announce indignantly that "the appeal of jazz" was directed to what he chose to call "the lowest part of our anatomy." In 1921, Clive Bell went even farther and blamed jazz for "breaking down discipline and exalting the unrestrained free spirit."

Two influences now attempted to pull jazz in opposite directions. The classical recognition of its potentialities extended not only to Stravinsky, but also to Ravel and Hindemith in Europe, and to Carpenter, Sowerby and Lane in America. Europeans particularly continued to be impressed by and to experiment with the new tonalities coming out of jazz. But the old-line dignitaries of the classics must have detected the voice of a musical Frankenstein in jazz, about whom the less said the better. For by 1925, when jazz's general pattern of tonality

had been absorbed, classical music returned to its old traditional way of cultivating dissonances.

Another direction was taken by the alumni of Tin Pan Alley. They sought to elevate the new music to the concert hall level, through the programming of taxi-horns, tugboat whistles and the nostalgia of Americans in Paris. "Gershwin's *Second Rhapsody*," one critic wrote, "originally called *Rhapsody in Rivets*, led me to reflect on the fallacious notion that since American life included jazz and riveting, the music which 'expresses' this life also had to include them."

This "arty" development of jazz was being perpetrated by white composers who, weary of the ballads of Broadway, looked with longing on the fresh ideas of Negroid music. And despite the fact that their symphonic treatments were received with as much controversy as the legitimacy of jazz itself, in 1924 these same symphonic stylists managed to endow the word jazz with comparative respectability. With one Gershwinian grunt it leapt onto the concert stage; and following Gershwin's lead, Ferde Grofé, Jerome Kern and Rube Bloom all turned to the production of "symphonic jazz." Paul Whiteman, ever on the scent of commercial success, conducted the premiere performance of *Rhapsody in Blue*, earning for himself the somewhat laughable title of King of Jazz. By 1925, the symphonic movement, afflicted with a mild touch of surrealism, had proceeded westward as far as Chicago, where another Whiteman concert featured Sowerby's *Monotony, a Symphony for Jazz Orchestra and Metronome!*

Meanwhile, honest jazz remained close to its origin, the people. And, thumbing its nose at Whiteman and his metronome, it flourished with particular vigor in Chicago. The exodus of Negro musicians from New Orleans, which began when the outlawing of the city's bawdy houses, in 1917, threw so many out of work, crystalized in the Windy City between the years 1918 and 1928. King Oliver's band made the Royal Gardens, Dreamland Cafe, and the Plantation Club the jazz-history equivalents of Elizabethan London's Mermaid Tavern, and also spawned Louis Armstrong and cut records now numbered among jazz's greatest classics. In 1921, a white group, the New Orleans Rhythm Kings made a jazz-shrine of the Friar's Inn, simply by playing there for eighteen months. Sidney Bechet, Jimmy Noone and others were in Chicago with small combinations. Erskine Tate's mighty band rocked the small Vendome Theatre nightly. And scores of other groups were making Chicago's south side reverberate as it never had before.

The reverberations reached out like a siren call, attracting such young men as Charles Ellsworth (Pee Wee) Russell, Eddie Condon, Joe Sullivan, Gene Krupa, Benny Goodman, Jess Stacy and Muggsy Spanier. They swarmed into the Loop's noisy spots to listen to Louis and Oliver and a thin, pale young cornetist from Davenport, Iowa, named Bix Beiderbecke and said that's for me. And, fired by what they heard, a group of Austin High School classmates—Dave Tough, Jimmy McPartland, Frank Teschemacher, Bud Freeman and Jim Lannigan—were organizing themselves into the Blue Friars band. It was, Armstrong has said, the happiest era he had ever known, "like seventh heaven and all that." Listen to Louis as he reminisced about "all that" back in the January, 1951, issue of *Esquire*.

That toddlin' town

When King Joe Oliver sent for me to leave New Orleans, in 1922, and join him at the Lincoln Gardens to play second trumpet to his first trumpet, I jumped sky-high with joy. The day I received the telegram from Papa Joe—that's what I called him—I was playing a funeral in New Orleans and all the members of the Tuxedo Brass Band told me not to go because Papa Joe and his boys were having some kind of union trouble.

When the Tuxedo boys told me that King Oliver and his band were scabbing, I told them the King had sent for me and I was answering, it didn't matter to me what he was doing. I was going to him just the same. So I went.

I arrived in Chicago about eleven o'clock the night of July 8, 1922, at the Illinois Central Station at Twelfth and Michigan Avenue. I'll never forget it. The King was already at work. I had no one to meet me. I took a cab and went directly to the Lincoln Gardens.

When I was getting out of the cab and paying the driver, I could hear the King's band playing some kind of a jump number.

Believe me, they were really jumpin' in fine fashion. I said to myself, "My Gawd, I wonder if I'm really good enough to play in that band." I hesitated about going inside right away, but finally I did.

When I got near the bandstand, King Oliver spied me. He immediately stopped the band to greet me, saying, "Boy, where have you been? I've been waiting and waiting for you." Well, I did miss the train that the King thought I should have been on, and I mumbled some kind of excuse. Then they went into another hot number. In that band, besides Oliver, there was Johnny Dodds, clarinet, Honore Dutrey, trombone, Baby Dodds, drums Bill Johnson, bass, and Lil Hardin, piano, who became Mrs. "Satchmo" No. 2 a little later.

When I joined the band on second trumpet I made the seventh member. Man, those were thrilling days I'll never forget. I went to work the next night and, first thing, King and I stumbled upon a little something that no other two trumpeters together ever thought of. While the band was just swinging, the King

Chicago: the precise, insistent sounds
of the banjo indicated that jazz had found a new home.

would lean over to me, moving the valves on his trumpet, making notes, the notes that he was going to play when the break in the tune came. I'd listen, and at the same time I'd be figuring out my second to his lead. When the break would come, I'd have my part to blend right along with his. And the crowd would go mad over it!

King Oliver and I got so popular blending that jive together that pretty soon all the white musicians from downtown Chicago would all gather 'round us after their work was done and stay until the place closed. Sometimes they would sit in with us to get their kicks. Lillian was doubling from Lincoln Gardens to the Edelweiss Gardens, an after-hours place. After work I'd go out there with her. Doing this, she and I became regular running buddies, and we would go to all the other places when we had the time. She knew Chicago like a book. I'll never forget the first time she took me to the Dreamland Cabaret on 35th and State to hear Ollie Powers and Mae Alix sing. Ollie had one of those high, sweet singing voices, and when he would sing songs like *What'll I Do*, he would really rock the whole house. Mae Alix had one of those fine strong voices that everyone would also want to hear. Then she would go into her splits, and the customers would throw paper dollars on the floor, and she would make one of those running splits, picking them up one at a time.

I asked Lil if it was alright to give Ollie and Mae a dollar each to sing a song for me. She said sure, and called them over and introduced me to them as the new trumpet man in King Oliver's band, and they wouldn't take my money. Gee whiz! I really thought I was somebody, meeting those fine stars and all that. I followed Ollie Powers everywhere he sang, until the day he died. At his funeral I played a trumpet solo in the church where they had his body laying out for the last time. Oh what a sad day that was.

In 1923, Papa Joe moved us all over to the Sunset. Chicago was really jumping at that time. The Dreamland was in full bloom. The Lincoln Gardens, of course, was still in there. The Plantation was another hot spot. But the Sunset, my boss' place, was the sharpest of them all, believe that. A lot of after-hours spots were groovy, too. There was the Apex, where Jimmy Noone and that great piano man, Earl Hines, started some of the finest stuff there ever was. They made history right there in the Apex. The tune *Sweet Lorraine* used to gas everybody there nightly. I was one of the everybodies. Then there was a place on State Street called the Fiume, where they had a small ofay band, right in the heart of the South Side. They were really fine. All us musicians, nightlifers, everybody, plunged in there in the wee hours and had a grand time. I used to meet a lot of the boys there.

But soon King Oliver received an offer to go on the road and make some one-night stands at real good money. Ump! That got it. The band almost busted up. Half of the boys just wouldn't go, that's all. The same situation hits band leaders square in the face all the time. So the King replaced every man that wouldn't go. As for me anything the King did was all right. My heart was out for him at all times. And the tour was great. We had lots of fun and made lots of money.

Along about the end of 1923, I received a telegram to go to New York and join the great Fletcher Henderson orchestra. *Great* was how I felt about "Smack" Henderson, years before I had seen him in person, from recordings he'd made for years, both by himself and with Ethel Waters and Revela Hughes. He had the first big colored band ever to hit the road and tear it up. When I explained to the King that it was my one big chance to see New York, where people really *do things*, he dug me. I knew he would, and he released me so I could knock it.

When I arrived in New York I had to go straight to rehearsal. And don't you know that when I got into that rehearsal, I felt so funny. I walked up to old "Smack" and said, "Er, ah, wa, I'm that boy you sent for to blow the trumpet in your band." And "Smack", all sharp as a Norwegian in the hard-hitting steel gray suit he had on, said, "Oh, yes, we're waiting for you." That's all. I said, "Yassuh," and went on up on the bandstand with my eyes closed. When I opened them I looked square into the faces of Coleman Hawkins, Don Redman, Kaiser Marshall, Long Green, Escadero, Scotty, Elmer "Muffle Jaws" Chambers and Charles Dixon.

They all casually looked out of the corner of their eyes. You know how they do when a new man joins a band, they want to be real friendly right off the bat. But they'd rather hear you play first. I said to myself these boys look like a bunch of nice fellows, but they seem a little stuck-up. That was the opinion I had of them right off the reel. I guess they had theirs about me, too.

Where I had come from I wasn't used to playing in bands where there were a lot of parts for everyone to read. Shucks, all one man in the band had to do was to go to some show or hear a good tune someplace. He keeps it in his head until he reaches us. He hums the number a couple of times, and from then on we had a new song to throw off when the band was advertising in the wagon on the corner the following Sunday. That's how we stayed so famous down in New Orleans. We had a new number for the customers every week.

Now I was in New York getting ready to join the biggest band in the city. We played the first number down, it was *By The Waters of Minnetonka*. I had the third trumpet part which was so pretty. Still nobody said anything. Finally, we got to mugging on *Tiger Rag*, which gives the boys a chance to hear me really tear out. After that, believe me, it was on. I'd made it with them.

Our engagement at the Roseland was great. Our road tour was the same. I stayed with "Smack" Henderson until way up into 1925. Then Lil, who was my wife at the time and who had the band at the Dreamland Cabaret in Chicago, suggested that I come home because it would be nicer for us to starve together than be apart so long. I was a little homesick, too. So I cut out from those fine boys who had treated me so swell.

Back in Chicago we had some fine moments at the Dreamland. Some real jumping acts. There was the team of Brown and McGraw. They did a jazz dance that just wouldn't quit. I'd blow for their act, and every step they made, I put a note to it. They liked the idea so well they had it arranged. About that time,

King Oliver Creole Jazz Band
By Robert Andrew Parker

too, a boy by the name of Benny Goodman used to come out and set in and help us tear up the joint every once in a while.

Then Professor Erskine Tate asked me (ahem) to join his Symphony Orchestra at the Vendome. I wouldn't take a million for that experience. The Professor played hot music as well as overtures.

Things were jumping so around Chicago at that time, there was more work than a cat could shake a stick at. I was doubling from Dreamland to the Vendome for awhile. Then I stayed single at the Vendome about a year, until Carroll Dickerson persuaded me to double from the theater to his band at the Sunset Cafe. After the show, I'd go over to the Sunset and swing there with them until the wee hours. 'Twas great, I'll tell you. In that band there were *the* Earl Hines, Darnell Howard, Tubby Hall, Honore Dutrey and Boyd Atkins, who wrote the tune called *Heebie Jeebies*.

The Sunset had Friday night Charleston contests and you couldn't get into the place, unless you got there early. We had a great show in those days with Buck 'n' Bubbles, Rector and Cooper, Edith Spencer and Mae Alix, my favorite entertainer, and a gang of now famous stars. We had a finale, too, that just wouldn't quit.

In this finale, four of us band boys closed the show doing the Charleston. That was really something. There was Earl Hines, as tall as he was; Tubby Hall, as fat as he was; little Joe Walker, as short was he was; and myself, fat as I was at the time. We would stretch out across the floor doing the Charleston as fast as the music would play it. Boy, oh boy, you talk about four cats picking them up and laying them down—that was us. And we had to stay there until old boss man got tired of laughing at us.

Things began to move out further on the south side of Chicago. The Metropolitan Theatre was running in full bloom with Sammy Stewart's orchestra out of Columbus, Ohio, holding sway and featuring my boy Zutty Singleton. After Sammy came Clarence Jones' orchestra, with which I did a turn. Then there was the Savoy Ballroom, drat it.

The time the Savoy opened, in 1927, Earl Hines, Zutty and myself had just leased the Warwick Hall, around the corner from the Savoy. But the Savoy had such a jumpin' opening that we never did get a chance to open our own place. Ump! There we were with a year's lease on our hands and no place to get the rent. We decided to hustle. We gave a dance on the West Side of Chicago and had a big success. After all, the three of us had a popularity. After playing in those famous bands such as Erskine Tate's, Dave Payton's and Clarence Jones' in those big theaters, the folks came around to hear us dish that mess out.

Then Earl went back to the Apex and Zutty and I, not being able to lick him, joined Carroll Dickerson at the Savoy Ballroom. The place was jumping, as was the Apex, and the three of us managed to pay off the Warwick Hall lease. The real estate people gave us a break and threw the whole thing out for a hundred and fifty dollars. We could breathe again.

I stayed at the Savoy until 1929, when my agent sent for me to come to New York to join that big show which was in rehearsal at that time called *Great Day*. It sort of choked me up to leave. All in all, looking back, in Chicago from 1922 to 1929 I spent some of my finest days, maybe even my best."

When Louis left Chicago in 1929 the basic structure of jazz had been laid down and was well on its way toward the polishing and refining stage. One influence at work on its refinement was being fostered by a group of white musicians like Red Nichols, Miff Mole, Frank Trumbauer and Bix Beiderbecke, who were playing a sort of chamber music in a hot vein. Another influence was being exerted by Eddie Condon, Bud Freeman, Frankie Teschemacher, Jimmy McPartland and the other musicians who were shaping what has come to be known as "Chicago style" jazz.

The small "jam" combinations of King Oliver and the New Orleans Rhythm Kings had, of course, already set the pace for the many jam units which came later. Duke Ellington's installation at New York's Club Kentucky (1923) marked the beginning of a distinctly characteristic kind of jazz—a style which the Duke and his band always pursued. McKinney's Cotton Pickers, with impetus from Don Redman and John Nesbit, developed the full band ensemble playing, with interspersed solos, later used by the swing bands. And finally, during this period Fletcher Henderson, Erskine Tate, and Charles "Doc" Cook greatly enlarged the vocabulary of jazz as they brought their superb bands to an epitome of expressiveness.

Meanwhile, the opposition kept sniping. Although *Bookman* magazine had begun a regular department of jazz record reviews its critic, Abbe Niles, could still note that "one of the unwritten mottos of sensational pulpiteers runs 'when in doubt, denounce jazz'."

The following year the Depression hit Chicago, and what has been called the Golden Age of Jazz came to an abrupt end. That city, after 1930, was only a gutted shell of its former self. Sweet music took over completely: Jan Garber was grooming himself for the role of "idol of the airwaves," Wayne King and Guy Lombardo schmaltzed their way to fortunes. Depression-ridden, confused, dispirited, the overwhelming majority of Americans who could pay for music preferred sentimental other-worldliness to any expression of the real life they sought to forget. Drenched in their own blues, they turned their backs on blues music.

No better proof that jazz ties into the mainstream of life can be found, nor a better answer given to those who claim that jazz itself is escape-music, than its complete neglect during the escapist years of the early Depression. Frank Teschemacher could say categorically, "You can't play jazz and make a living at it." Ben Pollack, head of a combination of some of the greatest names in jazz, and a great drummer, also took up crooning. Between 1929 and 1932, Bix Beiderbecke, Frank Trumbauer, Joe Venuti, Eddie Lang, Jimmy and Tommy Dorsey, Red Norvo, Mildred Bailey and others kept the wolf from the door by joining Paul Whiteman. Although Duke Ellington and

McKinney's Cotton Pickers managed to get by, most musicians had to scrape for sustenance. Many of the best soloists were scattered, some destitute. Still others were forced into radio and theater pit orchestras, their talents obscured and unrealized. Jazz itself became localized. Ellington and Henderson were confined to New York City; Benny Moten and Andy Kirk to Kansas City; while McKinney had to hibernate in Detroit's Gravstone Ballroom. By 1932, Joe Marsala had done time as a truckdriver; Jack Teagarden, Miff Mole, Ned Nichols and a host of others had succumbed to the lure of radio money; Leon Rappolo was in the madhouse; Bix, Teschemacher and Lang were dead.

Nevertheless, jazz survived. In a period when the opposition was triumphantly proclaiming its death—completely overlooking the Depression as a factor—jazz went underground and stayed alive, kept so by the men who played it and almost no one else. This was the time when, it's been said, jazz was almost exclusively the concern of the boys in the backroom, when if you were a Bix devotee, say, you felt a little as if you were a member of a secret society.

Around New York, jazzmen kept their interest alive by jamming for the love of it, recording with pickup bands, and jobbing on one-nighters whenever they could find work. Many of them ruined their health, but they kept jazz breathing simply because its breath was in them, and even if they had to play it for nothing they couldn't stop playing it entirely.

At the same time, oddly enough, jazz was making further inroads in the ranks of the intelligentsia. In 1930, a feature article on jazz appeared in the highbrow publication *Symposium*. Two years later, Robert Goffin, a Belgian lawyer, brought out his *Aux Frontiers du Jazz* in Brussels, and in 1934 Roger Pryor Dodge contributed *Harpsichords and Jazz Trumpets* to the celebrated literary journal *Hound and Horn*. The same year Hugues Panassié wrote his French edition of *Hot Jazz*. Jazz clubs began to spring up in Europe and America, and in 1934 *Down Beat* was born; *Metronome* was switching to swing, and jazz won recognition in a general magazine with the publication in *Esquire* of Charles Edward Smith's *Collecting Hot*.

Larger bands now began to make a significant appearance. Although Erskine Tate's Vendome Orchestra, Fletcher Henderson's Orchestra and McKinney's Cotton Pickers had all been large organizations whose recordings sometimes reveal a precocious similarity to the swing ushered in by Benny Goodman in the '30's, jazz up to this time had been principally identified with small combinations. Mainly a New York influence, the large swing-band idea now began to look attractive to hot musicians.

In 1934, Goodman persuaded some of the men to follow him out of the backrooms, theaters and radio studios into a large band that would be dedicated to the playing of real jazz. After months of trials, he obtained work at Billy Rose's Music Hall in New York and proceeded to make some headway. In 1935 he moved into the sedate Joseph Urban Room of Chicago's Congress Hotel and miraculously became the first band to bring the place popular success as a nightspot. At the end of six weeks

he was re-engaged for seven months, and his rise to national fame was assured. In 1934, the Dorsey brothers had struck out for themselves and organized a swing band which, amoeba-like, split into two bands a year later, Jimmy and Tommy going their separate ways to prominence. In 1935 the Ben Pollack group was reorganized into a swing orchestra under the leadership of Bob Crosby.

Swing began to take on the proportions of a national craze in the spring of 1937, when Goodman played the Paramount theater in New York. Extra police had to be called in to handle the audience which screamed and danced in the aisles and scrambled over each other to get closer to the band. Ballrooms, theaters and hotels, eager to cash in on the craze, began clamoring for swing bands. Gate receipts soared. At the Astor Hotel in New York, Tommy Dorsey would break all attendance records, attracting 4,000 people in two nights. The Saturday and Sunday performances of Goodman at the Paramount drew 29,000 persons, shattering all existing records for that theater.

In January, 1938, Goodman presented his now historic Carnegie Hall concert. During it, the audience, 3,000 strong, stomped its feet to the rhythm, shouted, jumped up and down, and generally demonstrated that hallowed Carnegie Hall had no appreciable sobering influence on it.

The whole country was rocking to swing, and the big bands were riding high, higher than they ever had before or ever have since. It was a memorable period, and much of its mood was recaptured by George Frazier in September, 1953 as he reminisced about and lamented the passing of the big bands.

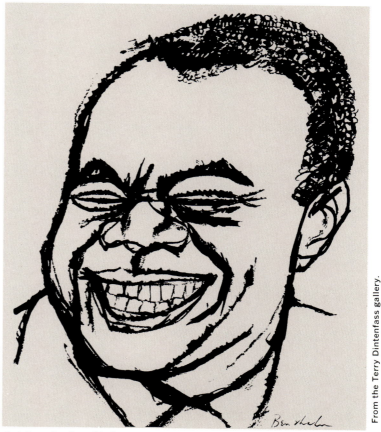

Satchmo by Ben Shahn

Benny Goodman and his Swing Era

Although years have passed since Benny had them shagging in the aisles, as the expression so quaintly went, he is still, at least on records, the most popular band leader in the world. As evidence, consider the sales rung up by his 1938 Carnegie Hall Concert album following its issue in 1958, and the sales of his current album, *Mission To Moscow.*

There are two obvious inferences to be drawn from the fact that a dance band as old as Benny's has proved more appealing than any contemporary group. One is that the Goodman band had authentic greatness. It did. The other is that the dance-band business has fallen upon lean times. It has. It is a real pity, of course, that Goodman no longer appears in ballrooms, but there is easier money to be made today on concert tours, and the music is still on records for all to hear, and it is miraculous and lovely and abiding and always, even though from so far out of the past, *ave* as much as *vale*. What seems far more deplorable is that Goodman's semiretirement has contributed toward rendering the dance-band business all but extinct.

Dance bands are Nostalgia and in the memory of their rhythms is one's youth—whether it was spent, like Scott Fitzgerald's, tea-dancing to *Poor Butterfly* and all the other bittersweet refrains that haunt his pages; whether up in Harlem at breakfast dances or at debutante parties with the stag line ready and willing; whether in the big hotels, like the Ambassador in Atlantic City, where a very Michelin-tire-advertisement of a man named Paul Whiteman used to play in 1920, and the Biltmore in New York, where five years later a multimillionaire's scion named Roger Wolfe Kahn offered such current favorites as *Room with a View,* or in the cabarets, like Reisenweber's in Columbus Circle, where, about the time of our entry into World War I, the Original Dixieland Jazz Band tore the roof off with a quadrille called *Tiger Rag,* and Gogi's Larue, on East Fifty-eighth Street, where Ted Straeter salvaged the departed years with show tunes like *Manhattan* and *The Most Beautiful Girl in the World;* whether in the ballrooms, like the old Cinderella in New York, where in 1923 the Wolverines, six pieces at $1250 a week, featured the silvery explosions of a young and tragically destined cornetist named Leon Bismarck Beiderbecke, or in lakeside dance pavilions, with moonlight dappling the water, the muffled sound of a canoe and someone's paddlin' Mad'lin home, the scuffing of feet on the dance floor, and the swelling brassiness of the bands—bands like the Casa Loma, which was big and meaningful and absolute class in the early Thirties, what with, among other enticements, a portly man named Pee Wee Hunt to sing Hoagy Carmichael's *Lazybones* and a darkly handsome one named Kenny Sargent to croon *For You* or *Under a Blanket of Blue.* And always there were the college gymnasiums on warm nights in long-vanished springtimes, and up on the bandstand the celebrated likes of Isham Jones, with an elf of a vocalist named Eddie Stone, or Ozzie Nelson, whose special treats were a pretty girl named Harriet Hilliard and a number called *It's Dark on Observatory Hill,* which was ineffably haunting and probably always will be.

Benny Goodman in the 30's, when the swing craze took hold.

In the band business, the resonant years were the Thirties and early Forties, which is to say after Goodman emerged as the King of Swing, the idol of a generation, the prophet of an era. This was the golden time, with fine, exciting bands at every turn of the dial late at night and with everybody making the big money. There has never been anything like it, neither before nor since, and more than likely there never will be again. But the band business goes back behind Goodman.

There were individuals like Art Hickman, who got things under way in 1914, when he had the flabbergasting boldness to add a saxophone section to his band in San Francisco and went on presently to enthrall the dancers on Ziegfeld's Amsterdam Roof; Paul Specht, who had a band that featured a small hot combination—The Georgians—as early as 1922 and made more than 3000 records for the Columbia label; Abe Lyman, an unfrocked drummer; Gus Arnheim; Ted Weems; Smith Ballew; Larry Funk ("and his Band of a Thousand Melodies," no less); George Olsen, who did things like *The Varsity Drag, Lucky in Love,* and *Who* to the considerable enrichment of both himself and the Victor record people; Jan Garber ("The Idol of the Air-Lanes"); Irving Aaronson's Commanders; Russ Morgan, once a coal miner; Carlton Coon and Joe Sanders ("The Ol' Lefthander") and their Kansas City Nighthawks; Ace Brigode, Charlie Dornberger, Don Bestor, Jack Denny, Ted Fiorito—all of them once upon a time very big; Jean Goldkette, whose weekly payroll was more than $3500; Ben Bernie ("The Old Maestro") and his "Yowsah, yowsah, yowsah"; Vincent Lopez ("Lopez speaking"), who is still active; Paul Tremaine; Ted Lewis, who became a leader in 1917 and who, for all his palpable corn, gave gainful employment to the jazz likes of George Brunis and Muggsy Spanier; Bernie Cummins, converted football player; Rudy Vallee ("The Vagabond Lover"); Johnny Hamp's Kentucky Serenaders; Joe Haymes; Ben Pollack, a great drummer who, with a personnel that included dedicated improvisers like Jack Teagarden, Jimmy McPartland and Benny Goodman, had the best white band prior to Goodman's own; Anson ("Dancin' with Anson") Weeks; Fred Waring, who, in 1918, had his Banjo Band; Horace Heidt, who featured, of all things, a German police dog in his band; the inspired Negro outfits like Duke Ellington's, Claude Hopkins', McKinney's Cotton Pickers; Benny Moten's, Don Redman's, which had a singer named Harlan Lattimore, and Fletcher Henderson's, with a roster of geniuses like Coleman Hawkins, Buster Bailey, Tommy Ladnier, Joe Smith, Charlie Green, and Louis Armstrong; and—of course—Paul Whiteman, who was a substantial man in more respects than his girth and weight.

A whole generation responded to Whiteman's Victor recordings of *Whispering* and *Japanese Sandman* and to the swelling strains of his trade-mark, *Rhapsody in Blue.* Today it is thought fashionable to scorn Whiteman, but his music had golden moments—Bunny Berigan's few impassioned bars in *It's Only a Paper Moon,* Beiderbecke's insinuating necromancy in treasures like *Sweet Sue* ("the rip up the middle of Sweet Sue," as a highly proper young lady from *Vogue* described it, once and for all) and *Melancholy Baby,* and many another as well. And Whiteman recognized and loved the dignity and frailty of men as musicians.

When, for example, poor, sick Beiderbecke quit the band for a year in an effort to regain his health, "the old man" kept him on the payroll record at his full salary. "The old man," one of his musicians once said, "was never a boy to cast the first stone." There was an evening out in Iowa when his hand was so shaky after a prodigious night-before that he inadvertently shaved off his celebrated mustache, and the outraged ballroom operator cut his fee. The old man refused to preach what he himself abstained from practicing.

And Edward Kennedy Ellington—or, as he is customarily known, The Duke—who opened with his band at the now-defunct Cotton Club in Harlem on December 4, 1927. In the years since then, there has never been a time when he was anything less than the leader of a magnificent ensemble—rich, inventive, and always the voice of one man and that man a genius.

Ellington has written a thousand songs, many of them resounding hits, rehearsed his men meticulously, arranged, played piano, recorded, and gone without a wink of sleep for days and nights at a stretch. He does it without stimulants, year after year. In the history of the band business, Ellington's longevity as a top-flight leader is unchallenged except by one man, Guy Lombardo, the son of a London, Ontario, tailor. Lombardo, who had a six-piece band as early as 1922, brought his Royal Canadians into the Hotel Roosevelt in New York seven years later, at almost the precise moment that Wall Street was laying its egg, and has remained a beguiling and thriving attraction ever since.

One year, Lombardo's gross income from radio, records, and personal appearances amounted to more than a million dollars, a figure exceeded only by Vaughn Monroe ("The Man with Hair on his Tonsils"), whose plurality of some $200,000 comes from playing on the road more often than Lombardo, who prefers the less remunerative but less exhausting job at the Roosevelt Grill. What makes the Royal Canadians a genuine phenomenon is that they have maintained their popularity without ever altering their original style, which is described, perhaps euphemistically, as "the sweetest music this side of Heaven." Other leaders frantically twisted their idioms as a young bespectacled clarinetist from Chicago rocked the world with his brilliant new band, but Lombardo stood firm. Of all the groups which persisted in playing sweetly, only the Royal Canadians continued to attract huge crowds. The dazzling slash of Benny Goodman's clarinet was irresistible from the moment it cut through the air in the Palomar in Los Angeles on the night of August 21, 1935.

Now the age of swing was under way and the dance-band business was booming and the heroes in the land were youngsters named Benny and Gene and Teddy and Jess and Bunny—and never any necessity to identify them further, because everybody knew that they were, respectively, Benny Goodman, Gene Krupa, Teddy Wilson, Jess Stacy, and Bunny Berigan. Presently, even the staid British were unbending, even though, only a few months before, a reviewer from the *Melody Maker* in London had written testily about the use of nicknames. Referring to Wilson as Theodore Wilson, he said, "I am not sure that I approve of the familiarity of 'Teddy.' It's rather like talking of 'Wally' Gieseking or 'Nat' Paderewski."

Benny Goodman, who was one of twelve little Goodmans born

in the Chicago ghetto, began his career as a professional clarinetist at the age of twelve by doing an impersonation of Ted Lewis, participated in many of the Red Nichols and Ben Pollack records cherished by hot enthusiasts, played in New York pit bands and radio studios, formed a large combination and went into Billy Rose's Manhattan Music Hall in 1934 and was featured, a few months later, on the Let's Dance program broadcast over NBC on Saturday nights, and considered himself a failure as a leader until his wild reception at the Palomar. When he opened at the Paramount Theatre in Times Square at 8:15 a.m. on January 26, 1938, he faced a crowd of 1500 people; many of them had been standing in line since five in the morning waiting for the doors to open. The first note from the band showed the truth of Samuel Taylor Coleridge's observation, "How inimitably graceful children are in general—before they learn to dance."

"From that moment on," the World-Telegram reported that afternoon, "things went loudly nuts. Couples started to shag in the aisles and the ushers couldn't do anything about it. When the aisles got too crowded, the couples marched on stage and continued their peculiar movements . . ."

Goodman's success, built partly on Fletcher Henderson's simple, swingy arrangements, produced profound, pervasive, and manifold changes. Leaders who merely waved a baton and smiled toothily at their listeners were replaced by instrumentalists on the high order of the Dorseys, Harry James, Bunny Berigan, and Count Basie, who featured their own talents, often building arrangements based on their own styles of playing. Swing bands offering jazz classics became the rage, while sweetish ones along the lines of the late Hal Kemp's suffered disastrous losses. Everybody who played an instrument raced to get in on the gold rush. Artie Shaw formed a band in 1937, and there is a story about the night Goodman dropped into the Lincoln Hotel to hear it. After listening to Shaw, who also played clarinet, lead his men through a set of Goodmanesque arrangements, Benny is reported to have turned to his companion and said, "All Artie needs are my glasses." Within a few years, however, Shaw became so satiated with the hysterical adulation of his fans that he publicly branded them "morons." By 1939 the situation had grown so repulsive to him that one day he abruptly quit his band and took off for Mexico on what turned out to be the most celebrated hegira in 1,317 years since Mohammed's flight to Medina. Instead of being wracked with uncontrollable grief, however, some of the musicians turned to Tony Pastor, an engaging vocalist, experienced instrumentalist and remarkably cheerful and considerate leader, who kept them near the top for a little longer.

The year of Shaw's desertion marked the first conspicuous success for Glenn Miller, who had been building his band since 1937. A trombonist who had played with Goodman in Ben Pollack's band and had arranged for the group of American musicians whom Ray Noble, the Englishman, used during his engagement at the Rainbow Room in 1935, Miller opened at the Glen Island Casino in the Spring of 1939 and was immediately installed as an idol. Within ten months he was playing to bigger audiences than any other band in the country. A few years later, when he was at the head of an Air Force band abroad, he was

lost during a flight over the English Channel. Meanwhile, swing was making big money for others—Jimmy Dorsey, Tommy's older and less excitable brother; Les Brown, a personable young Duke University graduate; Woody Herman, who inherited the leadership of the Isham Jones band in 1937; Harry James, a former circus trumpeter who had also worked for Goodman; Count Basie, a sparkling pianist who had migrated from Red Bank, New Jersey, and in Kansas City started his own band, which included some of the old Benny Moten group; Bob Crosby, a former vocalist with Anson Weeks and no musician (and, as such, an anomaly in an age of instrumentalist-leaders) who served as an amiable "front-man" for a group of gutbucket performers; Jimmie Lunceford, who had been a leader since 1929; and a great many others. Furthermore, some of the musicians (or, as they are known in the profession, sidemen) and female vocalists—notably a small, dark, vivacious girl named Helen Ward, who sang with Goodman—became celebrities in their own right.

Goodman featured the electrifying percussion performances of a handsome young Chicagoan named Gene Krupa, who had once studied to become a Jesuit and had arrived with Goodman by way of Mal Hallett and Buddy Rogers, a young man known as "America's Boy Friend" who, according to critics, "played all instruments, equally lousy." Every reader of Down Beat and Metronome, the two leading jazz journals, knew that Krupa was supposed to mutter "Lyonnaise potatoes and some pork chops!" over and over again while playing, opened doors with his left hand because he regarded it as undeveloped, and was studying tympani with Saul Goodman of the New York Philharmonic. Musicians were becoming figures of folklore, the stuff of legend.

Millions believed that Bix Beiderbecke carried his cornet in a brown paper bag, that one of his intimates was Babe Ruth, who found the doors of the Beiderbecke apartment so small that he used to take them off their hinges and set them aside whenever he wished to go from one room to another, that musicians who wanted to leave Joe Venuti, a man of bull-like strength and probably the most exciting of all hot violinists, were expected to earn their release by fighting him bare knuckles, that Goodman was referred to by his men as "The Ray" because of his habit of glaring at them when they played indifferently, that Tommy Dorsey had once, in a rage, broken his brother's instruments, that Muggsy Spanier, the eloquent cornetist, had a finger missing from his right hand, that when Eddie Condon, "dying" of a pancreatic infection in a private room in a hospital, was given a rectal injection of brandy, he looked up brightly and quipped, "See what the boys in the ward will have," and that the roughest of all band leaders, at least physically, was a fabulous Southerner named Blue Steele, who had a steel plate in his head and who lost his first fist fight when one of his musicians hit him with a microphone.

And along with the folklore, of course, there was West Fifty-second Street in New York. The places were the Onyx and the Famous Door and the Hickory House (and the Three Deuces and Kelly's Stables in Chicago), where, on Sundays, musicians had breakfast around four o'clock in the afternoon and then proceeded to "sit in" on some of the most stirring jam sessions in history. These were shrines and on their bandstands inspired

Music

By Philip Evergood

men took hot choruses that will probably never be duplicated. Now, of course, it's all gone. West Fifty-second Street is all big skyscrapers and the bands don't broadcast late at night the way they did in the blessed, barrelhouse years when Ellington's jungle would be on one network, Earl Hines' supple piano on another, and Fletcher Henderson's genius on a third, and all at the same time. The *aficionados* like the small groups, and if they want to hear the big bands they go to concert halls. Nobody dances in ballrooms any more."

Few bands swing as they used to, either. For, as usual, a good thing was overdone. By 1940 the market was awash with swing bands, most of them feeble imitations of the Goodman ensemble, with uninspired musicians who copied their betters note for note. As usual, too, when a good thing is overdone a reaction sets in. In this instance, the public grew tired of listening to nothing but swing at about the same time a great many musicians grew bored with playing it. Both were sated because, with the perfection of swing, jazz had reached a harmonic and melodic stalemate. It had begun repeating itself over and over again, with monotonous regularity.

Yet, again as usual, when a movement dies of its own weight another is always waiting to replace it. Even as the swing band leaders were wondering why they were no longer able to fill a ballroom, a group of rebellious and experimental musicians were laying the groundwork for a new music that was destined to lead jazz out of the blind alley into which it had unwittingly turned. These rebels were the founders of bop, and their Mecca was Minton's Playhouse, in South Harlem.

Trumpeter Harry James (opposite page) drummer Gene Krupa (top) and vibraphonist Lionel Hampton, three graduates of the Benny Goodman band who were among the most popular instrumentalists and band leaders during the big band swing era.

Setting for a revolution: Minton's, 1941

To contend that a revolution was wrought solely by one group of musicians, playing in one cafe, would oversimplify the matter, even romanticize it. No one could deny that many other musicians, playing in many other nightspots, made significant contributions to bop. But the fact remains that Minton's was far and away the most important single setting in the bop revolution. Every jazzman of importance in the movement played there at one time or another. And many, many more converts to the cause were won over at Minton's than at any other half-dozen spots. Indeed, considering that jazz today is a by-product of the revolution fomented at Minton's in the early Forties, it may well be the most important single shrine in the world of jazz.

Fortunately, the full story of Minton's Playhouse has been told. Ralph Ellison, amateur musician as well as jazz historian, was there, and his January, 1959, eyewitness report on manners, morals and music at Minton's in the pregnant days of the bop revolution is a classic of jazz literature.

It has been a long time now, and not many remember how it was in the old days; not really. Not even those who were there to see and hear as it happened, who were pressed in the crowds beneath the dim rosy lights of the bar in the smoke-veiled room, and who shared, night after night, the mysterious spell created by the talk, the laughter, grease paint, powder, perfume, sweat, alcohol and food—all blended and simmering like a stew on the restaurant range, and brought to a sustained moment of elusive meaning by the timbres and accents of musical instruments locked in passionate recitative. It has been too long now, some twenty years.

In the wee hours at Minton's, musicians came and went. Almost any jazzman who was anybody made his pilgrimage to the Harlem night spot to sit in and jam.

Above the bandstand there later appeared a mural depicting a group of jazzmen holding a jam session in a narrow Harlem bedroom. While an exhausted girl with shapely legs sleeps on her stomach in a big brass bed, they bend to their music in a quiet concatenation of unheard sound: a trumpeter, a guitarist, a clarinetist, a drummer; their only audience a small, cockeared dog. The clarinetist is white. The guitarist strums with an enigmatic smile. The trumpet is muted. The barefooted drummer, beating a folded newspaper with whiskbrooms in lieu of a drum, stirs the eye's ear like a blast of brasses in a midnight street. A bottle of port rests on a dresser, but it, like the girl, is ignored. The artist, Charles Graham, adds mystery to, as well as illumination within, the scene by having them play by the light of a kerosene lamp. The painting, executed in a harsh documentary style reminiscent of W.P.A. art, conveys a feeling of musical effort caught in timeless and unrhetorical suspension, the sad remoteness of a scene observed through a wall of crystal.

Except for the lamp, the room might well have been one in the Hotel Cecil, the building in 118th Street in which Minton's Playhouse is located, and although painted in 1946, sometime after the revolutionary doings there had begun, the mural should help recall the old days vividly. But the décor of the place has been changed and now it is covered, most of the time, by draperies. These require a tricky skill of those who would draw them aside. And even then there will still only be the girl who must sleep forever unhearing, and the men who must forever gesture the same soundless tune. Besides, the time it celebrates is dead and gone and perhaps not even those who came when it was still fresh and new remember those days as they were.

Neither do those remember who knew Henry Minton, who gave the place his name. Nor those who shared in the noisy lostness of New York the rediscovered community of the feasts, evocative of home, of South, of good times, the best and most unself-conscious of times, created by the generous portions of Negro-American cuisine—the hash, grits, fried chicken, the ham-seasoned vegetables, the hot biscuits and rolls and the free whiskey—with which, each Monday night, Teddy Hill honored the entire cast of current Apollo Theatre shows. They were gathered here from all parts of America and they broke bread together and there was a sense of good feeling and promise, but what shape the fulfilled promise would take they did not know, and few except the more restless of the younger musicians even questioned. Yet it was an exceptional moment and the world was swinging with change.

Most of them, black and white alike, were hardly aware of where they were or what time it was; nor did they wish to be. They thought of Minton's as a sanctuary, where in an atmosphere blended of nostalgia and a music-and-drink-lulled suspension of time they could retreat from the wartime tensions of the town. The meaning of time-present was not their concern; thus when they try to tell it now the meaning escapes them.

For they were caught up in events which made that time exceptionally and uniquely *then,* and which brought, among the other changes which have reshaped the world, a momentous modulation into a new key of musical sensibility; in brief, a revolution in culture.

So how *can* they remember? Even in swiftly changing America there are few such moments, and at best Americans give but a limited attention to history. Too much happens too rapidly, and before we can evaluate it, or exhaust its meaning or pleasure, there is something new to concern us. Ours is the tempo of the motion picture, not that of the still camera, and we waste experience as we wasted the forest. During the time it was happening the sociologists were concerned with the riots, unemployment and industrial tensions of the time, the historians with the onsweep of the war; and the critics and most serious students of culture found this area of our national life of little interest. So it was left to those who came to Minton's out of the needs of feeling, and when the moment was past no one retained more than a fragment of its happening. Afterward the very effort to put the fragments together transformed them—so that in place of true memory they now summon to mind pieces of legend. They retell the stories as they have been told and written, glamourized, inflated, made neat and smooth, with all incomprehensible details vanished along with most of the wonder—not how it was as they themselves knew it.

When asked how it was back then, back in the Forties, they will smile, then, frowning with the puzzlement of one attempting to recall the details of a pleasant but elusive dream, they'll say: "Oh, man, it was a hell of a time! A wailing time! Things were jumping, you couldn't get in here for the people. The place was packed with celebrities. Park Avenue, man! Big people in show business, college professors along with the pimps and their women. And college boys and girls. Everybody came. You know how the old words to the *Basin Street Blues* used to go before Sinatra got hold of it? *Basin Street is the street where the dark and the light folks meet*—that's what I'm talking about. That was Minton's, man. It was a place where everybody could come to be entertained because it was a place that was jumping with good times."

Or some will tell you that it was here that Dizzy Gillespie found his own trumpet voice; that here Kenny Clarke worked out the patterns of his drumming style; where Charlie Christian played out the last creative and truly satisfying moments of his brief life, his New York home; where Charlie Parker built the monument of his art; where Thelonius Monk formulated his contribution to the chordal progressions and the hide-and-seek melodic methods of modern jazz. And they'll call such famous names as Lester Young and Ben Webster, Coleman Hawkins; or Fats Waller, who came here in the after-hour stillness of the early morning to compose. They'll tell you that Benny Goodman, Art Tatum, Count Basie, and Lena Horne would drop in to join in the fun; that it was here that George Shearing played on his first night in the U.S.; of Tony Scott's great love of the place; and they'll repeat all the stories of how, when and by whom the word "bop" was coined here—but, withal, few actually remember, and these leave much unresolved.

Usually, music gives resonance to memory (and Minton's was a hotbed of jazz), but not the music then in the making here. It was itself a texture of fragments, repetitive, nervous, not fully formed; its melodic lines underground, secret and taunting; its riffs jeering—"Salt peanuts! Salt peanuts!" Its timbres flat or shrill, with a minimum of thrilling vibrato. Its rhythms were out of stride and seemingly arbitrary, its drummers frozen-

though we know that ideally anything is possible within a democracy, and we know quite well that upper-class Europeans were seriously interested in jazz long before Newport became hospitable.) All this is too much for memory; the dry facts are too easily lost in legend and glamour. (With jazz we are not yet in the age of history, but linger in that of folklore.) We know for certain only that the strange sounds which they and their fellows threw against the hum and buzz of vague signification that seethed in the drinking crowd at Minton's and which, like disgruntled conspirators meeting fatefully to assemble the random parts of a bomb, they joined here and beat and blew into a new jazz style—these sounds we know now to have become the clichés, the technical exercises and the standard of achievement not only for fledgling musicians all over the United States, but for Dutchmen and Swedes, Italians and Frenchmen, Germans and Belgians, and even Japanese. All these, in places which came to mind during the Minton days only as points where the war was in progress and where one might soon be sent to fight and die, are now spotted with young men who study the discs on which the revolution hatched in Minton's is preserved with all the intensity that young American painters bring to the works, say, of Kandinsky, Picasso and Klee. Surely this is an odd swing of the cultural tide. Yet Stravinsky, Webern, and Berg notwithstanding—or more recently, Boulez or Stockhausen—such young men (many of them excellent musicians in the highest European tradition) find in the music made articulate at Minton's some key to a fuller freedom of self-realization. Indeed, for many young Europeans the developments which took place here and the careers of those who brought it about have become the latest episodes in the great American epic. They collect the recordings and thrive on the legends as eagerly, perhaps, as young Americans.

Today the bartenders at Minton's will tell you how they come fresh off the ships or planes, bringing their brightly expectant and—in his Harlem atmosphere—startlingly innocent European faces, to buy drinks and stand looking about for the source of the mystery. They try to reconcile the quiet reality of the place with the events which fired, at such long range, their imaginations. They come as to a shrine; as we to the Louvre, Notre Dame or St. Peter's; as young Americans hurry to Café Flore, the Deux Magots, the Rotonde or the Café du Dôme in Paris. For some years now, they have been coming to ask, with all the solemnity of pilgrims inquiring of a sacred relic, to see the nicotine-stained amplifier which Teddy Hill provided for Charlie Christian's guitar. And this is quite proper, for every shrine should have its relic.

Perhaps Minton's has more meaning for European jazz fans than for Americans, even for those who regularly went there. Certainly it has a *different* meaning. For them it is associated with those continental cafés in which great changes, political and artistic, have been plotted; it is to modern jazz what the Café Voltaire in Zurich is to the Dadaist phase of modern literature and painting. Few of those who visited Harlem during the Forties would associate it so, but there *is* a context of meaning in which Minton's and the musical activities which took place there can be meaningfully placed.

The Mood of Minton's by Robert Andrew Parker

Jazz, for all the insistence of the legends, has been far more closely associated with cabarets and dance halls than with brothels, and it was these which provided both the employment for the musicians and an audience initiated and aware of the overtones of the music; which knew the language of riffs, the unstated meanings of the blues idiom, and the dance steps developed from and complementary to its rhythms. And in the beginning it was in the Negro dance hall and night club that jazz was most completely a part of a total cultural expression; and in which it was freest and most satisfying, both for the musicians and for those in whose lives it played a major role. As a night club in a Negro community then, Minton's was part of a national pattern.

But in the old days Minton's was far more than this; it was also a rendezvous for musicians. As such, and although it was not formally organized, it goes back historically to the first New York center of Negro musicians, the Clef Club. Organized in 1910, during the start of the great migration of Negroes northward, by James Reese Europe, the director whom Irene Castle credits with having invented the fox trot, the Clef Club was set up on West Fifty-third Street to serve as a meeting place and booking office for Negro musicians and entertainers. Here wage scales were regulated, musical styles and techniques worked out, and entertainment was supplied for such establishments as Rector's and Delmonico's, and for such producers as Florenz Ziegfeld and Oscar Hammerstein. Later, when Harlem evolved into a Negro section, a similar function was served by the Rhythm Club, located then in the old Lafayette Theatre building on 132nd Street and Seventh Avenue. Henry Minton, a former saxophonist and officer of the Rhythm Club, became the first Negro delegate to Local 802 of the American Federation of Musicians and was thus doubly aware of the needs, artistic as well as economic, of jazzmen. He was generous with loans, was fond of food himself and, as an old acquaintance recalled, "loved to put a pot on the range" to share with unemployed friends. Naturally when he opened Minton's Playhouse many jazzmen made it their own.

Henry Minton also provided, as did the Clef and Rhythm clubs, a necessity more important to jazz musicians than food: a place in which to hold their interminable jam sessions. And it is here that Minton's becomes most important to the development of modern jazz. It is here, too, that it joins up with all the countless rooms, private and public, in which jazzmen have worked out the secrets of their craft. Today jam sessions are offered as entertainment by night clubs and on radio and television, and some are quite exciting; but what is seen and heard is only one aspect of the true jam session: the "cutting session," or contest of improvisational skill and physical endurance between two or more musicians. But the jam session is far more than this, and when carried out by musicians, in the privacy of small rooms (as in the mural at Minton's) or in such places as Hallie Richardson's shoestring parlor in Oklahoma City—where I first heard Lester Young jamming in a shine chair, his head thrown back, his horn even then outthrust, his feet working on the footrests, as he played with and against Lem Johnson, Ben Webster (this was 1929) and other members of the old Blue Devils orchestra—or during the after hours in Piney Brown's old Sunset Club in Kansas City; in such places as these with only musicians and jazzmen present, then the jam session is revealed as the jazzman's true academy.

It is here that he learns tradition, group techniques and style. For although since the Twenties many jazzmen have had conservatory training and were well-grounded in formal theory and instrumental technique, when we approach jazz we are entering quite a different sphere of training. Here it is more meaningful to speak, not of courses of study, of grades and degrees, but of apprenticeship, ordeals, initiation ceremonies, of rebirth. For after the jazzman has learned the fundamentals of his instrument and the traditional techniques of jazz—the intonations, the mute work, manipulation of timbre, the body of traditional styles—he must then "find himself," must be reborn, must find, as it were, his soul. All this through achieving that subtle identification between his instrument and his deepest drives which will allow him to express his own unique ideas and his own unique voice. He must achieve, in short, his self-determined identity.

In this his instructors are his fellow musicians, especially the acknowledged masters, and his recognition of manhood depends upon their acceptance of his ability as having reached a standard which is all the more difficult for not having been rigidly codified. This does not depend upon his ability to simply hold a job but upon his power to express an individuality in tone. Nor is his status ever unquestioned, for the health of jazz and the unceasing attraction which it holds for the musicians themselves lies in the ceaseless warfare for mastery and recognition—not among the general public, though commercial success is not spurned, but among their artistic peers. And even the greatest can never rest on past accomplishments for, as with the fast guns of the old West, there is always someone waiting in a jam session to blow him literally, not only down, but into shame and discouragement.

By making his club hospitable to jam sessions even to the point that customers who were not musicians were crowded out, Henry Minton provided a retreat, a homogeneous community where a collectivity of common experience could find continuity and meaningful expression. Thus the stage was set for the birth of bop.

In 1941 Mr. Minton handed over his management to Teddy Hill, the saxophonist and former band leader, and Hill turned the Playhouse into a musical dueling ground. Not only did he continue Minton's policies, he expanded them. It was Hill who established the Monday Celebrity Nights, the house band which included such members from his own disbanded orchestra as Kenny Clarke, Dizzy Gillespie, along with Thelonius Monk, sometimes with Joe Guy, and, later, Charlie Christian and Charlie Parker; and it was Hill who allowed the musicians free rein to play whatever they liked. Perhaps no other club except Clarke Monroe's Uptown House was so permissive, and with the hospitality extended to musicians of all schools the news spread swiftly. Minton's became the focal point for musicians all over the country.

Herman Pritchard, who presided over the bar in the old days, tells us that every time they came, "Lester Young and Ben Webster used to tie up in battle like dogs in the road. They'd fight on those saxophones until they were tired out, then they'd

put in long distance calls to their mothers, both of whom lived in Kansas City, and tell them about it."

And most of the masters of jazz came either to observe or to participate and be influenced and listen to their own discoveries transformed; and the aspiring stars sought to win their approval, as the younger tenor men tried to win the esteem of Coleman Hawkins. Or they tried to vanquish them in jamming contests as Gillespie is said to have outblown his idol, Roy Eldridge. It was during this period that Eddie "Lockjaw" Davis underwent an ordeal of jeering rejection until finally he came through as an admired tenor man.

In the perspective of time we now see that what was happening at Minton's was a continuing symposium of jazz, a summation of all the styles, personal and traditional, of jazz. Here it was possible to hear its resources of technique, ideas, harmonic structure, melodic phrasing and rhythmical possibilities explored more thoroughly than was ever possible before. It was also possible to hear the first attempts toward a conscious statement of the sensibility of the younger generation of musicians as they worked out the techniques, structures and rhythmical patterns with which to express themselves. Part of this was arbitrary, a revolt of the younger against the established stylists; part of it was inevitable. For jazz had reached a crisis and new paths were certain to be searched for and found. An increasing number of the younger men were formally trained and the post Depression developments in the country had made for quite a break between their experience and that of the older men. Many were even of a different physical build. Often they were quiet and of a reserve which contrasted sharply with the exuberant and outgoing lyricism of the older men, and they were intensely concerned that their identity as Negroes placed no restriction upon the music they played or the manner in which they used their talent. They were concerned, they said, with art, not entertainment.

But they too, some of them, had their own myths and misconceptions: That theirs was the only generation of Negro musicians who listened to or enjoyed the classics; that to be truly free they must act exactly the opposite of what white people might believe, rightly or wrongly, a Negro to be; that the performing artist can be completely and absolutely free of the obligations of the entertainer, and that they could play jazz with dignity only by frowning and treating the audience with aggressive contempt; and that to be in control, artistically and personally, one must be so cool as to quench one's own human fire.

Nor should we overlook the despair which must have swept Minton's before the technical mastery, the tonal authenticity, the authority and fecundity of imagination of such men as Hawkins, Young, Goodman, Tatum, Teagarden, Ellington and Waller. Despair, after all, is ever an important force in revolutions.

They were also responding to the non-musical pressures effecting jazz. It was a time of big bands and the greatest prestige and economic returns were falling outside the Negro community —often to leaders whose popularity grew from the compositions and arrangements of Negroes—to white instrumentalists whose only originality lay in the enterprise with which they rushed to market with some Negro musician's hard-won style. Still there was no policy of racial discrimination at Minton's. Indeed, it was very much like those Negro cabarets of the Twenties and Thirties in which a megaphone was placed on the piano so that anyone with the urge could sing a blues. Nevertheless, the inside-dopesters will tell you that the "changes" or chord progressions and the melodic inversions worked out by the creators of bop sprang partially from their desire to create a jazz which could not be so easily imitated and exploited by white musicians to whom the market was more open simply *because* of their whiteness. They wished to receive credit for what they created, and besides, it was easier to "get rid of the trash" who crowded the bandstand with inept playing and thus make room for the real musicians, whether white or black. Nevertheless, white musicians like Tony Scott, Remo Palmieri and Al Haig who were part of the development at Minton's became so by passing a test of musicianship, sincerity and temperament. Later, it is said, the boppers became engrossed in solving the musical problems which they set themselves. Except for a few sympathetic older musicians it was they who best knew the promise of the Minton moment, and it was they, caught like the rest in all the complex forces of American life which comes to focus in jazz, who made the most of it. Now the tall tales told as history must feed on the results of their efforts."

Dizzy Gillespie, one of the high priests of the Minton era.

A new cool generation

The bop revolution was, of course, an even more shocking departure from the past than the revolution that marked the change from ragtime to classic jazz. For example, collective improvisation, basic to swing, required stable chord lines. But the bopsters broke violently with this concept, to go adventuring outside the standard, accepted chord progressions. In addition, they instigated the still-continued search for longer and freer melody lines, greater harmonic resources, fresh contrapuntal ideas, and new rhythm concepts that is now freeing jazz of the monotony of two-beat Dixieland and four-beat swing.

Unfortunately, though, in the first, or bop, stage of this search, radical departures from past norms were often treasured more for their radicalism than for their validity, and many of the early searchers were far too inclined to exploit technique and forget content. As a result, bopsters were too often instrumental exhibitionists ("I can do more with an eighth note than Armstrong can with a quarter one"). And their music was often only a loud and frenzied misinterpretation of the new musical language introduced by Parker, Gillespie, and the other inspired innovators who broke ground for today's jazz.

Under the circumstances, a conservative reaction was inevitable, and it appeared in the Fifties in the form of "cool" jazz, a movement which still has its adherents. In the mid-Fifties, critic Arnold Shaw made an analysis of the nature and content of cool jazz. To his way of thinking, the differences between hot and cool jazz are as vivid as the contrast between live steam and dry ice. This is a new generation in full, earnest revolt against the generation of twenty years ago. The musicians call themselves *hip* to make certain that you won't confuse them with the Dixieland *cats*. They disapprove of exhibitionism, and the hunger for audience approval. "Moldy fig" is the term of opprobrium that they hurl at the hot fans. Then they retreat to a jazz played for one's self instead of an audience, played for listening and not for dancing, played without a beat to express many moods, some of them thoughful and uneasy.

Hot jazz, Dixieland and swing, was (and is) happy music. It had bounce, spirit, movement, kaleidoscopic colors. The cats who played it grimaced, sweated, contorted, shouted, stamped, worked themselves into a lather. The dancers hopped about like crazy, screamed approval, urged the boys on, and went frantic. Hot jazz was (and is) a music of action, excitement, confusion, but, above all, of release.

In violent contrast, cool jazz is introspective. It is a state of numbness. The musician—Lennie Tristano at the piano, Stan Getz on tenor sax, or Cal Tjader at the vibraphone—is a study in still life. At the peak of "coolness" he betrays no emotion whatever. This is the musical mind seeking order out of chaos and fearful of discovering only a void. "That's cool, real cool," alto saxist Lee Konitz might say of a guitar solo by Billy Bauer. But the very expression is restrained. For this is a cult of passivity, contemplation, uneasiness, withdrawal.

"Hot" tone was (and is) racy, raucous, off center, and frequently downright dirty. The clarinet giggled. The tenor sax growled. The alto was suggestive and nostalgic. The trumpet piped, barked and chittered. In contrast, cool tone is calm, collected and controlled.

In appearance, "hot" jazzmen presented the mobile picture of people enjoying themselves. Like the dancers whom they exhorted and stimulated, they leaped about, "bent" with their notes, and vibrated with the beat. Center of this violent display was the hide-beater—a Gene Krupa, Dave Tough, Cozy Cole, Buddy Rich, or Big Sid Catlett—a contorted mass of bouncing ergs, the mouth hanging open, the jaws grinding convulsively.

The "cool" crowd presents the contrasting picture of a group of bank clerks immersed in their digital operations. The bodies are relaxed and the faces run the gamut from quiet concentration to apparent indifference and apathy. In the earliest stage of cool jazz, say 1950, the musicians made a fetish of wandering on and off stage as if they had forgotten something and were not sure where to find it.

Cool jazz aims at the mind and heart, rather than the feet. It is heavier—more complex and intricate—than Dixieland or swing. Cool musicians do not believe in the supremacy or omnipresence of "the beat." They substitute what we might call a "listening beat" for the dance beat. Neither do they limit themselves to the conventional forms of the popular song or the blues. Nor do they stick to the traditional instrumentation of the Dixieland combo—clarinet, trumpet, trombone, piano, bass and drums.

A cool quintet, for example, may consist of piano, vibraphone, guitar, bass and drums. Quite naturally, it produces music that is soft, insinuating and tender, and usually cerebral. Variations of accent spice the melodies subtly and coolly in standard tunes like *Don't Blame Me* and *September in the Rain*. Modern chords flavor ensemble choruses with the whole-tone impressionism of a Debussy or the tart harmonies of a Stravinsky. Improvised solos are delicately thought-out studies in tone color. And the little smile of George Shearing lights up his face as an accolade of a soloist's cool artistry.

Improvisation, the essence of all jazz, plays a significant role with the cool contingent. Only instead of being an expression of excitement, as it was with the Dixieland and swing bands, it now expresses a musician's sense of structure, color and form. Chords and counterpoint have become basic, instead of rhythm. Reason

Pianist Lennie Tristano, intellectual exponent of the Progressive movement.

and knowledge count, not feeling. And the elaboration of a musical idea to its logical conclusion is considered the highest achievement. (No wonder a customer can't talk!)

The over-all contrast of hot and cool jazz is well delineated in recent statements of two top jazz musicians. "We want to bring back that old roar [of the Herman Herd]," Chubby Jackson said, in speaking for the hot jazz of the new Jackson-Harris quintet. "There's been too much coolness in jazz. We want to bring back that old feeling when music was anything but cool, when it was exciting. Dynamics have been fluffed off too long. Suppose I talk to you all the time in a monotone? And we have humor. Tongue-in-cheek humor. We poke fun at ourselves and we entertain."

To which Dave Brubeck, brilliant cool pianist, retorts with a big, wide smile full of upper teeth: "Makes me sick to see a young kid playing Dixie . . . if that's all he can play . . . Now take a group like Lennie Tristano's, which added onto the feeling of freedom in Dixie, made it atonal, the chord progressions more intriguing and challenging. . . . But for a young kid to become a two-beat musician? Well, that's like a concert pianist studying Bach all his life, ignoring Bartók, Schönberg, Hindemith, Stravinsky, Milhaud."

If this contrast of cool and hot jazz suggests that the cool boys are on the studious side, it is not without point. Austin High School in Chicago was the breeding ground of many of the top hot musicians of the Thirties and Forties, among them Jimmy McPartland (cornet), Dick McPartland (guitar), Frank Teschemacher (clarinet), Bud Freeman (tenor sax). The cool crowd tends to be college-trained. Pianist Dave Brubeck received his B.A. degree at the College of the Pacific and wrote a string quartet toward his thesis for his M.S. at Mills College. Lennie Tristano received his Bachelor of Music degree at the American Conservatory in Chicago and completed all requirements for the M.A. except the final exams. Cool jazz also shows the influence of both modern art and music. Brubeck has studied with the French longhair composer Darius Milhaud. Clarinetist John LaPorta has been a student of the German modernist Ernst Toch. Saxophonist Lee Konitz spends many hours with the canvases of modern contemporary painters.

Perhaps the most colorful and influential individual in the cool school is pianist Lennie Tristano, who was born in Chicago in 1919. His eyesight, weak at birth, was dimmed by a severe attack of measles. By ten, when he was sent to a state institution for the blind, Lennie's natural aptitude for the piano had developed to a point of high skill. Despite the serious limitations of the institution, Lennie flourished both as a student of music and mathematics. When he was ready for college, he entered the American Conservatory in Chicago, and secured his Bachelor of Music degree in three record-breaking years.

From the moment he stepped out on his own, Lennie avoided the obvious path of commercial band music and orthodox jazz. Even though he had the technical proficiency to surpass many of the most successful jazz pianists, Lennie chose to pursue his own promptings toward a new type of jazz. It was not an easy path to follow. Lennie was fired from a number of jobs and drove several nitespot managers crazy with such innovations as playing in several keys at once. Nevertheless, Lennie was not to be distracted from his calling and surrounded himself with

a group who played important roles in launching cool jazz.

Some of these—Lee Konitz (alto), Warne Marsh (tenor), Billy Bauer (guitar), Arnold Fishkind (bass)—and Lennie may be heard on a number of records, including *Intuition*, made as an experiment in which Lennie and his disciples recorded the spontaneous interplay of their musical ideas. The resulting music is complex, contrapuntal and polyrhythmic—a wedding of crewcut feeling and longhair thinking—in short, cool jazz. Other records include *Subconscious Lee* and *Judy* (with Lennie, Konitz, Bauer, Fishkind and Shelly Manne); *Speculation* and *Through These Portals*, with Lennie, Bauer, Fishkind and John LaPorta.

"All the devices of serious music," Dave Brubeck has said, "can be incorporated into jazz." As an instance, Dave cites his arrangement of *The Way You Look Tonight*. "First comes the intro—two horns just playing counterpoint; then, still with the two horns playing counterpoint, I put in *The Way* on the piano.

"In the bridge, I changed the chords 32 times in a row, just to keep it moving harmonically. And then at the end of the tune, to make it have more unity, I put the first eight bars and the bridge together.

"That's a trick as old as Mozart in classical music, and one used by Stravinsky, Milhaud, Bartók and other contemporaries."

When a record company released an LP disc to highlight the Battle of Jazz *Hot vs. Cool*, they selected Dizzy Gillespie as one of the leaders of the cool contingent. While Lennie Tristano would applaud the musicianship of Diz, he would be vaguely troubled by the choice. There is no question that "bop," with which word John Birks Gillespie of Cheraw, South Carolina, is largely synonymous, was the first stage of the cool revolt against Dixieland and swing. But bop, which was at its peak in 1947, was largely regarded as a corpse in 1950 when the cool crowd was beginning to ride high.

Lennie Tristano himself early paid tribute to the fresh stream of ideas that bop poured into jazz (and incidentally articulated some of the ideas that were to become basic in his own later brand of cool music). "Bebop is diametrically opposed," he said, "to the jazz that preceded it (swing as applied to large groups and Dixieland as applied to small ones). Swing was hot, heavy and loud. Bebop is cool, light and soft. The former bumped and chugged along like a beat locomotive; this was known in some quarters as drive. The latter has a more subtle beat which becomes more pronounced by implication."

From a technical standpoint Lennie approved the boppers. They improved the melodic line by adding new chords to the jazz vocabulary. They contributed new ideas by emphasizing scales rather than arpeggios (an arpeggio limits melodic invention by merely restating the underlying chord). They made it possible for a soloist to invent while he played because the rhythm section used chordal punctuation instead of pounding. "A chorus of bebop," Lennie explained, "may consist of any number of phrases which vary in length. It may consist of one or several ideas. The music is thoughtful."

Some of these qualities of Dizzy's style may be heard in the M-G-M platter *Hot vs. Cool*. Gillespie and his Birdland Stars' treatment of four tunes—*How High The Moon, Muskrat Ramble,*

The Saxophonist

By Larry Rivers

The Modern Jazz Quartet; standing, (l. to r.) John Lewis, Percy Heath, Kenny Clarke, sitting, Milt Jackson; epitomize the cool detachment of modern jazz.

Battle of Blues and *Indiana*—is immediately contrasted with hot versions played by Jimmy McPartland and his Dixieland stars. These contrasting versions make clear that boppers opened the door to the cool cohorts by their assault on two- and four-bar riffs, their use of inverted rhythms (powerful upbeats instead of conventional downbeats), and their introduction of new chords and intervals, particularly the flatted fifth.

But bop early became the image of one man and his music. Tristano himself commented at Dizzy's prime on what he called "the little monkeymen" who were stealing Dizzy's phrases note for note. "Whether they play drums, saxophone, piano, trombone or glockenspiel," he wrote, "it still comes out Gillespie." And a triplet used by Dizzy in an early solo, *Salt Peanuts* became the oft-repeated "eel-ya-da" of bop. The first and third notes of the triplet were an octave below the second, and the accent—unlike triplets generally—fell away from the first note and landed on the second and third.

The ascendancy first of bop and then cool jazz occurred in the years after World War II. These were years that were also marked by a strange but steady decline of the dance bands. The war years (1941-45) had been a lush period for dance music, with the nation jitterbugging to band grosses as high as $145,-000,000 a year. The end of the war suddenly saw the process go into a reverse spin. This is a signal change emphasizing that "coolness" is the keynote, not merely to a musical cult, but to the generation that came to maturity in the postwar years.

The fact is that by 1949 the demand for dance music had sunk to such a low that hundreds of bands, including outstanding aggregations such as those of Benny Goodman, Harry James and Gene Krupa, were compelled to fold. Ballroom operators as well as band leaders began crying the blues. Teenagers were not going to dances. And when they went, they did not dance. They just stood around the bandstand, hands in pockets, and listened. Or they sat around and talked and drank pop, while the middle-aged folks—the dancers of the Thirties—took to the floor.

Down Beat once devoted an entire issue to the still-unsolved problem of the dance-band decline. "We lost a generation of dancers a few years ago," said Freddy Martin, who has ridden out the rug-cutting depression. "The kids who were born in the early Thirties when reaching their teens were listeners instead of dancers. They had been brought up on a diet of vocals and bop. Now, in their early twenties, few of them can really dance..."

Harry James, whose swing band folded, had a similar explanation: "Today's younger generation doesn't dig the dance jive. Until a big, fat majority of young people get the urge to dance again, instead of standing in a trance watching a singer, there won't be any appreciable upswing in the dance business..."

But what has happened to the urge to dance? And what has caused it to deteriorate? A clue is, perhaps, to be found in a statement of cool pianist Dave Brubeck. "The important thing about jazz (cool, that is) right now," he said, "is that it's keeping alive the feeling of the group getting together. Jazz, to make it, has got to be a group feeling and a group feeling for everyone concerned at the time.

"In other words, when we're playing well, I consider the audience as important a factor as the guys on the stand...It's too bad that they don't dance to jazz any more so that it becomes a complete group expression."

From this statement one might deduce that swing music and dancing were at their peak when group feeling was most unified, when a sense of unity in the group was at its peak. With the decline of that sense—with a breakdown in group feeling—the urge to dance has deteriorated. Thus, the isolation and detachment of listening have replaced the emotional unity of dancing.

The plain fact is that the generation which has come to maturity in the years since the end of World War II is puzzled, troubled and confused. Buffeted by fierce winds set in motion by the atom bomb, it has yet to find its direction. Codes of conventional conduct have been shattered by previous generations. Sex taboos are gone. Standards of decency and morality have yielded blatantly to "big-money" yardsticks. New concepts of time and space have destroyed traditional ideas of man's place in the universe. New instruments of motion and communication have changed conventional concepts of home. And in the face of new weapons of destruction, the danger of another world holocaust persists.

In this troubled time, the young generation is like an army going into a battle from which it will not flinch but which it is not prepared to fight. To cover its uneasiness, it tries to muster a hard, tough exterior. Internally, it seeks to cultivate a compensatory attitude of withdrawal and reserve. In a world of uncertainty, numbness is the perfect state. Don't plan, don't hope, don't feel—and you won't be disappointed.

The Lost Generation also faced a world of mounting tensions and a future of tremendous uncertainty. But the young people of the Twenties somehow had the capacity to lose themselves in dizzy flights from reality. The cool generation is more uneasy, more concerned, and apparently too troubled to laugh it off. When its efforts to remain calm, collected and cool break down, it turns to marijuana to narcotize its fears.

These turnings and churnings of the younger generation are well documented in a number of recent books. A novel, *Corpus of Joe Bailey*, depicts the decline in sexual morality and the increase in alcoholism of a generation that has little faith in the future and no sense of direction in the present. The terrible sense of being unable to take control of this jet-plane world, hurtling God knows where, is brought out in a statement by Joe Bailey's wife. "We're all caught," she says. "Maybe somewhere along the line our children's children's children won't be, but we are."

Like the cool musicians daring an audience to like them, the cool generation is fighting neglect with neglect. Fearful that it may be turned down, it will make no bid for acceptance. Convinced that it will be taken, it will not commit itself emotionally to anything. Uneasy and cynical, it tries to be, like the new jazz, detached, calm, and withdrawn. In a word, cool—real cool, man."

Today, things are no longer as cool as they once were. The cool musician's disdain for his audience and the self-conscious pose of aloofness his audience adopted have been recognized for what they largely were—pretentious affectations—and rejected by all but the most intransigent diehards. Nevertheless, the

Pianist Horace Silver, devout modernist, plays Progressive jazz with the passion of a revivalist.

cool movement has been of immeasurable value. Whatever their excesses, its musicians destroyed the myth that jazz is by its very nature a visceral music. In their somewhat frantic pursuit of the cerebral and the elusive, the cool men proved that scholarly musicianship is a rich asset to a jazzman, and that "thinking" on an instrument and improvising in a contemplative mood can produce fresher and more exciting new sounds than any ever born of gin and marijuana.

Furthermore, while the modern musical language introduced by Parker and Gillespie still continues to dominate jazz, the cool musicians were the first to demonstrate how infinitely flexible this language can be. In a sense, then, they blazed the beginnings of the path into the new musical terrain further explored by the cultists who soon succeeded them—the "hard bopsters" like Horace Silver, Art Blakey, the Adderley brothers, and Sonny Rollins and John Coltrane, who often tried to weld a modern technical approach to the blues and other primitive jazz forms; the neo-classicists like John LaPorta, Charlie Mingus, Lennie Tristano, the Sandole brothers, and others who have endeavored, in part, to strike some sort of a balance between jazz concepts and twentieth-century classical music; the neorockers like Miles Davis, Herbie Hancock, Chick Corea

and Freddie Hubbard, whose use of electronics won over young, theretofore non-jazz record buyers and concert goers; and "the new thing" musicians like Ornette Coleman and Don Cherry and others whose atonal search for "musical freedom" has won them wild applause and shrill derision in about equal parts.

Much of today's *avant-garde* jazz may sound to some, especially to musically untrained listeners and jazz diehards, like technical exercises, with the more tolerant perhaps applauding the spirit of the adventure while decrying its musicality. But the listener would be wise not to dismiss these new sounds with prejudice; a few receptive listens might reveal traces of true jazz hidden under that technical veneer.

On the other hand, many of these experimenters should realize that many a young student can write a fugue, alter chords to make them polytonal, manipulate rhythms to accent offbeats, assemble a piece in two- or three-part counterpoint, etc. But making music that is meaningful—be it modern or traditional, cool or hot—is another matter entirely. At stake is the enrichment of jazz, not its alteration into an entirely new form of music. Duke Ellington's admonishment will always hold sway: "It don't mean a thing if it ain't got that swing!"

Part Three

The Giants of Jazz

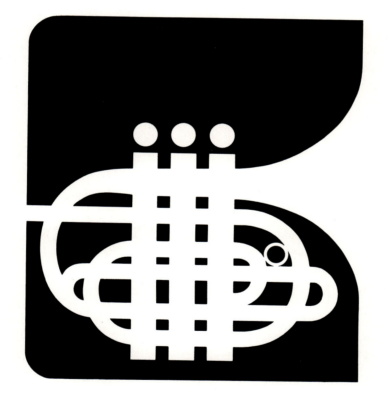

The three faces of Satchmo

Louis Armstrong was that rarest of rare things, a living legend in his own time; the most talked of, written about, imitated, and revered figure in the entire history of jazz. Of all the giants of jazz, he is probably the only one whose story is known to every jazz-minded individual in the world. Yet there are facets of Louis that still remain little-known, as Leonard Feather revealed in March, 1955.

Louis Armstrong has been around for sixty-three years, but there are very few people who know all three of him. The world's best-known jazz musician, the man I think of as Louis II, is familiar to record collectors, music students and historians as someone whose influence among his contemporaries has been incalculable, whose magistral horn and nutmeg-grater throat have been enjoyed in person by audiences from Tokyo to Stockholm. Even better known is Louis III, the show-business personality, the symbol to whom the adjectives "beloved" and "inimitable" are invariably applied, the clown whose antics were immortalized when Hollywood made a character actor out of him in movies such as *Pennies From Heaven*.

The least-known of Satchmo's three personalities is Louis I, the human being, the Negro, among his own people, born and raised "Back O'Town" in New Orleans' toughest years; Louis the family man, the idol of his friends and neighbors.

The real Louis, partially exposed to the American public when Prentice Hall published his autobiography *(Satchmo: My Life In New Orleans)*, has been more clearly visible to those who have been with him in his home town during the Mardi Gras celebrations.

One Mardi Gras Eve, Mayor "Chep" Morrison of New Orleans, entertaining Louis III as guest of honor, made a short speech bestowing on him an honorary citizenship and the keys to the city.

"I understand," said the mayor, "that all you wanted to do was fulfill your ambition to be King of the Zulus in the Mardi Gras parade, and you'd be ready to die. Is that true, Satchmo?"

"Yes, Mr. Mayor," replied Louis III, "but there ain't no sense of the Lord taking me literally!"

A few minutes later, the wisecracking front was down and he became Louis I again, preparing to realize an ambition he had once described in a letter to a friend:

The Zulu Social Aid and Pleasure Club was the first colored carnival club to get together in New Orleans. The club has been together for generations and consists of the fellows in my neighborhood. The members were coal-cart drivers, bartenders,

waiters, hustlers, etc.—people of all walks of life. Nobody had very much, but they loved each other . . . and put their best foot forward in making a real fine thing of the club. I am a lifelong member and it was always my ambition to be elected King of the Zulus some day.

Perhaps Louis' first dream of becoming king began to mature while he watched the kings of the white section of the parade:

I'd see them get off their fine launches in the Mississippi, looking like a million—which most of 'em had. And the king would get up on his float, which was waiting for him by the river, and the parade would be on.

When he made the picture *New Orleans* in 1946 and was invited to attend the world *première* in New Orleans during the following year's Mardi Gras, he came close to realizing his ambition, as he later reported:

The day of the parade—I was right in the middle of that mess —b'lieve that. . . . On that day—you know—the Zulu King arrives in the New Basin Canal. . . . This year they had around six or seven floats. . . . The king rides in the first float. . . . I was on the float with the king and they really did gas me no end. . . . You should have seen me bowing and waving to the folks and cats as they cheered at the sight of me (their home boy). . . . Oh, it's only great. . . .

They were serving the king nothing but champagne . . . and every time he raised his elbow—I raised mine right along with him. . . . And—er'wer-ump—I gotten so full of champagne until I thought I was seeing two floats with a gang of kings and Satchmos on it . . . Haw Haw Haw. . . .

Two years later, in 1949, Louis himself was King of the Zulus.

Shrove Tuesday fell on March 1. Two nights earlier, the Zulus presented Louis and his group (featuring Earl "Fatha" Hines, Jack Teagarden, the late Sid Catlett and Velma Middleton) in a concert at Booker T. Washington Auditorium. During the show several dignitaries of the Zulu Social Aid and Pleasure Club, after a series of fluorescent speeches, crowned Louis king, while Bernice Oxley, buxom, brown-skinned ticket taker at a local theatre, became queen. It was the first time in the thirty-three-year history of the club that the Zulus, whose objectives included the provision of a decent burial for dues-paying members, had reached out to bring a nonresident member home for coronation, instead of the customary local merchant, porter or undertaker. This year's king was the boy who had started in New Orleans on the Fourth of July in 1900 and had gone out to conquer the world.

To the Zulus it was Louis I who was being honored. To the mayor who gave Louis the keys to the city (without specifying where they would and would not admit him), it was Louis III, a personality for whom the parade's logical theme song would have been *There's No Business Like Show Business*, rather than a a rollicking New Orleans march.

There were many local citizens who made sure that the trumpet king would live his Louis I life on the visit. A motley group paraded to his hotel room on the morning of the parade, making it fairly clear that their visits, in the most tattered clothes they could find, had a motive beyond courtesy. I recalled what Louis had once told me about the many benefactions that were in-

evitable corollaries of every trip home:

I always lay a little scratch on grandma—alongside of the long line of cousins and stepbrothers and sisters I have down there. . . . And there's my real sister Beatrice (Mama Lucy) Armstrong . . . I greases her mitts real heavy.

While Louis took care of the indigent well-wishers, the parade streets were lining solidly with Negro citizens and an occasional white. The balcony in front of the Gertrude Geddes Willis funeral home, a major stop en route, was packed to the last square inch, since it overlooked the grandstand that was to receive the king and queen.

A little later the babble in the streets grew slowly to pandemonium as the parade drew up and Louis' float came into full view.

Louis I, now King of the Zulus, was an unforgettable sight. The Armstrong features had been caricatured almost beyond recognition, converted into a travesty of music-hall blackface through huge white circles around his eyes and mouth. He wore a crown, a long black wig, a red-velvet tunic trimmed with gold sequins, a yellow cellophane-grass skirt, black tights and high golden shoes. He had a big cigar in his mouth and carried a silver scepter in his left hand. Never in history, ancient or modern, had any man looked less like a king.

As Louis made his way slowly to the upper echelons of the funeral home, a frail little old lady edged her way through the crowd to receive a royal hug. It was Mrs. Josephine Armstrong, Satchmo's grandmother, bearing her ninety-one years with pride as she embraced her triumphant grandson. Newsreel cameras whirred as reporters clamored and Zulu acolytes tendered *canapés*. The spirit of the celebration had reached its height and Louis I was in his glory. This was not Broadway's King Louis, nor the Louis who had played for Europe's royalty, nor the Louis for whom they had lined the streets of Tokyo with flowers. This was the coal-cart-running kid they used to call Dippermouth before he went up to Chicago to join Joe (King) Oliver's band and start on the road to fame back in 1922. This was the king who had returned to his own castle and was its elected, honored master. . . .

Louis II needs no such colorful setting as a Zulu parade. He is more at home around a phonograph, or a small gathering of serious-minded fans. Louis II, the jazzman, the purists' idol, is the personality most of his foreign audiences expect to see, and it was this Louis, almost unspoiled, who appeared on his first European tour in 1932. In subsequent visits Louis III began to peek in more and more often from behind the curtains as novelty songs like *Ol' Man Mose* and *Brother Bill* began to edge out the old *echt*-jazz favorites of the *West End Blues* and *Tiger Rag* variety.

Many of his fans in Germany and France, where the jazz cult reaches its most fantastic extremes, refuse to recognize any but their esteemed Louis II when Satchmo comes to town; to them "My Satchmo, right or wrong" has become a cry of battle.

Fifty policemen had to be called in to quell an incipient disturbance in Hamburg; and when Louis played Toulouse, the rival jazz factions started a three-way riot between the

The gay, clowning personality of Satchmo fails to obscure the most elegant jazz mind in history.

"squares" who had come to see Louis III clowning, the purists who were there to study Louis II, and an anomalous third party that seemed to be at loggerheads with both.

Louis II has been a storm center in the past decade as a result of the split between traditionalist and progressivist jazz fans. Casting his lot with the old-timers, he has come out volubly against the beboppers and all modern musicians who play what he calls "jujitsu" music.

Recently a visitor to the modestly comfortable house in Corona, Long Island, where Louis lives with his fourth wife, Lucille, a former Lew Leslie chorus girl, found him engrossed in a Guy Lombardo record. Purist fans of Louis II are constantly embarrassed by his sincere affection for Lombardo, whom he ranks along with the late Bunk Johnson and Joe (King) Oliver as one of the true musical idols of his life. It is as if e.e. cummings were to come out for the poems of Nick Kenny.

"People ask me what's my favorite band," he said as he took the record off, "and when I tell 'em Guy Lombardo they won't believe me. I've been a Lombardo fan ever since he started back in Cleveland in the 1920's. When we were working in Chicago we'd always rush back home to catch the late-night Lombardo broadcast.

"Man, those Lombardos are keeping music alive—helping to fight them damn beboppers. They're my inspirators! When I had my big band twenty-five years ago we tried to get our sax section to sound like Lombardo's—listen to our records of *When You're Smiling* and *Sweethearts on Parade*."

After he had shown the visitor through his library of tape recordings (he is an avid collector and has transferred hundreds of jazz records to tape, including many broadcasts of his own band), Louis was persuaded to listen to some records of modern jazz.

"Now that's what's causing music today to go bad," he said, after studying a performance by Shorty Rogers, a trumpeter who reflects the far-out influence of Miles Davis. "Didn't any of those guys end up their solos on the nose? They tried to be out of this world. They're played for musicians."

This sounded like Louis III trying to take over. Louis II liked nothing better than to play for musicians during his halcyon years; but when Louis III plays, the whole world tunes in.

The split personality became more evident when Louis went to work one day during mid Fifties at Basin Street, a night club off Broadway.

In the dressing room at the club that evening Louis II sprawled on a wooden chair. He had a patch of cotton over his mouth, another over one eye, and an eyecup over the other eye. His head was inclined far back as he bathed the eye while "Doc" Pugh, his dour-faced Negro valet, prepared his clothes.

"I'm tired today," said Louis. "Been down to Columbia Records. They had some nice open spots on the tapes, where I could fill in behind my vocals—dub in some horn accompaniment." He hummed a few phrases and chuckled. "Man, a cat came in from Columbia and said we gotta make some more of these. It was an album of W. C. Handy's blues. Mr. Handy came in too and listened to all the records.

"They're perfect—they're my tops, I think. I wouldn't call them Dixieland—to me that's only a little better than bop. *Jazz music*—that's the way we express ourselves." He picked up his horn and blew a long, lingering legato phrase. "You know what this is?" he said. "It's *Duna—little stars of Duna call me home.* I remember playing that with Erskine Tate back at the Vendome Theatre in Chicago. I like to warm up my chops with things like that—it brings back memories of those pit-band days. One day," he recalled as Pugh helped him to struggle into his jacket, "they offered me an extra $25 to do that number on stage, and I was too scared to do it."

It was almost time for Louis' first show and the dressing room by now was crowded with intruders: an Argentine newspaperman, a photographer from a Negro magazine, and a drunken woman who had been standing in a corner listening.

"Go on talking, don't stop," said the woman. "I just love to hear you talk. Isn't he just superb?" she said to nobody in particular.

"Come on, let's get the pictures," said Louis a little impatiently to the photographer.

It was clear that Louis II's time was running out and that Louis III had to do a show.

Satchmo conferred hastily with Pierre "Frenchy" Tallerie, a corpulent white man who has been his capable road manager since 1942, then he got up from his chair and strode out of the dressing room and walked on stage as the crowded club applauded him.

It was Louis' opening night at Basin Street; Red Buttons, the comedian, was there, Betsy von Furstenberg and John Hodiak and Don Budge and all the big shots from Decca and Columbia were there, Aly Khan was there with Joan Fontaine. They had all come to see Louis III, and that was just what he gave them.

He played his theme, *When It's Sleepy Time Down South*, and then told the audience, "We're gonna lay some of them good ol' good ones on ya," and pretty soon he had clarinetist Barney Bigard taking a vocal, and then he introduced Billy Kyle, his pianist, as "Liberace in Technicolor," and the audience loved it. He grinned and mugged, and exchanged pleasantries with members of the audience—"Old Braud out there, he was playing bass when I was selling newspapers!"

This was the Louis III who wrote in his book, "I have always loved my white folks," and proved it by giving them just what they expected; the Louis of whom Murray Kempton once said, "He endures to mix in his own person all men, the pure and the cheap, clown and creator, god and buffoon." It was the Louis who, guest-starring on the Dorsey Brothers' television show, had said over a network microphone, "Don't play it too fast, and not too slow—just half-fast." It was the Louis III who, signed for a joint concert tour with Benny Goodman (by someone who was under the impression he was signing Louis II), insisted on having Velma Middleton do the splits when they played at Carnegie Hall, and followed it up with an unprintable joke. This was Louis the Inimitable Personality—"Louis, like the River

Satchmo in Sunset

By Art Kane

Mississippi," as Kempton said, "pure like its source, flecked and chocked with jetsam like its middle, broad and triumphant like its end."

But when he put his horn to his lips, there was still enough of Louis II to please the minority segment of the audience. The minority comprised those who were here to see the man who had shaped jazz and set it on its global path—the man of whom it was said, "No matter how a jazzman may play, there's a little bit of Armstrong in all of 'em."

Louis Armstrong's three lives have merged and overlapped many times, but it is clear to anyone who has studied all of them that the greatest of these three is Louis II—the real Satchmo, the man who blew the horn heard around the world, before Louis III found out the world was listening."

Clarinetist Edmond Hall and Satchmo "chase" each other in scat-singing chorus.

Tragic young man with a horn

Most would argue that following Armstrong, the next ranking legend in jazz is that of Bix Beiderbecke. The tragic tale of this shy, introverted, self-taught cornet player whose genius was recognized while he was still in his teens, and whose untimely death at 28 was due to a combination of alcoholism and pneumonia, is now firmly entrenched in the folklore of jazz. Myths have even grown up around his name—for instance, because he sometimes carried his horn in a corduroy draw-string bag we now have the fable that Bix habitually carried his cornet in a grocer's brown paper bag in order to give his indispensable bottle of gin the full protection of his instrument case.

In addition, there are two versions of the legend where Bix's alcoholism is concerned. One claims that his death was simply the end product of excessive carousing, of his uncontrolled appetite for willing wenches and bathtub gin. The second version is more sophisticated. It makes a point of the unhappy fact that for most of his musical life Bix was forced to play with sweet bands in order to earn a living. For example, with Paul Whiteman, who hired him because he could play so much. Actually he was asked to play very little and could rarely indulge in the inspired improvised solos which were the breath of life to him. Consequently, he was driven to drink by artistic frustration. As his frustration mounted he drank more and more, until, in the end, he destroyed himself.

Which version comes nearer the truth? Was Bix no more than a debauchee? Or was the sad young man who spent the last year of his life in a dingy hotel room, playing the piano and stumbling out at intervals to get another bottle, one more in the long line of defeated artists whose inability to adjust to reality drove them down the path of self-destruction?

A few years ago, Belgian jazz historian Robert Goffin made a trip to Lake Forest Academy, where Bix briefly attended school, to learn what he could of Bix's behavior during the crucial, formative years of his short life. It was a unique piece of historical research, and on the basis of Mr. Goffin's findings there seems to be little doubt as to which version of the legend is correct. Obviously music was all that ever mattered to Bix. All else was incidental as Mr. Goffin's portrait of Bix as a teen-ager revealed in March, 1944.

The Academy of Lake Forest, Illinois, is a beautiful red brick edifice near the Lake Michigan shore, about thirty-five miles from Chicago. In 1921, when new pupils were entering school, the old students and the professors looked around at the new faces with a kind of doleful curiosity. One, a professor by the name of R. P. Koepke, who had been born in Strassbourg, had studied in Paris and Berlin and now taught French and Spanish, was energetic as well as curious and circulated from group to group.

He approached a group of three more or less bewildered new students chattering in a corner. He noted one of them especially —a boy with an open face, hair pulled straight back, a striped tie and a sports jacket with patch pockets. "What's *your* name?" asked Koepke.

"Bix," replied the boy.

"What, 'Bix'?"

"Bix. That's my Christian name. My full name is Leon Beiderbecke."

"Where do you come from?"

"I live in Davenport, Iowa, 1934 Grand Avenue."

"What's your father's name?"

"Bismarck."

The other students smiled then and Koepke looked up sharply.

"Yes, Bismarck Beiderbecke!" the boy repeated.

Koepke hesitated a moment. "Have you a hobby?" he said at last.

"Yes. Music!"

"Very good! I'll put you in the college orchestra. What do you play?"

"The cornet."

"Can you play Sousa's marches?"

"No!" said the boy firmly. "I prefer jazz."

Everyone laughed—except one senior named Walter Earnest Welge, from Evanston, Illinois.

Thus young Bix Beiderbecke entered the second year at Lake Forest Academy—that is, the Lower Middle Class. Next morning he found himself before Latin teacher Arthur Edgington, with exactly thirty other students. Most of them came from Illinois. Bix immediately found two students who came from Iowa: John Graydon, Jr., and Howard Strahan. During recreation periods they were often seen together, but very soon Bix made other friends who, like himself, were crazy about music.

There was the young Welge, who was called "Cy" and who played the drums; and above all, there was the fellow who became Bix's best friend—Samuel Sidney Stewart, Jr., from Flint, Michigan. Both were students in the Senior Class and, at the end of the year, in 1922, when the class elected the best musician of the year, Stewart got eighteen votes, Bix three, and Welge two.

According to the testimony of Arthur Edgington, the only professor who knew Bix and is still at Lake Forest Academy, it was obvious from that first day in school that Bix had little interest in academic studies. Two things were necessary to his existence: sports and music. At the opening of the school year, the Orange and Black baseball team was decimated by the departure of the Senior Class. They needed new members. *Caxy,* the school annual, later reported:

"As the date of the first game approached, the one finally decided upon consisted of Magnuson or Lipe.... Pattison and Welge won their right to roam the pastures, and Beiderbecke and Covert became the recognized utility men."

There were two football clubs, one "Orange" and the other "Black." Stewart played in one, Bix in the other. Thus music came to the rescue of sport.

That year music took on considerable importance in the Academy. Professor Koepke was an energetic organizer and he got together a symphony of forty players. Bix played the cornet.

In midwinter they gave a grand concert. I've seen the program and it begins with *Lake Forest, Go!*, a double-quick march composed by leader Koepke. He was interested in classical music and therefore didn't consider Bix very brilliant for, when there was a cornet solo, it was conferred not on Bix but on another pupil by the name of E. Parker, who rendered *In Old Madrid*.

Bix was already specializing. His technique was too individual to be accepted by a conservatory amateur like Koepke. Where Bix stood without peer was in the little dance orchestra composed of two violins, Sargent and S. Smith; two cornets, Parker and Beiderbecke; three saxophones, Stewart, Haysen and F. Wagner; one trombone, Rising; and a drummer, Cy Welge.

Bix lived in the northwest corner of East House, on the second floor. It was a very natty little room but little by little his love of music transformed it into a conservatory. When he wasn't busy in football or baseball practice, Bix exercised with his friends in his room and they often kept it up at high pitch until the neighbors complained. Then Stewart would be quiet, Cy would keep time very gently on the study table and Bix would stuff the bell of his trumpet with a handkerchief or hand towel. And when night came and it was impossible to play an instrument, Bix would open his old portable phonograph, stop up the loudspeaker with a towel and in almost totally smothered tones he would play some record of the Original Dixieland Band. Bix would close his eyes and keep time until he was tipsy with rhythms and counter-rhythms — the rhythms which came to govern his life and lead him into immortality.

Should someone drop in, Bix would light up one last cigarette and go down to the first floor where he tried to play tunes on the piano which wouldn't be heard all the way up to the sleeping quarters. At that time it was the slow melancholy of *Margie*, the magic of *St. Louis Blues*, the speed of *Tiger Rag*, the improvisations of *Nobody's Sweetheart*—and in the course of his various visits to dance halls, Bix had heard a tune which bewitched him and which he transformed little by little into a melancholy composition called *In a Mist*.

One evening at a dance in Evanston a young man in the crowd was amazed at Bix's solos and came to talk with him during the intermission. It was Milton Mezzrow. He discussed the power of this new music which had swept over Chicago. He spoke of the Original Dixieland, King Oliver, and especially the New Orleans Rhythm Kings and the fine high frenzy they created each evening at the Friar's Inn.

The next morning Bix talked it over with Cy and they decided that one night a week they would sneak out of the Academy after supper, look up Mezz in Chicago and hear this new orchestra in which the trombonist, George Brunis, and the clarinetist, Leon Rappolo, were musical divinities.

They saved their last pennies and when they finally arrived at the Friar's Inn they sat dumbly behind their wine glasses while the Kings—the Nork, as they were called—played the new tunes: *Angry, That Dada Strain*, and *Shimme-Sha-Wabble*. It was the small hours when Cy went back on the North Shore Electric. The huge, bare trees of Lake Forest shivered in the cold damp wind blowing in from Lake Michigan. The boys slid along behind the bushes, reached the back door which they had taken care to leave open, and arrived at the Academy just in time for the rising bell!

From that day on Bix's life was changed. Not only did his courses in science and mathematics hold no more meaning for him; George F. Sisler, the history professor, described the beauties of Egyptian inscriptions in vain, for Bix was dreaming of the cornet solo of Paul Mares in *Swanee* or the gurgling of the trombone in *Aggravating Papa*.

Even sports, which had been so important to him, no longer interested him. The director of physical education, Ralph Robert Jones, who had hoped to make a star of Bix, forgot him completely, and even today when a certain "Bix" is mentioned Jones can't remember him. The immortal cornetist has been washed from his memory by twenty-five school generations of baseball and football players.

Little by little, Bix dedicated all his time to jazz. He skipped physical exercise to play the cornet; the Academy coach was especially piqued about it, because he often took saxophonist Stewart or drummer Cy Welge along with him.

When none of his pals would allow themselves to be seduced away, Bix the siren, crazed by jazz, would sit alone at the old piano and practice the then-popular tunes of Jelly Roll Morton; or else he would improvise music which no one could have recognized.

The report in "Social Events" of *Caxy* noted that on October 29th, "Bix Beiderbecke, one of our 'home talent', furnished the music which was declared to be unexcelled by his fellow students."

On November 26th a dance was held in honor of the victorious football team. The same magazine again mentioned the excellence of the music in its notice:

"The gym was very appropriately decorated in orange and black with multicolored Japanese lanterns giving a rainbow of light. L.F.A. banners, pennants, and pillows were, of course much in evidence while on the wall facing the entrance to the gym, a huge black paper football with the inscription *Champions 1921* served to increase the spirit of celebration.

"Under the leadership of two L.F.A. students, Beiderbecke and Stewart, the orchestra turned out feats of musical skill which everyone declared excellent. As a privilege, the pianos were allowed to be moved from the balcony, where they generally are to a corner of the dance floor. This greatly increased the tone and pep of the music and was well appreciated."

At the next party the appearance of *Bix-Wally Orchestra* was noted again, while on the 17th of February, for a third big ball *Caxy* briefly, but pleasantly, said:

"Bix-Wally's music lived up to their reputation by turning out wonderful music."

Between times, Bix was a member of the Academy in theory only. He had formed, with Cy Welge, an orchestra called *Cy-Bi*

Orchestra in which young musicians from Chicago played. Several times a week they went to Evanston or Waukegan or Milwaukee, thus collecting the dollars which enabled Bix to flee each evening to Chicago where the gods of jazz breathed into genuine trumpets and trombones of gold. At the Academy, Bix's room became nothing more or less than a record library. Students knew that the room in the northwest corner was a temple of hot music and counterpoint.

Bix often skipped classes, study periods and morning exercises and when he did appear, usually after spending the night on a dance engagement or improvising, his sound sleep was disturbed only by the recitation of his fellow students. The school principal soon noticed Bix's frequent absences. Bix was told to appear before John Wayne Richards, the Headmaster. Mr. Richards gave the young sophomore a round scolding and informed him that at the first recurrence of such absences he would be summarily expelled from the Academy.

After this warning Bix looked up Stewart and Cy and the three held an earnest counsel of war. He showed them his list of coming dance engagements in neighboring villages. Stewart submitted meekly to the school's ultimatum while Cy and Bix decided to live the adventure out.

The month of April arrived. The editors of *Caxy* entered an agreement with Bix through which he paid them to publish this advertisement to appear at the end of the school year in June:

FOR YOUR DANCE
CY-BIX ORCHESTRA
• • •
CY WELGE
711 Central Street
Evanston, Illinois
• • •
BIX BEIDERBECKE
1934 Grand Avenue
Davenport, Iowa

On May sixth, 1922, there was the big celebration of the Junior Prom, but on that day Bix and Cy had a paying engagement in Gary and couldn't appear at the Academy. Somewhat huffily, *Caxy* reported that "Bill Green and his Northwestern orchestra supplied the best music that had been heard at the Academy for a long time."

This write-up appeared in June alongside Bix's advertisement. Then a farewell party was held in the Academy court. Members of the Senior Class were celebrating their graduation. Stewart and Cy were there but Bix, brave sophomore, was not. He who had rallied the sporting spirit of the professional corps, he who had been a good companion if not a good student, he who had brought school dances to life, was no longer a student of the Academy of Lake Forest.

It happened thus:

About the middle of May, the Headmaster learned that Bix was leaving the Academy every night to play dance engagements. On May 17th, he tried to call Bix into the office but, as a crowning misfortune, Bix was away from school on that particular afternoon. That evening, John Wayne Richards, returning from a party about midnight, went to see for himself what was going on in Bix's room. The room was empty.

Two days later, Bix again failed to answer a summons. On the 20th, he slept all day, not appearing at a single class or school meeting. So, on the 21st of May, Bix, with his eyes still half closed, marched unhappily into the office of the Headmaster who told him furiously that he was no longer a member of the Academy. Bix didn't cry. He became a little paler than he already was and left the office whistling *Aggravating Papa*.

Returning to his room, he met Stewart and Cy and told them the news. He gave one big sigh and began to pack up his records and books. He thought, said Bix, that that evening he would go to hear a trumpeter who had just come to Chicago: Louis Armstrong!

Thus it was that in June Bix was not among his friends. He had been expelled from the Academy. But the school annual had been printed and it was too late to cut out the name already bound for immortality.

The teacher, Ed Arpee, who showed me the rare and treasured documents, added:

"This just proves that the best way to become an excellent collegian is sometimes to leave college. But that's a recipe only for geniuses. It's best that the others do their regular four years in the Academy."

Oscar Pettiford by Bruce Mitchell.

More than flying fingers

Of all the jazz greats mentioned so far, Art Tatum is in all probability the one least appreciated by the general public. He made few records for the major, well-distributed companies; was seldom heard on the radio or in concerts; and appeared mostly in small clubs, where his speed alone impressed the square listeners.

But as his fellow musicians recognized, Tatum was far, far more than a "fast" piano player. To them he was one of the true wonders of the musical world, possessing a fantastic technique and an unbelievable harmonic originality. At the time of his death in 1956, in fact, among musicians he was almost universally regarded not only as the world's finest piano player but also as the unexcelled jazz soloist of his day, regardless of instrument.

Some idea of Tatum's greatness, and of the awe that he inspired in lesser pianists, is conveyed in Leonard Feather's October, 1944, description of a visit he made one night to the Three Deuces, to hear Tatum play:

"Step inside," yelled the fat little doorman, "and hear the world's greatest pianist."

I stepped inside and found the dark little 52nd Street club crowded with pianists, breathlessly watching the man they all call the world's greatest—Art Tatum.

The admirers who sat watching him were unstinting with their superlatives. Sitting over in a corner, Duke Ellington declared himself too entranced by the music to offer a comment. Soft-voiced Mary Lou Williams, at a front table, asserted, "Tatum does everything the other pianists try to do—and can't." Bill Roland, Raymond Scott's pianist, said, "I can't talk —I'm shaking with excitement."

"Man, I better not come in here too often," murmured Eddie Heywood. "That man plays so much piano it sounds impossible. The more I hear him, the more I want to give up the piano forever and drive a milk truck." Said Teddy Wilson, sitting with Heywood, "Art was great when I first heard him, in 1928, but his style is more rhythmic, better integrated today. He's not only the greatest jazz pianist ever—there are very few concert artists who have his abilty."

"There are only two ways you can take him," Clyde Hart summed it up. "You can be nuts about Tatum, or you can be jealous as hell of him."

There are many good reasons why musicians hold these truths about Tatum to be self-evident. He is the apotheosis of jazz; he is the art of modern rhythmic music, of hot jazz, swing, syncopation, at its ultimate. His genius is so apparent that even those who have no musical understanding of what he does are content to be dazzled by his technique. What makes Tatum great, however, is *not* his technique; it's the incredible flow of brilliant rhythmic and harmonic ideas that this technique enables him to express.

How Tatum reached this pinnacle is anybody's guess. His background is not remarkable. He was born and raised in Toledo, and was the only musician in his family. After studying several years with one Overton G. Rainey, a local teacher, he planned on a career as a concert pianist, but was counter-influenced by hearing Fats Waller and Lee Sims on the air. Some experience at a local radio station, WSPD, was followed by his first trip to New York in 1930, accompanying a singer, Adelaide Hall, with whom he made his first records (*I'll Never Be the Same, This Time It's Love.*)

In January, 1943, he joined Tiny Grimes, an electric guitarist, and Slam Stewart, the fabulous bass player who improvises endless choruses *con arco* and simultaneously hums them in a supernatural voice. This trio was as great collectively as its leader was singly. There was a welding of ideas, a blending of the instruments' tone colors, and an understanding between the three men that few jazz trios have equaled. All three had a sense of musical humor that expressed itself in the form of quotations from odd sources, inserted as part of the variations on another theme. The fact that you might hear snatches from *Yankee Doodle, It Ain't Necessarily So* and *The Campbells Are Coming* during the Tatum version of *The Man I Love* does not add to his greatness, though sometimes he subjected these tunes to fascinating harmonic and melodic changes in order to fit them into the pattern of the main theme.

More important is the fact that Art had a touch of unbelievable lightness. The tone he produced from a piano, the agility of his right-arpeggios, the magnificent rhythmic underlinings of his bass work all owe as much to this deftness of touch as to his natural feelings for jazz style and phrasing.

Tatum had neither the manner nor the appearance of a great artist. His hoarse voice, his loping gait, his infinite capacity for taking beers give no hint of the delicacy and fitness of his work. He has the reputation of being temperamental, though surely it would be surprising if he showed no sensitivity about the drunks who blabbed while he played, or the squares who asked for *Flying Home* after he had just played it for seven minutes.

Variously described in the press as half-blind (*Time*), three-quarters blind (*Le Jazz Hot*), blind (*Colliers*, etc.), his left eye was completely closed and he saw dimly out of the right. His vision was impaired in an accident at birth, and he never read music. Most of his front teeth were missing. Down from 230 to 180 pounds in his recent years, he retained a healthy appetite but ate irregularly. After getting through work at 4 a.m., he was likely to wander to some obscure Harlem house party and play until noon.

Like many great jazzmen, Tatum had a set routine on most of his numbers. A series of ideas which he improvised or worked out on *Sweet Lorraine* or *Body and Soul* may stay the same, note for note, night after night, but they retain the same rhythmic spirit as if they were improvised. On the other hand, his Blues records with Joe Turner, which are among his greatest performances, were almost completely extemporized.

Tatum has been compared with, and in some cases admired by, such people as Horowitz and Godowsky. Oscar Levant's *A Smattering of Ignorance* tells of a party given by Gershwin to exhibit him before several prominent guests. But the praise that has most significance is the praise of fellow jazzmen. They know that Mary Lou Williams' comment hit the nail on the head.

Art Tatum, greatest virtuoso of the jazz piano.

The
diligent
Duke
As a musician, leader, arranger and composer, Duke Ellington exerted more influence on more phases of jazz than any other person in history, and it is doubtful that anyone else will ever match his prodigious contributions.

He is also one of the most misunderstood jazzmen of our day. Thanks to some possibly well-meant but certainly mis-informed stories, the impression has gotten abroad that the Duke is simply a half-primitive genius who scribbles his music on scraps of paper and lets his band finish the composing in a wild-free-for-all at rehearsals.

To set the record straight, here is an authoritative profile of the Duke, by biographer Harry Hess.

Out of the maelstrom of good and bad, of honest and phony that has stamped the brief history of jazz music, few personalities have emerged to match the sincere, inspired musicianship of Duke Ellington. The Duke is at once alive and a legend. His cult of admirers clings to music in the Ellington fashion with a tenacity as constant as the Gulf Stream. Unlike the mercurial tribes of hot-music addicts who worship first at one swing altar and then at another and who sometimes desert the just cause to sing hymns of praise for the merchandisers of schmaltz, Duke's fans are stayers. If anything, their admiration for Ellington grows deeper and more mellow with the years.

Duke is one of the rare quadruple-threat men in jazz; he is outstanding as pianist, arranger, leader and composer. But for all his merit in the first three of these occupations, it is as a composer that he makes his bid for permanence in the music world.

Since tossing off his first composition as an adolescent back in Washington, D.C., he has written more than two thousand songs. A few of these like *Black and Tan Fantasy, Mood Indigo, Solitude* and *Reminiscing in Tempo*, are landmarks in jazz history. Most of the others, like *Blue Celley*, which was written to commemorate Duke's hiring a new band manager named Al Celley, are not well-known to the general public.

Because he has written an average of approximately one hundred tunes a year for over two decades, Duke has acquired a reputation as a musical speed merchant. Many of his fans visualize him ripping off compositions in a few minutes while waiting for trains or resting between stage appearances. Actually his best tunes are the result of much hard work and thought, although the theme of a song may come to him on the spur of

(Top to bottom) Harry Carney, Johnny Hodges, Russell Procope, Paul Gonzales

the moment. By the time the new song is ready for his band to play, Duke, the members of his band, and nearly everyone else remotely associated with him have labored long and lovingly. Even then his tunes are always in the process of being rearranged to include some new effect discovered during rehearsals or performance. In his first recording of *Mood Indigo*, Duke went so far as to write an arrangement that utilized a slight humming sound made by early carbon microphones, and his friends freely admit that if he thought it would add to his music, he could find a use for almost any sound including that of a flight of honking geese. His ceaseless drive toward perfection and his willingness to experiment have kept his band at the top ever since they moved into New York's Cotton Club in 1927.

Although Duke is certainly no formula composer, the birth of an Ellington tune invariably occurs in one of two ways. Either he sees something he thinks ought to be expressed in music, or some member of his band noodles a few inspired bars that remind him of some experience he felt deeply. The sight of a forlorn little girl sitting in her window waiting for a playmate who didn't come inspired *Mood Indigo*, and a few bars of improvised melody that Juan Tizol, a former valve-trombonist with the band, played while he was practicing between shows, developed into *Caravan*. *Sophisticated Lady* evolved from a character Duke dreamed up. "She's a Harlem schoolteacher," he says in describing her. "Colored, sure . . . but she's been to college. Maybe she's done some graduate work. Her father is a doctor. One summer he gives her money to go to Europe. She comes back cultured . . . likes to visit art museums and go to concerts. So I try to put all that in the music. I make her sophisticated but I keep her a little bouncy and ragged around the edges."

Once Duke has released an emotion in a three- or four-bar phrase, he may whip the idea into a composition at one sitting. More often, though, he allows the original phrase to ferment in his mind, enlarging on it, changing tempo and key, cutting and adding, listening for usable passages from his men, and asking the advice of anyone who can offer an intelligent opinion. The mental fermentation may go on for hours or days, even weeks or months. Then suddenly Duke has what he wants and he hurriedly writes out the song complete with melody and harmony. *Solitude* was written in twenty minutes while Duke and his band were waiting to get into a recording studio. But no one knows how long the germ of the tune thrived in his mind before he entered that studio.

An Ellington composition isn't wrapped up until it has been arranged for his band. That explains why Duke's stuff never sounds quite right when performed by another band. Duke explains this by saying: "When I write a tune I write it for *my* band to play. I write to my musicians' style. A musician's style is his boundary. There's a definite person behind every instrument and unless you keep him in mind when you're writing he loses his perspective."

The musicians themselves have the final word. They get their say in a jam session that can best be likened to a conference where the conferees talk on trumpets, wood winds, strings and percussion.

These sessions usually take place early in the morning after

A pensive Duke pauses at rehearsal while musicians (opposite page) await his new idea.

the band has finished an engagement. When Duke arrives he is welcomed by the unrestrained sounds of his men running the scales, practicing tricky passages, or just noodling. He calls for order and if he's lucky he gets it within ten or fifteen minutes. Then he passes out *his* arrangement. As each musician receives his copy of the music he begins to experiment. By the time the last sheet is on the last music stand, a wild ruckus has broken out and that takes another ten or fifteen minutes to subside.

Then Duke gives them a four-bar intro on piano and the band plays through the arrangement for the first time. Invariably it satisfies no one and touches off another series of verbal explosions. Duke yells for order in a high-pitched voice that sounds like an adolescent handicapped by a quinsy throat. One by one the musicians play suggested revisions for passages they don't approve of. Phrase by phrase they tear the arrangement apart and put it together again. Each revision brings fresh objections. Perhaps by the time the sun is well up in the sky, the band has reached a tenuous agreement and a basis is laid for the library arrangement. Before long even that arrangement will be annotated with numerous changes resulting from a continual stream of suggestions voiced or improvised every time the band plays the number. Actually Duke worries that someday he may become completely satisfied with something.

Once a piece is in the band's repertoire, Duke temporarily loses interest in it and begins working on something new. Although his methods of composing and the environment in which he writes are highly colorful and would make good material for a romantic story on the life of a composer, Duke refuses to engage in self-dramatization and is inclined to regard the picturesque version of a composer as the stuff of which Hollywood shorts are made.

Duke Ellington was born in Washington, D.C., on April 29, 1899. His parents named him Edward Kennedy, and it wasn't until his teens that high school companions nicknamed him Duke because of the haberdashery he affected. The Ellington family lived comfortably on the income of Duke's father, a naval blueprint expert with the government, and Duke remembers the affable surroundings of his boyhood with considerable pleasure, having celebrated it numerous times in music. By the time he was seven his mother had arranged for a woman he alternately recalls as Mrs. Klingsdale or Mrs. Klinkscale to give him piano lessons. But it developed that his interest in piano was confined to inventing strange chords that excited him with their weird off-tone, minor qualities, and Mrs. K at last abandoned her losing battle to make young Ellington practice legitimate exercises. Time proved that Duke was on the right path, for his dissonant

banging was the foundation of a nonconformist style that later was to distinguish his music.

When he entered high school, Duke was far from an accomplished pianist but he had invented enough chords to combine them in a composition of his own. In honor of getting a part-time job as soda jerk in a local hangout, called the Poodle Dog Café, he titled his improvised theme *Soda Fountain Rag*. Students who frequented the Poodle Dog and heard him play it on a reluctant piano in many different rhythms and keys thought he was a pretty sharp musician.

Duke was a good student, showing such talent in art that he was offered a scholarship to a commercial art school upon graduation. But he rejected the scholarship in favor of a job with a Washington band leader who used a combination of five pianos in a sixty-piece orchestra. Duke had learned enough about music since his Poodle Dog days to hold the job, but his exuberant improvisation during orchestrated rests got him fired. He wandered from band to band, searching for an outfit that would allow free play to his urge for hot improvisation. Finally he gave up and formed a five-piece hot band of his own.

The Ellington hot five, known as the Washingtonians, found their name city unfriendly if not definitely hostile to jazz. After unsuccessfully trying to change the musical tastes of capital café society, the Washingtonians pulled stakes and moved to New York. Manhattan swallowed them and for approximately six months their fame was limited to a select group of Harlemites who frequented "rent parties" or "parlor socials." These were midnight-'til-dawn affairs held for the very practical purpose of paying the host's rent through the generous donations of his guests. Generosity was stimulated by hot piano music and prohibition spirits. The "rent party" pianists were semi-professional musicians whose economic status put them on an equal plane with the Washingtonians, and whose virtuosity was limited only by their capacity to remain conscious. Duke, who prides himself on being able to recognize genius in a Harlem gin mill as well as in Carnegie Hall, assiduously studied their many styles and added immeasurably to his vocabulary of hot phrases and tempos.

It was during these lean months that Duke began to add to his knowledge of musicology by an eclectic process of begging information from anyone who had it. Without time or funds to study formally, he sought out musicians, song writers, pit orchestra men, singers, and occasionally private teachers to tell him what he needed to know. His most dependable and prolific sources were a famous Negro violinist named "Doc" Perry, and Will Marion Cooke. Duke's payments for Doc's tutoring sessions were long taxi rides in Central Park during which Perry conducted the class by humming phrases and chord components which he then asked his charge to rearrange for desired effects. At nights, the theoretical knowledge acquired during afternoons of touring through Central Park was tempered in the hot furnace of the rent parties.

The Washingtonians' six-month Manhattan interlude of the empty purse and full soul ended with the hot five accepting a spot in a Times Square bistro called the Kentucky Club. This engagement lasted four years, during which Duke increased his band to its present size, and managed to meet and impress most of the notables of the entertainment world. One thing led to another and by December of 1927, after the band had recorded a number of Duke's original compositions and made several radio broadcasts, the Cotton Club waved a contract. The Washingtonians, who had long since dropped their name in favor of none at all, arrived in style. Since then Duke and his band have been constantly in the public eye.

It is difficult to consider Duke Ellington the composer without also considering Duke Ellington the band leader. His band is a constant source of inspiration; without it his music would lose flavor. This partly explains why Duke doesn't drop his band and devote all of his time to composing. Each of his sixteen musicians is a master of his instrument and as a unit they make up the most versatile jazz band in the world. They consistently lead or place high in polls conducted to determine the nation's best hot musicians, and have constantly astounded listeners by their ability to play far beyond the usual limits of their instruments. When Duke and the band toured Europe in 1933, 1939, and again in 1950, critics sang their praises in ecstatic columns that purported to find an infinity of sublime nuances and eternal truths in their music. These European critics, who accord jazz the same deference most American critics reserve for the classics, found it hard to believe that in his own country Duke and his musicians divided their time playing five to seven shows a day at vaudeville houses, and playing night clubs, dance halls, private parties and recording engagements.

Ellington has a relatively small but fanatically loyal set of fans. They include college professors, politicians, movie actors, dry goods clerks, streetcar conductors and ferryboat captains.

Duke's records sell so regularly that they enjoy somewhat the same prestige as a book-club selection—they are practically subscribed in advance. Unlike some band leaders, Duke feels a personal attachment to each of his admirers and has been known to spend several hours at a stretch answering questions for the faithful.

As a show-business figure, Ellington is fortunate in being the kind of man who is everything to everybody. To those of his admirers and associates who expect him to be the prototype of the Negro jazz musician as popularly conceived, he is gay, carefree and "sharp." He dresses well, owning an extensive wardrobe of clothes that mostly combine good taste and flash. His suits have been estimated to number as low as forty and as high as two hundred, and if they've never helped him to write a note or play a lick, at least they've given him a lot of publicity. He is a sucker for sartorial inspiration and will on occasion travel twenty miles to buy a different "big fat" knit tie. He talks like the layman's conception of a jazzman, too. His conversation can become so laced with jive talk that even a hep high school freshman cannot understand him.

Duke's more sanguinary fans are appeased by the constant disorganization of his life which borders on utter confusion when he plays a crowded schedule of one-night stands and five-a-day vaudeville engagements. (He'll add to this chaos now and then when he and his band will descend on an obscure hole in the wall and join the local band to play out the night and half

the next day in a wild jam session.) Reporters who like to prove that genius is eccentric are gratified to note that Ellington has an appetite which comes close to lacking control; that he goes to his doctor four times a year for a complete physical checkup with several interim visits for imagined ailments; that he has an abnormally low pulse beat; that he possesses a flamboyant attitude toward the "chicks;" that he cultivates a disregard for punctuality; that he will go without sleep for several days at a time; and that he will spend hours developing a tune and balk at spending a few minutes to write a thirty-two bar lead sheet.

On the other hand, those of Duke's fans who stress the deeper aspects of a man's personality are not disappointed in Ellington either. They find him to be well educated, with an insatiable curiosity for further knowledge. He reads extensively in history, poetry, music, literature and religion. He has a simple, unshakable belief in God, has gone through the Bible on an average of once a year, prays every night, and wears a plain gold cross around his neck, a habit that several of his musicians have been inspired to copy. He often writes poetry and imaginative prose and, when circumstances dictate, he drops the jive idiom in favor of carefully-phrased sentences that combine a wide command of words with the spontaneity of his dressing-room conversation. When he speaks of something he feels deeply, he achieves the cadenced music of poetry, and he has developed a mature philosophy of quietude and acquiescence to the turmoil and intolerance of the world that permits him to enjoy life to the fullest while catching few of its punches. Friendliness surrounds him like an aura and he is equally at home among the impecunious relatives of one of his musicians or among the habitués of one of Europe's prewar salons. He believes in democracy, living it himself. His manners know no dividing line of race, nationality or creed, and in his dressing room between shows an heiress might find herself sitting next to a tattered little colored boy from PS-89.

Like many composers who have achieved success writing popular music, Duke Ellington nurtures an ambition to compose serious works. He long has considered writing an opera tracing the history and struggles of his race. This, however, is still in the planning stage. But otherwise he has notably fulfilled his ambition. Over the years he has introduced many tone poems and concertos at his many Carnegie Hall concerts, among them *Deep South Suite, Black, Brown and Beige, Blutopia, Blue Bells of Harlem* and *Liberian Suite.* He also introduced a suite entitled *Harlem* at a Metropolitan Opera House concert in 1951. And his band was combined with the Symphony of the Air for the premiere of his *Night Creature* at Carnegie Hall in 1955.

A few years ago, Duke heard the siren call of Hollywood when a film company hired him to write the score for a serious movie on jazz. Nothing came of it though. After thirteen weeks at a thousand dollars per week, he had received no directions on exactly what was wanted, and he couldn't even locate the parties who hired him to tell them he had dreamed up sixty-four bars of music he thought they ought to hear. But he did enjoy the fabulous atmosphere of the movie capital and was gratified to learn that among his devotees were a good number of movie stars, including Orson Welles, Bing Crosby and Judy Garland. Incidentally, Duke was surprised to find that Orson Welles knew

Ellington was a big name in the heyday of the great Cotton Club revues of the 20's and still is today.

more about his history than he did himself, and he was flattered when Welles, in a generous mood, proclaimed him a genius.

Welles' sentiments are shared by men of considerable musical authority. Stokowski and Stravinsky not only believe Ellington is a contemporary genius, but they are willing to place him high in the ranks of all-time musicianship. Duke himself is extremely modest about his work and refuses to agree even that he has become a landmark in American music. At best he admits that he lives solely to write and play music in the Negro idiom; that his compositions have never been anything else but Negroid; that he has never apologized for their origin nor has he tried to polish away their simplicity; and that he has always tried to recognize musical excellence wherever he found it. He knows that his efforts have been sincere, but he is not sure that he has accomplished anything lasting.

Over-all, however, he acknowledges the slight probability of any one man achieving immortality through his art. "It's like this," he says: "There are plenty of fine songs and serious compositions that have been kicked around until they were lost. Maybe there were more Bachs and Beethovens and Brahmses than we'll ever know about. But something happened. Their music got shelved or lost. The way I figure, it's like a crap game whether people two hundred years from now are even going to know who I was. I've got a chance, sure. Just like in a crap game I got a chance to throw five naturals in a row."

Segue to today

As the decade of the Forties opened and the big band swing movement went into a drastic decline, Duke Ellington publicly and vigorously stated his belief that jazz was badly in need of something new, that it needed some sort of a musical blood transfusion to restore its waning vigor. At the time, the Duke's charge was held treasonable by those of his fellow titans who were smugly content with their music or too deaf to hear the anemic note that had crept into it. Yet anyone who cared to listen objectively could tell that jazz had fallen into a rut. Its harmonic, melodic and rhythmic potentials had been fully exploited and it was beginning to repeat itself with the metronomic monotony of the four-to-a-bar beat to which it was then shackled.

However, even as the Duke spoke, a change was in the making. A group of rebellious young jazzmen were already experimenting with a new musical language, practicing a new tongue, preparing to launch a new era in jazz. Chief among them were alto saxophonist Charlie "Bird" Parker and tenor saxophonist Lester Young, trumpeters Dizzy Gillespie and Miles Davis, guitarist Charlie Christian, pianists Thelonious Monk and Kenneth Kersey, Kenny Clarke on drums, and a handful of others. And, curiously enough, although they were employed in a wide variety of bands the rebels for a period of about five years conducted their experiments almost exclusively in one laboratory—Minton's Play House, in Harlem, with its extraordinarily permissive musical atmosphere.

At Minton's, the innovators found the ideal spot for gathering together after they had finished their regular jobs, to hold the historic jam sessions which were to revolutionize jazz. There they could work out without hindrance such then novel musical ideas as improving on a chord sequence rather than a melodic theme, employing ninths and augmented fourths, working from a tonic to a dominant chord through a progression of minor sevenths, and many other unheard-of departures from traditional jazz techniques.

It was 1945, however, before the rebels found their collective voice and could speak with authority. Then the roof blew off Minton's and the new school of jazz could be heard from coast to coast. It was of course "bop"—and with bop the jazz we know today got its cataclysmic start. For out of the iconoclasm of bop first came "cool" jazz, then the neo-Afro-Cuban, "experimental", "main stream", "progressive", and other splinter schools of jazz now in vogue.

Considering the corrosive ease with which the acidity of time destroys reputations, it is perhaps foolhardy to speak of any of the principal exponents of these fledgling schools in terms of greatness. Only with four of them is the risk truly minimal. For it is almost impossible to believe that Charlie Parker, Dizzy Gillespie, Miles Davis, and Thelonious Monk will fail the test of time. By all existing standards they are surely seminal figures—so much so that, louder than any of their contemporaries, their voices can be heard distinctly in all of the jazz played today.

The high priest of the quartet is unquestionably Charlie Parker. His musical genius in combination with his self-destructive dissipation has made him every bit as much of a legend as Bix Beiderbecke, and a votive hero of the beat generation equal in stature to James Dean and Dylan Thomas. So much of Parker's inventiveness has rubbed off on so many jazz musicians that it has been said, "If Parker wanted to invoke the plagiarism laws, he could sue anybody who's made a jazz record in the last twenty years."

Here then is Bird's tragic story, as set down in December, 1957, two and a half years after his death, by Arnold Shaw.

To the mythical jazz combo of all-time greats that would include such legendary figures as Bix on trumpet and Fats at the eighty-eight may now be added the name of the most brilliant improviser of our time, Bird, who, not unlike his predecessors, played like an angel, lived like a devil and died like a fool. Wraithlike Bix Beiderbecke, you will remember, treated a cold under an electric fan—it was a hot, humid day in August, 1931—until pneumonia set in and he was dead at the ripe age of twenty-eight. Fats Waller, just recovered from a ten-day siege of influenza and exhausted from a string of one-nighters, partied himself into insensibility in the club car of the Super Chief and was found dead of pneumonia as the train paused at Kansas City. It was December, 1943, and he was thirty-nine. The passing of alto-saxist Charles "Bird" Parker in March, 1955, which likewise interrupted a career of tremendous promise, was as poignantly senseless and much more involved. For one thing, he showed signs of being dangerously ill four days before he died, but did nothing to help himself. For another, he died in the Fifth Avenue apartment of a wealthy baroness related to the Rothschild banking family, who had him examined by her physician but who "did not have the heart" to force him to go to a hospital, as the physician urgently recommended. For a third thing, after Charlie's heart suddenly stopped beating while he watched the late Tommy Dorsey's television show, Baroness Nica de Koeningswarter called her doctor who pronounced him dead. The body was taken to Bellevue where the medical examiner established that Charlie had died of heart failure, lobar pneumonia and cirrhosis of the liver, and estimated Bird's age as fifty-three—which was how the papers reported it—although Charlie gave his birthday as August 29, 1920, which would have made him thirty-four.

The sensational circumstances in which he died probably resulted in a bigger press for Parker than he had reason to anticipate. Both the New York *Times* and the *Herald Tribune* carried well-proportioned stories and, although the *Times* said that "Mr. Parker was ranked with Duke Ellington, Count Basie and other outstanding Negro (sic) musicians," there was recognition of Charlie as a "jazz master," "one of the founders of progressive jazz," and "virtuoso of the alto saxophone." The *Mirror* even referred to Charlie as "Jazzdom's Bop King," a title usually

Almost alone, Charlie "Bird" Parker ushered in a new jazz era.

From the Terry Dintenfass Gallery.

Charlie Parker one year old An Impression In Bronze by William King.

reserved for Bird's colleague, Dizzy Gillespie, who was associated in the public's mind with innovations for which Charlie was basically responsible.

The truth is that brooding, sad-faced Charles "Bird" Parker was unknown to average newspaper readers at his death in 1955, although in 1949 a Broadway jazz cellar, then called The Clique and now recognized as the mecca of jazz fans the world over, honored him by changing its name to Birdland. But among jazz musicians and *avant-garde* jazz fans, Charles Christopher Parker became celebrated, during his abortive life, as the most original, the most brilliant and the most influential jazzman of our time. A few days after the Bird took off on his ultimate flight, an apocryphal tale had its beginnings. Musicians told of a recording session during which a bird was discovered squatting

in a corner of the studio. Uneasy that it might make noises that would be picked up by the sensitive mikes, engineers tried to shoo the feathery creature from the studio. The bird eluded them, however, flew up onto a lighting fixture, and there defied all efforts to dislodge it. Observed on its perch at various moments during the session, it vanished mysteriously by the end of the date. Other curious stories were told about the same time: one of a bird that was discovered haunting a hallway outside Charlie's Tavern, a musicians' hangout on 7th Avenue and 52nd Street, where Bird occasionally got drunk; another of a white feather that floated down from the roof of Carnegie Hall during a Memorial Concert.

True or concocted, these tales reflect the superstitious reverence that fellow musicians felt regarding the source of Bird's

genius. A sampling of comments on his musicianship yields an amazing array of superlatives. "He's a genius you can't fence in with words" (arranger-alto saxist Gigi Gryce). "Intrinsic in his line was perfect form. There never was an unresolved note. His music was pure in the same sense that Bach's was pure" (pianist Lennie Tristano). "A giant" (pianist Dave Brubeck). "A giant of giants" (critic Marshall Stearns). "Most of the soloists at Birdland had to wait for Parker's next record in order to find out what to play next. What will they do now?" (guitarist Charlie Mingus). "There is scarcely a young musician who has achieved any success in jazz since 1945 without consciously, or unconsciously reflecting the influence of Charlie Parker. From every standpoint—tonal, rhythmic, melodic, harmonic—his work set a new standard, not merely for saxophonists but for

progressive musicians irrespective of instrument" (critic Leonard Feather).

Nor was Charlie's renown limited to the American scene. André Hodier, the French jazz critic, wrote: "By his personality, the scope and diversity of his gifts and his influence, he dominated his period just as Louis Armstrong around 1930 dominated his." The English *Melody Maker* had this to say: "Duke, Hawk, Lester, Django . . . they all have their place. But Parker's influence far transcends that of his contemporaries. The young man they called the Bird—an alto player from Kansas City—did, in a brief span, leave more mark on present-day bands than the Duke had in twenty-five years. Coleman Hawkins was the great logician, the driving force; Lester Young, the man of restraint; Django, the musical poet. Yet one Charlie

Parker had a combination of all their talents."

In life as in death, the Bird flew true to the tabloid tintype of the jazz musician. A man of voracious appetites, he was a drug addict from adolescence, a compulsive drinker, a sensation seeker, and an easy lover. But he was also a man of great sensitivity, a human being who was tormented by his weaknesses and who struggled fiercely against them. Twice the anguish of living drove him to suicide attempts, from which he thereafter fought fitfully to reconstruct his life. Yet at his death most of his friends felt that Charlie had no will to live and that a continuing drive toward self-destruction left open only the dateline.

Kansas City originally nurtured Charlie's talent; later, New York's 118th and 52nd Streets proved it. Kansas City was a good, if accidental, choice; for it had been receptive to jazz from the days when New Orleans musicians were traveling the Mississippi river boats, and had been productive of many fine jazzmen, among them Count Basie and his driving aggregation. During Charlie's youth and adolescence, Kansas City was booming with the corruption of the Pendergast era, which provided a climate friendly to jazz and friendly to vice. Charlie succumbed to both. By the time he was fifteen, he was playing the alto sax—he had tried baritone horn earlier in high school—and taking heroin.

In the anecdotes Charlie repeated of his youth, there is an emphasis on shyness and sensitivity. Typical is the story of how he tried one night to show off and played a chorus of *Body and Soul* in double tempo. Somehow he fumbled and "everybody fell out laughing. I went home and cried and didn't play again in public for three months." During those months, however, Charlie literally slept with his instrument. Charlie left high school after three years, during which "I wound up a freshman," and began gigging around, playing with local combos, including Harlan Leonard and Lawrence Keyes. Recognition of his musicianship came quickly for he was just seventeen when he joined the band of boogie-woogie pianist Jay McShann, which was making a name for itself and which brought him up to New York. In April, 1941, he cut his first record sides with the McShann band. One side was a composition called *Hootie Blues*, credited to Parker and McShann. On his second recording date with McShann (July 2, 1942), Charlie cut *Sepian Bounce*, playing the famous chorus whose opening two-bar break was to be imitated by boppers and jazzmen the world over. It was this chorus, memorized by trumpeter Benny Harris and played by him as he sat next to Dizzy Gillespie in Earl Hines' band, that led to Dizzy's early excitement about the Bird.

Before Bird emerged as the leader of his own combo in 1944, he played professionally with a number of big-name bands, among them Noble Sissle (1942), Earl Hines, Andy Kirk and Cootie Williams (1943), and the original Billy Eckstine band (1944). With Hines and Eckstine, Bird occupied a tenor chair. Apparently he was outstanding. Ben Webster, still one of our finest tenor men, is reported to have said: "Man, I heard a guy—I swear he's going to make everybody crazy on tenor." Yet Bird never liked the instrument. "Man," he told Hines, "this thing is too big. I just can't get the feel of it."

During this theatre tour with the Fatha, Charlie began getting into trouble by missing shows. Excesses of one kind or another occupied his nocturnal hours so that he simply failed to get up in time. To prevent his being fired, members of the band began routing him out of bed. He managed to arrive early for one afternoon show at the Paradise Theatre in Detroit, but was found at the end of it sleeping under the bandstand. The rest of the time, he slept on the stand itself, wearing dark glasses to hide his eyes and somehow managing to keep his cheeks puffed as if he were playing. Once, he ran out in front of the band and soloed in his stockinged feet. He had been snoozing and the members of the sax section had failed to warn him in time.

To understand the Bird's originality and the revolutionary nature of his musicianship—as well as his breakdown in 1946—one must see the jazz scene as it existed when Charlie came charging into New York with the Jay McShann band. Riding high were the big white swing bands of Benny Goodman, Artie Shaw, Glenn Miller, Tommy Dorsey—all of whom were playing a highly stylized four-to-the-bar, commercial brand of jazz. Each tried in a small way to preserve the spirit of jazz by developing within the larger band a smaller combo that afforded freedom for improvisation to the individual soloist. But the big bands played written arrangements, in which the whole sax section or the entire brass section "swung" in carefully rehearsed choruses. Rhythm figures, harmony, melody—all fell into a limited number of readily assimilated and monotonous patterns.

Against this stylized jazz and against dull Dixieland, a group of young Negro musicians rose in conscious revolt. Minton's Playhouse, located in the old Hotel Cecil on West 118th Street, became the scene of early-morning jam sessions in which a new generation of jazzmen, some of them with conservatory training, sedulously sought new sounds and new forms of expression.

"We're going to create something they can't steal," said pianist Thelonious Monk, "because they can't play it."

"We'd play *Epistrophy* or *I've Got My Love to Keep Me Warm*," drummer Kenny Clarke confirmed, "just to keep the other guys off the stand because we knew they couldn't make those chord changes. We kept the riffraff out and built our clique on new chords."

"Everybody was experimenting around 1942," says clarinetist Tony Scott, "but nobody had style yet. Bird provided the push."

Kenny Clarke, who was responsible for the development of the bop drum style based on punctuation rather than beat-pounding, knew Charlie intimately in this period. "Bird wasn't at all talkative," he has said. "He was very meek, very reserved. I don't think he was aware of the changes in jazz he was bringing about. Or at least he didn't talk about it much. Dizzy was more aware of what was happening and of his part in it."

At the Minton jam sessions—and later when the boppers moved to 52nd Street—everything seemed to be in reverse. Instead of improvising on the standard pop hits, they turned to show tunes, hitherto by-passed by the Dixieland and swing bands. Even here, they completely disregarded the melody. Instead, they took the chord sequences and wrote new melodies so that *How High the Moon*, a favorite with the boppers, became

Charlie Parker in the post-Minton's period.

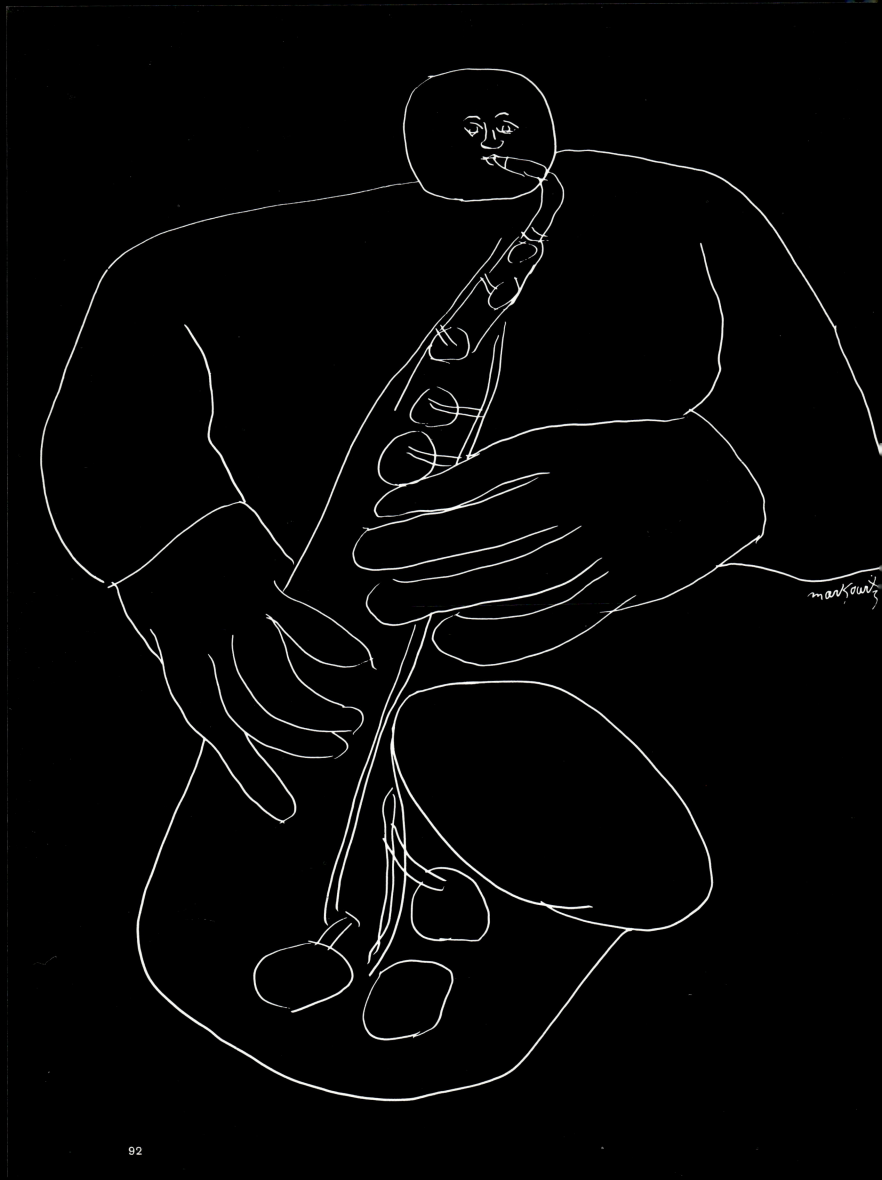

a new tune called *Ornithology* also *Bird Lore*. Romberg's *Lover Come Back to Me* became Parker's *Bird Gets the Worm*. Rhythmically, Bird, Diz, Monk, Charlie Christian, Tadd Dameron and Kenny Clarke departed from a dance beat and reached after offbeat and polyrhythmic patterns.

Even in the matter of musical manners the boppers turned things upside down. Let the late Davey Tough tell what happened when he and members of Woody Herman's first Herd visited a 52nd Street jazz club: "As we walked in, see, these cats (Gillespie-Pettiford Quintet) snatched up their horns and blew crazy stuff. One would stop all of a sudden and another would start for no reason at all. We never could tell when a solo was supposed to begin or end. Then they all quit at once and walked off the stand. It scared us."

The audience for bop grew slowly—and mainly in New York —so that 1945 was Bird's first big year. Leaving Eckstine, the last big band he played with, he found himself in demand along 52nd Street, and filled engagements with Ben Webster, with a Dizzy Gillespie combo, and with his own group at The Three Deuces. He was also sought after by the recording studios and cut discs for virtually all of the small jazz labels at the time.

With Dizzy he recorded the bop classics *Groovin' High, Salt Peanuts,* which gave us the "eel-ya-dah" triplet, and *Shaw Nuff,* Bird's own tune in honor of agent Billy Shaw. There were dates with Sarah Vaughan, Slim Gaillard (the *Flat-Foot Floogie* man) Red Norvo, and Bird's own first recorded group, "Charlie Parker's Be-Bop Boys." Releases of the last mentioned included four of his best compositions—*Ko-Ko, Now's the Time, Billie's Bounce* and *Thriving From A Riff,* a chorus of which in turn yielded another Parker classic *Anthropology.* All of these have recently been reissued under the title *Charlie Parker Memorial,* including not only the finished versions but the many preliminary takes as well. In May and June of '45 there were two Town Hall concerts, headlined by Dizzy Gillespie, who came to the fore as the showman of the boppers. Although these efforts to showcase the new music were not unmixed successes—*Down Beat* reported "Gillespie Bash Drags As Cats Fail to Show"— Bird was singled out by *Metronome:* "Charlie's solos almost never failed to get a roar from the audience," the reviewer wrote, "because of his habit of beginning them with a four-bar introduction in which the rhythm is suspended (as in a cadenza), then slamming into tempo, giving his listeners a tremendous re-

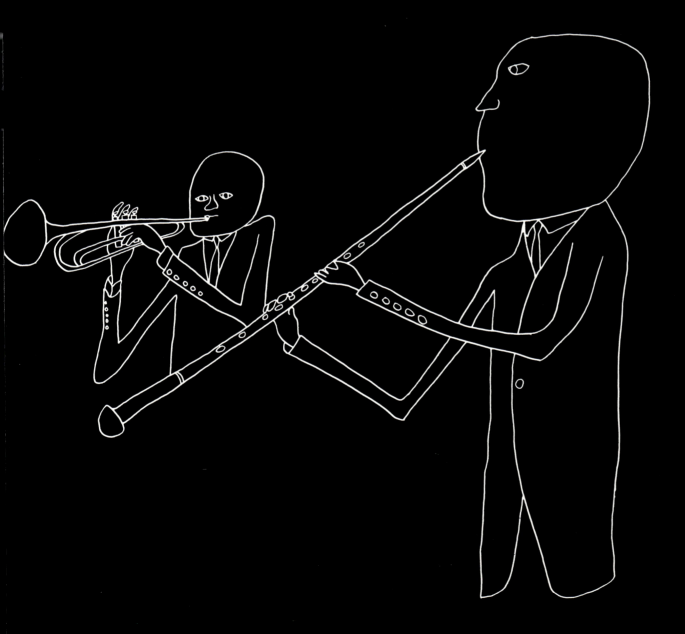

From the George E. Geisler Collection.

"The Bird" Sculpture In Stone by Julie MacDonald.

lease, an excited relief."

Mal Braverman, one of the sponsors of the 1945 concerts, offers a rather interesting backstage view of Bird's behavior. Apparently Charlie showed up at the concert early, but without his instrument. As curtain time approached he quietly volunteered the information that he didn't have his sax because he had pawned it. In consternation, the sponsors dispatched a messenger to the pawnbroker with the necessary money, delaying the beginning of the concert for almost half an hour. As the year wore on, Charlie's need of money, regardless of how much he made, became legendary. His failure to pay loans led to one of his friends' cracking: "To know Charlie, you have to pay your dues."

In 1945 Bird was on the way to becoming musically "the living legend of our time," as he was called in 1949. But then came the disastrous California trip with a Gillespie combo, which led to Bird's first suicide attempt. New York audiences were not unreceptive to the new jazz, but their attitude was not entirely friendly. Otherwise, why did the boppers adopt that air of boredom that they manifested on the stand? Partly, of course, as a reaction against Dixieland, "moldy fig" enthusiasm and swing's exhibitionism—remember Gene Krupa's openmouthed breathlessness and the grinding jaws?—but also, obviously, as

a defensive measure. In comparison, the Los Angeles audiences before whom the Gillespie combo performed were wicked. Dizzy, a much stronger personality than Bird, told later of how the boys conversed in whispers at Billy Berg's club and of how, feeling they were in enemy territory, they rented a dingy basement where they could play their music during off hours without being overheard. "They were so hostile out there," Dizzy said. "They thought we were just playing ugly on purpose. They were so very, very hostile! Man they used to stare at us so tough. Why does it have to be such a fight? If I ever get back alive to the Apple, I'll never leave it."

The Bird almost did not make it back alive. As the going got rougher and rougher, Bird's dependence on drugs increased. So did the resulting muscular tics. In March, he did a record session at which he cut his own tunes *Moose the Mooche* and the delicate *Yardbird Suite*, Benny Harris' *Ornithology* and Dizzy's *Night in Tunisia*. Then came the session of July 29, 1946, whose strange developments are so sensitively depicted in the remarkable story, *Sparrow's Last Jump*, by Elliott Grennard. (Appearing originally in *Harper's*, it was an O. Henry Prize Story of 1948.) The climax of this session came on the recording of *Lover Man*, so expressive in its melodic contortions of a man's inner agony that it led to Grennard's poignant paragraph: "His whole body began to twitch crazily and what he played was crazy in exactly the same way.... The boys stopped gradually, their music sort of trickling away, their eyes on Sparrow. He was still going, his twisted music and his tortured body all mixed up in one long insane convolution.... Yeah, Sparrow's last recording would sure make a collector's item. One buck, plus tax, is cheap enough for a record of a guy going nuts."

Unable to go through with the session (only two sides were completed, and Parker never forgave Ross Russell for releasing *Lover Man*), Bird rushed back to his hotel room. After trying desperately to go to sleep, he went beserk and set fire to his hotel room. Screaming uncontrollably, he ran naked through the hall and lobby. He spent the succeeding seven months recuperating at Camarillo State Hospital.

While Charlie was in Camarillo recuperating from his breakdown, Dizzy was basking in the sunlight of national publicity. (A few years later, when the public had developed a curiosity about the new music, *Life* did a story featuring Dizzy as the high priest of bop.) There can be little doubt that this was the beginning of a deep-seated resentment, which never came out into the open but which occasionally drove Charlie to try silly things. Once he rode into Charlie's Tavern on a horse and at another time to Birdland disguised as a hayseed farmer. These were unsuccessful attempts at clowning, which Charlie somehow could never carry off. He was no showman, as Dizzy and Slim Gaillard were, and he lacked the personality to bring off antics with which Dizzy garnered space. He was even too shy to be a good leader. As time went on, Dizzy, his beret, his heavy black glasses, and such other of his mannerisms as conducting with fancy motions of his rump became more and more the public face of bop. And though Charlie was the technical genius behind the movement, his renown remained for the most part inside musicians' ranks. That there was hurt and a sense of frustration is unquestioned.

On his return to the Apple, Charlie gave an interview to

Metronome in which he discussed his addiction to drugs with a frankness that required much more courage in 1947 than it would today. His statements are worth quoting at length. "Any musician," he told Leonard Feather, "who says he is playing better either on tea, the needle or when he is juiced is a plain, straight liar. When I get too much to drink, I can't even finger well, let alone play decent ideas. And, in the days when I was on the stuff, maybe I *thought* I was playing better, but listening to some of the records now, I know I wasn't. Some of the smart kids who think you have to be completely knocked out to be a good horn man are just plain crazy. It isn't true. I know, believe me."

Charlie's struggles against drugs and drink, which colored the remaining eight years of his life, reached climactic points again in 1950 and in the year before his death.

On his return to New York, he organized a sextet that made 1947 one of the best Parker years and yielded some of the greatest Parker sides. Accompanied by Miles Davis on trumpet, Max Roach on drums, and J. J. Johnson on trombone, Charlie cut a series of originals and standards for Dial re-released as *Charlie Parker All Star Sextet*. Among the standards are a breathtakingly beautiful treatment of *Out of Nowhere* and two remarkably different versions of *Embraceable You*, one a slow, classic ballad study and the other, called *Quasimodo*, a brighter, danceable variant. The originals include the Latin-flavored *Bird Feathers*, the weird *Klactoveedsedtene*, and the inventive *Scrapple from the Apple*. If one is to select a single album to represent the range of Bird's talents as instrumentalist, improviser and composer—also the melodic, harmonic and rhythmic felicities of bop at its best—this would doubtless be it.

In the fall of the year, Charlie appeared at Carnegie Hall in a concert, again under the aegis of Dizzy Gillespie, which featured Ella Fitzgerald. Whatever satisfaction he derived came again from the recognition he received inside the trade: "In the quintet numbers with Parker," *Down Beat* reported, "Gillespie was appreciably bested. Parker's constant flow of ideas, his dramatic entrances, and his perky use of punctuation were a revelation. . . ." There could have been no gratification in reading castigations by both *Down Beat* and *Metronome* of Dizzy's cheap showmanship, and the bad taste he displayed in an unending bid for the limelight—especially since, in July, 1948, *The New Yorker*, reacting to an increasing public curiosity about bop, profiled Dizzy. And toward the end of 1948 *Life's* story on Gillespie appeared. In a three-page picture story on bop, there was not a single shot of Bird.

But Forty-nine and Fifty brought Charlie a measure of increased recognition, chiefly among foreign jazz fans. In May of '49 he was invited by Charles Delaunay to bring his own group to the International Jazz Festival. A jazz pianist reviewing the festival reported that the Parker Quintet—with Max Roach, drums, Al Haig, piano, Kenny Dorham, trumpet and Tommy Potter, bass—brought the boppers to the edges of their seats.

Parker's new record releases during 1949 received only so-so reviews in the trade despite his coming in first in the annual *Metronome* poll, a position which he held for the succeeding four years. In 1950 Charlie was particularly hurt by adverse reactions to an album he did for Norman Granz with a string group. The fact that he was the first modern jazzman to attempt this successfully did not count with critics who accused him of "trying to go commercial." Once again, the pressures were building, tension in his personal life adding to the turbulence of his musical career. The appearance of a book by his friend Leonard Feather *Inside Be-Bop* did not help him either, for although Feather stated that "the musicians who saw the birth of the new jazz are almost unanimous" in paying tribute to Parker as "a real genius" and the man they consider responsible for its inception, Feather nevertheless gave only one chapter to Charlie and built his book around Dizzy Gillespie.

In the effort to beat the needle, Charlie began hitting the bottle. The result was an attack of bleeding ulcers, which almost took his life. While recovering from the near-fatal siege, he told friends: "I've had my last drink. The doctor told me if I don't quit drinking, I'll die."

In '53 and '54 he added the Critics' Poll to the awards he received from both *Down Beat* and *Metronome*. By this time he had split with tall Doris Parker, his third wife, and was married, apparently happily, to Chan, an attractive brunette, who bore him two children a girl Pree and a boy Laird. Then, suddenly, his little daughter Pree died of pneumonia. It provided a new and perhaps decisive peg upon which to pivot a never-ending search for oblivion. In September, '54, after an unbelievably bad performance at the jazz cellar named after him and after a ruckus in which he openly and vociferously quarreled with his sidemen while on stage, he went home and swallowed iodine.

Again there was a period of recuperation. In a desperate attempt to cope with his problems, he began visiting Bellevue regularly for psychiatric assistance.

At the doctor's suggestion, he moved Chan, his stepson Kim, and his son Laird to New Hope, Pennsylvania, to which he commuted daily.

But the adjustment was short-lived. This time there was nothing specific that set him off—just, perhaps, an inability, after years of dissipation, to accept the stresses and strains of living soberly, simply, normally. He stopped commuting. He started drinking heavily again. He went back to the needle. You can get an idea of what he looked like from a picture (taken earlier) which appears on the back of the record album *Charlie Parker Big Band*. By this time even his most sympathetic friends could not counter criticisms regarding his undependability, his constant quarreling, and his completely erratic conduct.

The week end before he died, Bird managed with difficulty to secure an engagement at Birdland. In the quintet were guitarist Charlie Mingus and pianist Bud Powell, who had also had a nervous breakdown in 1948 and was undergoing intermittent psychiatric treatment. During the first set, Charlie got into an open hassle about the choice of tunes with Bud Powell. When Powell stalked off the stand, Charlie went to the mike and, before a shocked audience that had grown fearfully quiet, he slowly intoned Bud's name, repeating it over and over and over again in the unbearable silence that filled the club.

A short while later he was seen by a friend at Basin Street, just around the corner. Drunk, he sat there with tears streaming down his eyes. "I need to have some friends around," he cried, "to see some kind faces." Returning to Birdland, he quarreled again on the stand with the other musicians. "If you go on like this," Charlie Mingus said, "you'll kill yourself." A week later Parker was dead.

Of Bird's remarkable endowments and achievements as a musician, many anecdotes have been told. Earl "Fatha" Hines, for whom Charlie played tenor in 1943, says that after one runthrough, Charlie always could play his part flawlessly from memory. Photographic recall is not, however, creative musicanship. Billy Bauer, whose fine guitar work backed Charlie on a number of records, has never stopped talking of Bird's split-second sense of timing. "This guy," Billy has said in his easy, hoarse voice, "could come in on beat, off beat, and between beats and, blowing up a storm of notes at whirlwind tempo, he could accent any note he chose—on beat, off beat, and between beats. Man, he was the beginning, the middle and the end!" No one who ever performed with Bird when he was in form forgot the experience. And the cats who played the 1948 Carnegie Hall concert with Diz and the Bird have never stopped talking about it. Dizzy, who is no slouch at off chord, off-beat improvisation, got into a solo-cutting contest with Bird, typical of that period of Bop. Naturally, Dizzy went as far out as he could go, reaching for the craziest chords, inventing the wildest rhythm patterns, and spilling a torrent of notes like a miniature Niagara. He was no match for Parker. Bird would come in on top of him, almost before the notes were out of Gillespie's horn, and in some instances duplicate Dizzy's solo lines note for note, in other spots duplicate and develop quick, sly variations. Musicians and critics alike were staggered by the remarkable performance.

What Bird did was to synthesize the discoveries of all the searchers for new sounds and, like the true innovator in an art form, show others how to put the off-beat, the far-out and the weird together so that they became aesthetically pleasing.

There has been a tendency in some quarters to portray Bird's musicianship as an untutored, intuitive type of achievement. To some extent, Parker may have himself prompted this idea since he spoke of bringing bop from "my mother's Kansas City woodshed." Billy Eckstine, with whom Parker played in 1944, also helped spread the idea: "Bird was responsible," he said, "for the actual playing of progressive jazz and Dizzy put it down." About this statement, Thelonious Monk recently commented: "Why should Bird get Dizzy to write something down? He could write it down himself." The truth is that, regardless of the actual length of his formal training, Bird was a serious student, not only of jazz, but of music generally; as time went on he developed a far-ranging interest in the works of the modern classicists. Not too long after his arrival in New York, Bird told friends: "I first began listening seven or eight years ago. First I heard Stravinsky's *Fire Bird Suite*. In the vernacular of the streets, I flipped. I guess Bartok has become my favorite. I did all the moderns." In 1947 Leonard Feather reported that Bird admired Debussy's *Children's Corner*, Stravinsky and Shostakovich, and that he had studied Schoenberg. Other friends have indicated that shortly before his death Charlie spoke of studying with Paul Hindemith at Yale and of commissioning Edgar Varese to write a rhythm background for him.

Although one thinks of Parker primarily as a performer, he was in fact an accomplished jazz and blues composer with a long list of works to his credit. These range from the later, familar *Now's The Time*, through the tender and lyrical *Yardbird Suite* and the rhythmically truncated *Klactoveedsedstene*, to the intense and exciting *Air Conditioning* and *She Rote*. Parker's first recording date with the Jay McShann band in 1941 included an original blues, and he wrote many as time went on. Perhaps the most interesting group of compositions are those which were developed on the chord lines of pop standards: *Quasimodo, Confirmation, Scrapple from the Apple,* and the tremendous *Ko-Ko*. These works suggest that Bird's drive as a composer was a further projection of his unexcelled genius as an improviser.

Whitney Balliett of the *Saturday Review* has said that Parker was "during all of his career a very hot jazzman." While this is basically true, it is subject to misunderstanding when offered by way of contrasting Parker's direction with that of be-bop, which, Balliett states, "evolved into a cool, oblique and somewhat hairless music." The fact is that Bird provides a link between the polytonalities and polyrhythms of the modern classic composers, like Stravinsky, Bartok, Prokofieff, and Schoenberg, and the cool musicians of today. The fact, too, is that Bird could do things with slow ballads that surpass anything other jazzmen have attempted. Listen to his versions of *Embraceable You, Don't Blame Me, My Old Flame* and *Lover Man* in *The Magnificent Charlie Parker*, and it is evident that he added a kind of heat to the pretty ballad which is his own unique signature. The overwhelmingly beautiful turn of phrase that he imposed on the original melodies is given an unexpected intensity by sudden gusts of cascading notes, hot rhythm figures that crash into slow passages, and the interpolation of big, new, exciting chords. While Charlie began his study of jazz saxophone under the deep influence of Lester Young's cool, lag-along tenor, his own frenetic personality soon found expression in a soaring style that is well typified by the nickname Bird.

The pattern of the abortive jazz career, drenched in alcohol, narcotized by drugs, and squandered in loose living, is hardly a new one. Enough talented young men have flashed across the musical horizon and burned themselves out overnight to suggest that the jazzmen themselves seem to confuse debauchery and genius.

While Charlie had the misfortune to be introduced to the needle as an adolescent, the search for thrills and Nirvana did not stop with his teens. Charlie remained a man of insatiable physical appetites. That these activities were in part compulsive, used as an escape when things were not going right, is apparent.

Charlie was an unhappy child of the early opposition to bop. Like most of the jazzmen during the late Forties and the early Fifties, he was a character in search of an audience. But in trying to draw the line between self-responsibility and socially destructive forces, one must note that other boppers rode out the storm and that Dizzy, in whose shadow Bird constantly walked, only recently scored a **really** great triumph. He made jazz history with a spectacularly **successful** ANTA tour of the Middle East.

There is a tendency in some quarters to believe that jazz itself is a destructive force. This is clearly as fallacious as the converse concept. Jazz is seldom enough to save a man from weakness of character or self-indulgence. The grave danger in the jazzman's pattern of existence is that he may immerse himself in music to such an extent that he develops no other values to live by. If anything goes wrong with his music,

he's a dead duck.

That's what happened to Bix when his inability to read notes well caught up with him. That's what happened to little Davey Tough when he became embroiled in the conflict between Dixieland and bop and as a consequence did not know which way to turn.

The greatness of Bird as a musician and the tragedy of Charlie Parker as a man make it inescapably clear that if showmanship is required in addition to musicianship, a jazzman also needs a concept of life and society in addition to his art."

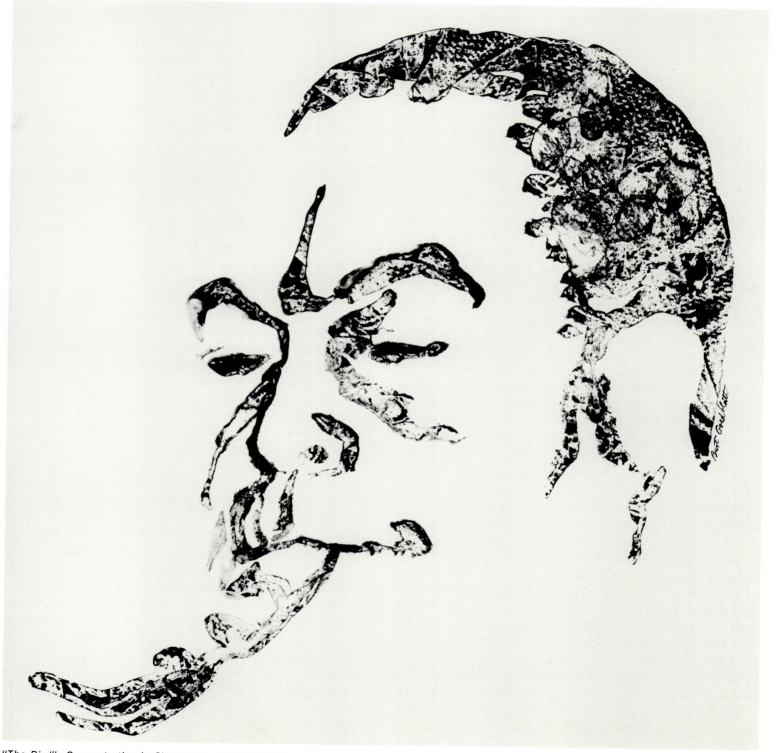

"The Bird"—Concentration in Charcoal by Burt Goldblatt.

For Bird, an Elegy

The following piece of jazz memorabilia is the logical footnote to Arnold Shaw's moving portrait of the Bird. It was written in October, 1958, by Jean Stein, who visited Parker's home town, Kansas City, to uncover what she could of his early years. In effect, what she discovered is the sad and revealing prologue to his tormented death.

As Ms. Stein revealed, "Kansas City still contains a few silent landmarks of Charlie Parker, from the seedy saloons on Twelfth Street to his gravestone, which reads:

SON
CHARLES PARKER, JR.
Aug. 29, 1920–Mar. 12, 1955

Two carved birds rest above the inscription.

Charlie Parker worked for various bands then, but mostly for Jay McShann, who still plays around town with a small group. I called on McShann at his house one afternoon recently. I found his personal manager sleeping by the front door. McShann was lying on a couch in the darkened living room wrapped in a patchwork quilt, avidly watching a quiz show on his TV set. He kept up a pleasant, sporadic conversation while staring at the program. Here's what he sounded like:

"I first met Bird in about 1935 when the guys would get together and jam. We'd have a spook breakfast about five in the morning after our gigs and blow and outdo each other. Bird had been playing about three years and when he'd sit in the guys would fall out. The neck of his sax was always coming unscrewed, and he played everything offbeat. He had it in his head long before he could put it together. I think that his not being wanted around made Bird more of a loner than ever. He never felt sure of himself at the beginning of his career. One morning about fifty musicians were packed into the Reno Club jamming and Charlie started to play. Jo Jones threw his cymbal over Bird's head. He was 'ringing the bell,' which means the guy didn't make it. The musicians laughed, but Bird said, 'I'll be back.' He went home and cried and didn't play the sax again for months.

"Bird knew he was getting nowhere in Kansas City, so he decided to 'go to the woodshed.'

"He left with George Lee's combo for a small summer resort at Eldon, Missouri, in the Ozarks. This was the end of 1936 when he was sixteen. He slept with that horn in the Ozarks and learned about chords in all keys from Effarge Ware, who was the guitarist in the group.

"When he returned about five months later, he was right. Nobody could believe it was the same guy blowing. Bird said it was his co-ordination.

"Bird started working with me about September of 1937. We played mostly at Tutty's Mayfair. We'd set a tempo to play. Bird would never come in with the others. We'd start and someone would have to nudge him, but he would come in when he wanted to.

"Bird slept so on the job that one night the others were playing blues, and Bird woke up and started blowing *Lady Be Good*. The band switched quickly so the audience wouldn't notice.

"Often he might not show the next night. He was already on narcotics. Sometimes his mother would call and ask me to bring her his pay directly. Either that, or he'd have his horn in pawn or his band suit or laundry in pawn—sometimes all three.

"I let him go the end of 1937. He hoboed his way to New York. He was always looking for adventure. Bird was almost eighteen then.

"When Bird got to New York he headed immediately for the Savoy. He stood in the snow and stared at it for three or four hours. He washed dishes in Jimmy's Chicken Shack in Harlem for a few months, while out front Art Tatum was gassing everybody. Charlie picked up $9 a week and meals.

"Several months later he got a job with a group at Monroe's Uptown House. He got forty or fifty cents a night; if business was good, he could make up to $6.

"By the end of 1939 he hoboed back to Kansas City. He kind of straightened up then and wanted to work with my band.

"Bird stayed pretty straight; at least he was controlling it. We were then thinking of having a big band. So in 1940 we added more horns. Bird made good time there.

" 'Man, that cat is late,' he'd say of other musicians.

"He'd rehearse the reed section for me.

"Bird's reading was slow then. The other alto man, John Jackson, read better, so Bird said, 'I'm going to woodshed this. That cat's reading all around me.'

"When I called a rehearsal next, Bird said he couldn't make it because of woodshedding, but told me, 'If I miss one note you have the privilege to fire me.'

"Then in 1939 we went on the road for the first time, leaving Kansas City behind. We were traveling along to Lincoln, Nebraska, when the car Charlie was in ran over a chicken.

" 'Man, let's stop this car and go back and pick up this yardbird,' he told the driver. So he picked up the chicken from the highway and when we got to the next roominghouse, he made the landlady cook it for dinner. And that's when we started calling him Bird."

One of the famous clubs around Kansas City in those days was Tutty's Mayfair, run by Tutty Clarkin. Tutty is recognized among the jazz musicians as a guy who's in the know about everybody and as the friend Bird could always count on. Tutty has retired from the night-club business and is now "custodian" of every stray animal and bird in the area around his home at Lake Latowana. I found him in his back yard binding the leg of a crippled duck. He rapidly told me the following in a sharp Midwestern twang:

"Charlie first worked at Tutty's Mayfair in 1937 for $2 a night when he showed. He was one-half to two hours late every night. But you could tell he was feeling/thinking, 'Why are those cats playing when I haven't arrived yet?' He always wore an old black slicker and an old black suede hat propped low on his head, and he carried the sax under his arm.

"He had an old sax, made in Paris in 1898, that was like nothing. It had rubber bands and cellophane paper all over it, and the valves were always sticking and the pads always leaking. The reeds didn't make any difference. They were usually broken or chipped. He had to hold it sideways to make it blow. He'd hold up the band hammering away at it in the kitchen with the help of the cook. No food would appear, and I'd scream at Charlie to leave the cook alone. He wore the cook out.

"I figured if Bird was great with a broken-down horn, he'd be sensational with a new one, so I threw his old sax into the snow and told him to meet me in front of the music store the next day. He was there on time, and I bought him a sax for $190. Bird cried and said, 'Man, I'll never be late again.' He didn't show for two days. Then I went looking for him. I found him where those cats hang out around 18th and Vine, but his new sax was in hock. I always took him back. You could tell: if the sax wasn't under Charlie's arm, it was in the pawn shop. He hocked it every week.

Parker first worked at Tutty's Mayfair in Kansas City in 1937 for two dollars a night. Eighteen years later, at age 35, he was dead of dissipation.

"When I first knew Charlie, he was getting high on nutmeg. One day I ran into the grocer who said, 'Tutty, you sure must be making a lot of pies over there with all the nutmeg your club is ordering.' I knew something was wrong and rushed back to the club to check up on the cats. I searched around, but couldn't find any trace of the spice. Finally, I looked under the bandstand and found the floor littered with empty cans of nutmeg. Later Charlie told me, 'Another sax player and I would chew spices and laugh at each other and our heads would enlarge and shrink. And if we didn't play, there'd be no more reed section.'

"From nutmeg Bird went to Benzedrine inhalers. He'd break them open and soak them in wine. Then he smoked tea and finally got hooked on heroin. He was the only man I knew who could drink with heroin. He'd come back late from a fix for the second show and say to my wife, 'Miss Leanor, I'm all put out.' A drummer called Little Phil was his dope connection. He's now in the insane asylum in St. Jo. Dope infected his mind. Little Phil lived on the Paseo, and after the fix Bird usually went into the Park with some friend, and they'd blow and blow and blow through the night.

"Bird often slept on a table in the club. We'd wake him up at night. Once after three days of living this way I looked out the window and thought the ground was covered with snow. In fact the ground was covered by empty white Benzedrine inhalers.

"The only way I could keep Charlie straight was to tell him his mother and half-brother were coming out. His mother watched him like a hawk. When Bird was sixteen he looked thirty-eight. He had the oldest-looking face I ever saw.

"In the later days he would work for me for $30 a night. In 1953 he came out to the club one night in an open convertible with some white girl he'd picked up in town. We got word somehow that she was trying to frame him on a narcotics charge for the government. He only had time to play eight bars of *How High the Moon* when we motioned him off the bandstand and helped him to skip town. I got up and said, 'The Bird goofed,' and the audience understood (later the girl framed two other musicians).

"If Bird ever got into trouble he'd call me from wherever he was. Every time he phoned he'd say at the end, 'Tell Mama I'm all right.' "

The person who was probably the most important influence in the Bird's life was his mother, Mrs. Charles Parker. She lives now in the seedy south section of Kansas City, in a house rising above a long series of narrow, broken-down stairs.

Mrs. Parker, a large, big-bosomed woman, works as a nurse at a state hospital from 3 till 12 at night.

Seated in a large rocking chair near a coal burner, with flourishing green plants covering the window sills, she said:

"I hope you're not going to write raggedy stories about my Charles like the other reporters, and please don't take any pictures. It's such a raggedy house. I'm ashamed of it. I take in roomers now upstairs. What shall I tell you about my son?

"Charles was all I had. Someday I might get over it. He was born August 29, 1920, in Kansas City, Missouri. When I met Charles' father, he was playing the piano and singing on the vaudeville stages around there.

"When he was only a child, Charles wanted to be a music-maker. He'd take my curtain rods and broom sticks and blow on them.

"My husband deserted us when Charles was ten. He went off to live with some woman in Baltimore. So I became mother, father, everything to Charles. He thought he was Mama's man. He never worked like the other little boys in the neighborhood. He wanted to carry newspapers, but I wouldn't let him. I thought I could take care of him until he was a man.

"Charles started on the tuba horn his last year in grade school. I didn't like it. It was too much to carry around. He was so little. Then he joined the R.O.T.C. band in high school. He first played alto horn, then went to baritone horn, and one day I bought him an alto saxophone from the pawn shop. It was white gold with green keys. I took it to a music store to have it padded. He practiced so loud in the house I'd go hide in the alley. I made a sack for his saxophone out of real heavy material. I'd wash and keep it white and pretty. He kept it for a long time.

"Charles got married to Rebecca when he was fifteen. He said he wasn't learning anything at Lincoln High School and his closest friend there, Robert Simpson, suddenly took sick and died.

" 'Mama, I want to leave school. Robert's gone. He was my only friend.'

"He never worked in high school—just music, music, music.

"Charles quit in his second year and put his age up four years to get into the musicians' union. Rebecca and he lived with me, and they had a baby. I worked then at Western Union from twelve till eight in the morning and had a day job besides. Sometimes he'd come home only in the morning.

"Charles got into serious trouble one night when he kept a taxi for six or seven hours and ran up a $10 bill which he couldn't pay. The taxi driver tried to snatch his horn, and Charles stabbed him with a dagger. They took him off to the farm. I told the police, 'How dare you treat my son like that. Bring him back!' He came home the next day. They'd taken the dagger away from him.

"There were too many of us in the house and I didn't like the crowd Charles was running around with, so I sent him away from Kansas City. He said he would go if I gave him the fare to Chicago. Rebecca didn't know till Charles was gone. She asked me how he got there. I said, 'How everybody got there.' She stayed around for a while, and then went home with the baby and divorced him. The boy is now in the Air Corps.

"You know, years later Charles married white girls—Doris and then Chan. We are in the South here in Kansas City, but in New York nobody knows the difference unless you look at yourself in the mirror.

"Charles came back to bury his father when he was nineteen. He always lived here when he returned. One night he wanted to take me with him to New York. He said, 'Parkie, let's fly,' but I said, 'Another time.' I go out to his grave on Memorial Day and on his birthday.

"I thought I'd have him always, but the Lord said different. You know, we come into this world to go."

SON
CHARLES PARKER, JR.
AUG. 29, 1920 - MAR. 23, 1955

Grave Marker and Sax Case

By Art Kane

Dizzy is
as
Dizzy does

In some quarters, the fruitless argument about whether Dizzy Gillespie or Charlie Parker started the bop revolution still continues, even though by now it should be obvious to all that neither of them was alone in fomenting it. At the most, they can only share honors as the revolution's principal agitators, as the leaders of the sizable band of progressive musicians who brought it to a head. It is equally pointless to continue the dispute about which of them had the greater influence on the other. The truth seems to be that they developed their novel musical ideas independently in the beginning, and ended up borrowing openly and freely from each other in a concerted effort to enlarge and refine the new musical idiom they were striving to create.

Actually, the most important single influence in Dizzy's musical life may well have been Roy "Little Jazz" Eldridge, whom Dizzy replaced in Teddy Hill's Savoy Ballroom Band in 1937. Roy is sometimes dismissed as being merely the link between Armstrong, who formed the style of almost all of the trumpeters (Eldridge included) of the twenties, and Dizzy, who influenced most of the trumpeters of the forties and fifties. But Eldridge is far more than a connecting link between two generations. He is a solidly original musician, highly inventive, with an occasionally unruly imagination and a wild and dancing style that produces solos which march from oblique beginnings to soaring, far-out climaxes. As one modern trumpeter said, "Roy may not always be hip but, Jesus, he sure fills that horn."

For years, Dizzy idolized and imitated Roy, and there can be no question but that "Little Jazz" played a major role in Dizzy's musical education and development. Yet in time, of course, Dizzy's own creative bent led him away from Roy into bop. And it is one of music's most curious paradoxes that Dizzy may well have done as much to help kill bop as he did to help found it.

Unfortunately for bop, Dizzy was its style-setter. And Dizzy, to put it mildly, had his eccentricities. He affected a wispy goatee. On the rare occasions when he wasn't wearing a visored beret he was wearing a coal miner's hat. He sported ostrich leather shoes and massive black, heavy-rimmed glasses. His language, if it could be called that, was indisputably his own. While it began in conventional English it quickly lapsed into coined words which were meaningless except to the "initiated," and all sentences were brought to an end with an artificial, forced, cackling laugh. Even his gestures were excessively mannered; most notably his highly stylized handshake.

As bop caught on, its followers began to play the sedulous ape to Dizzy in meticulous detail (some who had perfect eyesight even took to wearing heavy-rimmed glasses free of lens). At first his imitators were limited to the ranks of his fellow musicians. Then, as the vogue spread, "bopsters" began to deface the landscape from coast to coast. These were witless devotees of the new music who sought to prove their loyalty to its votive priest by imitating him, and who succeeded only in annoying the public with their ludicrous bereted-and-begoggled exhibitionism.

As if this wan't enough of a burden for bop to bear, the music itself began to suffer. While there was a great deal that was good in it, it had its bad aspects too. Its technical demands, for instance, were so great that few musicians could master them. Nevertheless, ill-equipped jazzmen turned to bop in wholesale quantities. And much of the music these "pseudo-boppers" produced was worse than worthless. Consequently, even the best-intentioned listener had so much difficulty telling good bop from bad that he finally threw up his hands in despair and turned away from it altogether.

When the audience for bop showed signs of shrinking, Dizzy,

who delighted in the glare of publicity, went to childish extremes to try and hold his auditors and keep the spotlight from wavering. In a desperate bid for popularity, he clothed his orchestra in orange jackets and purple berets. Even worse, he lapsed into ridiculous buffoonery as a leader, conducting largely with his rump and playing the goggle-eyed, leering clown for his audience. It was odious exhibitionism and the reaction was predictable—the people stayed away in droves, and the demise of bop was hastened.

All this scarcely makes Dizzy sound like a candidate for jazz's hall of fame. In exoneration, it must be explained that Dizzy's exhibitionism was only a passing phase. Like Orson Welles, Satchel Paige, Harpo Marx, and other zanies, with age he has mellowed. So much so, in fact, that he was recently seen walking towards his suburban home carrying an armload of groceries, as earth-bound as any other mortal. And perhaps his proudest possession today is a framed photograph showing him playing chess with Chief Justice of the Supreme Court Earl Warren. As the man says, he's grown as sober as a judge. What's more, in recent years he's developed into one of the most maturely satisfying jazz trumpeters alive. And, of course, the importance of his role in helping free jazz of its traditional shackles will never be forgotten.

Here, then, is jazz enthusiast Gilbert S. McKean's picture of Dizzy at the peak of the bop revolution, in 1947. While some of its details are dated, and although it may give Dizzy more credit than some feel is his due, it nevertheless captures much of the ferment and excitement of this vitally important transitional moment in jazz history.

The rehearsal studio was a long, unkempt hall of a place with walls painted a rather out-of-place baby blue. At one end of the room a bandstand backed by dingy gold drapes suggested the atmosphere of a dime-a-dance palace. On the stand a group of musicians crouched around the pianist who made sporadic notations on a music sheet as he fashioned the phrases on the keys. The piano man paused, grimaced and then, smiling, penciled in the finale.

"That's it, man."

The trumpet nodded, the sax leaned closer and stared intently.

"Uh-huh. I got it," he said.

"You see," said the pianist. "It's *eee*-blium, *eee*-blium. Not iblium-iblium. Let's run through it together now."

It was a large, choice piece of bebop and the score or so of the beret-and-goatee clan that had assembled to listen displayed the satisfaction of connoisseurs sampling a brandy. When the instrumentalists broke into solos, it was frantic, harshly beautiful music, made of curt phrases, complex excursions that somehow resolved themselves satisfactorily. The melody, complex and bizarre to begin with, was further dissected and juxtaposed until there was a feeling of being pleasantly stunned—as by a recent Picasso.

"Hey! Slow down, man!" one of the listeners wanted to say. "There's too much going on. It's so delicious I want to drink it in slowly. I can't *listen* that fast! I can't dig that much stuff all at once. It scares me!" There was a little of the feeling a great

modern symphony fosters, the exultance which comes in knowing that here is something original and great to be sampled again and again.

This, then, is bebop, another leg in the long journey from the New Orleans folk music called jazz. Like any music worthy of the name it changes with the impact of new personalities, new ideas. Its mutations tend toward an intellectual and finished form as opposed to the sensuous appeal of the more primitive jazz. Bebop has had a greater effect on musicians than any jazz innovation since Kid Ory decided to leave the tail gate open and exercise his elbow more.

Although many had a hand in its origin, the person generally credited to be the father of this modern music is a neatly dressed, youthful chap of medium height and build, with a mustache and goatee. He wears thick spectacles of the dark-rimmed, straight-templed type so popular with the Museum of Modern Art set, not to mention many of us whose eyes are faulty. Born of Negro parents in Cheraw, South Carolina, he was christened John Birks Gillespie by his brick-mason father. Pop had music as a hobby and led his own band. He owned the instruments and kept them at his house when the band was not giving a concert—so that, it may be conjectured, they couldn't wander off and get themselves hocked. It seemed that there was practically every instrument kicking around the house except a trumpet, so John Birks had to start out venting his creative urge on the piano. By the time our hero was fourteen he was fronting his own high-school combo. One day he felt the desire for a trumpet and borrowed one from a neighbor. The rest is history.

When Dizzy was nineteen years old he toured England and France with Teddy Hill's band. In those days he was just a good brass man playing the second-trumpet book and sharing the solos with Shad Collins. When Teddy Hill had planned the tour and hired Dizzy, many of the regular men threatened to leave.

"They thought I was just a green kid—which I was, I guess. 'Who is he?' they wanted to know. 'Who did he ever play with?' You see they wanted somebody with a reputation." Then with a shy smile he adds, "But Teddy thought I had possibilities so he called their bluff. They hated to back down on the trip and we all stuck together."

The South Carolina kid had a wonderful time overseas. In London he used to sit in after hours in a little dive called "The Nest" where his idiosyncrasies must have amazed and delighted the small British band there. In Paris, the land of milk and honeys, while Dicky Wells and Russ Procope were the darlings of the jazz dilettantes, Dizzy was an unknown quantity and therefore pretty much ignored. And, with time on his hands, he ran the gamut from the Sacré Coeur to the Louvre, from Montmartre to Montparnasse and back again—as any good country boy should.

No longer an unknown in Europe, Dizzy's records bring as high as $12 apiece among English collectors and he is the rage of Paris. There his admirers copy down his solos from records and study them avidly. He is the reigning topic of conversation among the French musicians. Charles Delaunay, the French jazz savant, will launch into a discerning critique on bebop with slight provocation. When Django Reinhardt arrived in the United States his first question was, "Where is Dizzy playing?" Gillespie was on a date in Baltimore at the time and there Django, speaking no English, and Dizzy, speaking no French, sat and discussed bebop pro and con on their instruments.

After Dizzy returned from Europe he spent most of his time at Minton's, a Harlem bistro which might be called the bebop salon. It was in this spot that bebop was developed, with many musicians contributing their ideas. There was Thelonious Monk on piano, Charlie Parker on alto, Joe Guy and Gillespie on trumpet and Kenny Clark on drums. But Dizzy first thought of playing in the new style awhile before.

He had been rehearsing with Edgar Hayes' band and there was one bit in a Rudy Powell arrangement that sounded a little different and weird. "It really got me," he says reminiscently. "I played it over and over and realized how much more there could be in music than what everybody was playing. There was a lot there that nobody had been getting. After that, whenever I got the time, I used to sit down with Thelonious Sphere Monk

on piano and we'd play anything that came into our mind."

And so Dizzy began to make a name for himself. It wasn't easy. To a conservative swing band a bebop soloist was as welcome as Senator Taft at an A. F. of L. rally. His periods of unemployment were doubly irritating because many big-name bands dangled fat contracts before him. But it meant playing straight-ride choruses with no chance to develop as he pleased. He stayed in New York playing odd jobs and spending his spare time at Minton's blowing the notes that many would have sworn weren't there in the first place.

As he exerted more and more influence on musicians, a music-publishing house got the idea that a trumpet-instruction book by Gillespie would be desirable. They summoned a representative, Milton Shaw, and told him to collar Dizzy and give him the pitch. They became friends and for some time Milt was a sort of free-lance advisor to Dizzy on bookings, jobs, publicity, etc. Finally, Dizzy persuaded Milt to work for him full time as manager and that is the present status of their quo.

Milt is one of Dizzy's most slavish admirers, which is just as

"The Bird" and Dizzy. While an unperturbed Parker just played, Dizzy played and clowned.

well because one of a personal manager's duties is to be on hand nightly for the band's engagements. He has heard the arrangements many times and swears he still gets a lift out of them.

Milt confesses: "I used to want to be a great trumpet player—I was working hard at it. One night I heard Dizzy, went home and put my horn in moth balls. After hearing Diz, I figured I was in the wrong end of the business—you know?" The same thing happened to Billy Eckstine, whom Dizzy regards as the world's greatest singer. Billy was playing trumpet until he heard Dizzy. Now he concentrates on trombone.

Besides the Diz, probably the most illustrious of Milton's alumni is Charlie Parker, the great alto saxophonist. Oddly enough he and Dizzy played in the same big band years ago. "Neither one of us was playing bebop at the time," says Diz. "A long time later I ran into Charlie and he was playing bebop. Between the meetings both of us had begun the style without the other knowing it."

Charlie Parker, also known as Bird, had played and recorded considerably with Dizzy. They had their first sizable success at The Three Deuces Club on 52nd Street. According to Milt Shaw, "Dizzy would take a bebop solo and Charlie would stand off and watch him. Then Charlie would take one and Dizzy would watch. Then, I swear to God, they'd just *look* at each other and take off on a long unison passage that would scare the daylights out of you—something neither had ever dreamed of before!"

There is some debate over whether the new idiom should be called *bop, bebop* or *rebop*. However, such astute *aficionados* as Dizzy prefer bebop.

Dizzy's manager explains the origin more or less lucidly. "You know when Diz started playing bepop with a group, all their stuff was head arrangements—memorized material that wasn't written down. Well, the pieces didn't have a name, so Diz would give them the first phrases something like this—*bee—bop—bobba—doe—bobba—doddle—dee—bebop!* You know how many bebop choruses end in a clipped two-note phrase with the last note on an off beat? It almost sounds like the instrument is saying 'bebop'! And when Dizzy works with his group he tells the trumpets what to play, the rhythm and the reeds what to play in that *ah—boodle—dud—bebop* talk."

Diz lives for his music. His almost total detachment, his antic uninhibitedness, his habit of gazing into space have something to do with his nickname. When he wants to make a specific purchase, his wife doles out the money; but she won't let him carry any large sum ever, lest he give it away or spend it on some wild whimsy. Dizzy leads a rather quiet life, smoking moderately and drinking little other than copious quantities of milk. You feel that he is a happy man doing what he most wants to do—with that bliss known only to youthful artists as they survey their limitless domains from a new threshold.

Sometimes for a couple of weeks Milt Shaw won't see Dizzy except around the bandstand, never talking business. Then Milt will get a phone call from Dizzy.

"Hey, Daddy! What's happening?" he'll begin.

"What do you mean?"

"What are you doing for the band, man?" And then, as if overcome with worry, "Gee, I guess things are going bad for the band—it'll probably break soon . . ."

There is injected at this juncture a sound effect denoting the explosion of a personal manager.

"Look, Dizzy—for two weeks you've been having a ball without ever worrying for a minute about the band. I've been beating my brains out over it, worrying myself sick. Just before you called I was sweating out a Midwest tour for you—and you want to know what's going on—what's happening—what am I doing for the band!"

Dizzy is very fatalistic about this sort of thing. He shakes his head sadly and tells you: "Every time I call up the office, I wind up getting a lecture! Man, I ain't done nothing!"

Dizzy is a very lovable guy—it is said that he hasn't an enemy in the world. The Savoy Ballroom clique copy his walk, clothes, glasses, mustache and goatee, his laugh, his bizarre voice which often sounds off-pitch. It is startling to go to Harlem of late because you see a reasonably accurate facsimile of Dizzy everywhere.

His memory is legendary; he can play anything through after one hearing. He has perfect pitch and is a brilliant composer and arranger in spite of the fact that he never took a formal music lesson. His tastes in listening embrace Ravel, Stravinsky, Stan Kenton and Billy Eckstine. Practically every instrument has been mastered by Dizzy—his trombone is almost as fine as his trumpet—and he especially enjoys relaxing at the piano, developing ideas that lead to arrangements for his band. His big ambition is to have a large, augmented bebop group, replete with French horns, oboes, English horns, etc. Anything that will increase his scope of expression will find its place in the dream orchestra. For instance, Dizzy started listening regularly to Afro-Cuban bands, recognizing the possibilities of improvising against the everchanging accents of Latin rhythms. Here was a rhythmic abandon akin to his own melodic excursions. One evening he decided to bring three extra drummers to Harlem's Savoy Ballroom. Two of them played the little bongo drums, and one the large congo drum. It was such a success Dizzy decided to use them with his orchestra on concert engagements. Tadd Dameron, one of the first composer-arrangers to work in Dizzy's idiom, is now collaborating with the master on an Afro-Cuban suite, utilizing modern improvisation with the native rhythms.

Selling bebop to the public has been a rather rough proposition. As late as July, '46, Gillespie laid an egg in Detroit that a mama ostrich would have cherished. But the masses are coming around—in this same city last February they had to call out the police to control the crowds.

You will probably want a couple of exposures to this new music yourself. Bebop is something that takes a lot of open-minded listening because it is difficult to judge or compare closely with the swing or jazz you have been listening to. It takes concentration because so much is happening to the rhythm pattern, in the curt phrases of varying lengths and in the solos which utilize notes and chords in a manner heretofore practically unknown to improvised music. However, you remember how difficult the tuba-banjo New Orleans combinations were to take if you had been weaned on Benny Goodman, et al—yet how gratifying it was when you got so you could dig them. With this realization came a glimpse into the past of jazz and everything

from Bunk Johnson to Roy Eldridge fell into place in a more logical pattern.

A look into the future is as rewarding as hindsight. With a hearing of Bunk Johnson, Louis Armstrong, and Bix Beiderbecke you can tell where American music has been—listening to bebop you can tell where it's going. Bebop is a new direction in music. It is that change in expression and idiom which makes all arts absorbing because they are never the same. The loudest scoffers at bebop are those who cling to the New Orleans tradition. There is no argument here that New Orleans, Chicago and so forth are not only esthetically valid but are exquisite listening experiences. But to consider them the ultimate in improvised music, making little effort to assay the worth of new music forms, is to admit to a most unfortunate musical isolationism.

To say that a very considerable number of young musicians are on a bebop kick is as axiomatic as that pat little press release General Sherman put out concerning war. (The adjective "young" is used advisedly. The older musicians, after many years of playing jazz or swing as we have come to accept it, find it almost impossible to adopt the new style.) The present-day idols of the young tyros are Dizzy and Charlie and those they have influenced. While they respect and study old masters like Armstrong and Bechet, they strive to emulate Diz and the Bird.

Dave Lambert, one of the finer vocalists and probably first to experiment with a scat vocal à la bebop (*Perdido* and *Gussie G.*), has given a lucid side light on the style. "A bebop musician doesn't improvise in licks the way the jazz musician does. His phrases are any length whatsoever—from one beat ad infinitum —no more one-, four- and eight-bar licks and riffs. Now the musician has to count *one—one—one—one—one—one—one— one instead of one—two—three—four, two—two—three—four, two—two—three—four,* etc."

So Dizzy and the rest of the Minton coterie have changed the complexion of our music, exerting a force which has influenced countless young soloists. And jazz, having dutifully doffed its hat to Armstrong, Bechet, et al—having genuflected toward New Orleans and Chicago, nodded to 52nd Street and winked at Juilliard, moves on to creative changes intrinsic in any folk art. God knows where it is headed but it's going to be swell to watch."

Dizzy and his trademarks—bulging cheeks, a goatee, a horn on the bias, and an ingenious manipulation of chords.

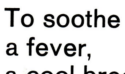

To soothe
a fever,
a cool breeze

By 1950, the bop vogue was over and done with. But since there can be no musical vacuums the emptiness was quickly filled with a new musical sound—a "cool" sound that is still heard today. Cool jazz, it seems obvious, was a reaction to the feverish, often over-taxing complexities of bop. Certainly, in contrast to bop's lush rococco tone and its torrential dotted-eighth-and-sixteenth-note rush, the cool style is soothingly quiet and unexcited, even dreamy. But even though it is a relaxed music, a seemingly lazy music, it still manages to convey a captivating feeling of swing.

The precursor of the cool movement was the late tenor saxophonist, Lester Young, who was known to his fellow musicians as the "President." Young, who acknowledged an indebtedness to both Bix and Frankie Trumbauer, a saxophonist of the twenties, began to be noticed as far back as 1936. Working with a Count Basie quintet at that time, when the rallying cry of the jazz fan was still "Get Hot!", Pres introduced an imperturable, easy-going, unhurried playing style unlike anything heard up to that time. As he said before his death in 1959, "I just lag along, relaxed-like, and don't bother hitting everything on the nose."

Actually, what the,"President" was doing was revolutionary. Before he came along it was taken for granted that you couldn't produce a jazz tone without sharp attacks, rough timbre, a hard touch and a full vibrato. But as French jazz critic Andre Hodier says, "Lester Young showed that it is possible to avoid almost all these features and still produce authentic jazz. Young's veiled sonority and his almost imperceptible vibrato, which disappeared completely in quick tempos, brought into being an unprecedented musical climate. But the indefinable charm that was all Young's own came chiefly from his astonishing relaxation.

"His influence, though it merely touched Charlie Parker and his disciples lightly, is evident today in the work of a whole group of young musicians who regard the "President" as their spiritual father. For a long while, Young was believed just to have given the tenor sax a new style; actually, what he did was to give birth to a new conception of jazz—to the style that has been labeled 'cool'."

Among the "President's" more notable descendants have been trumpeter Miles Davis, trombonist J. J. Johnson, pianists

Miles Davis; a fresh, clear, cool sound.

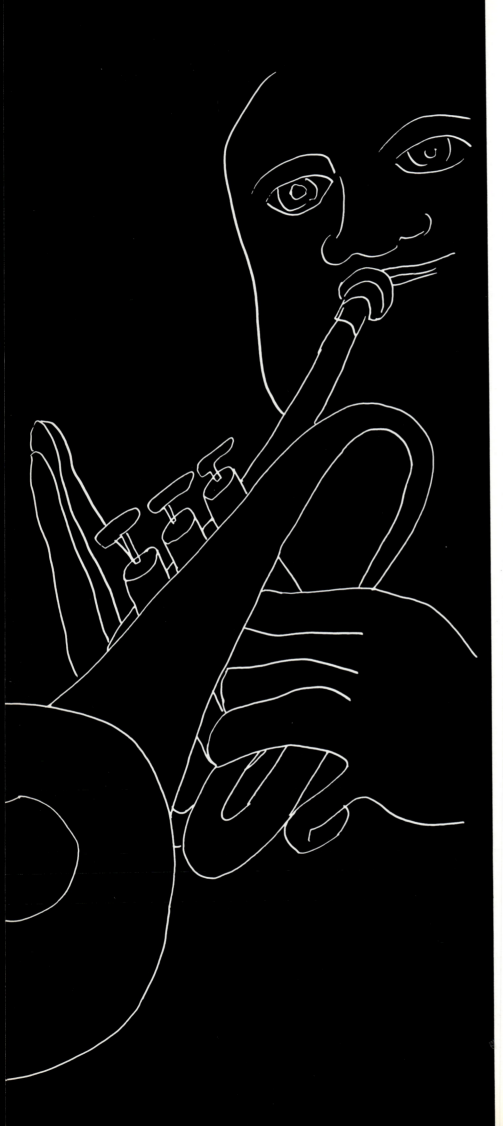

John Lewis and Lennie Tristano, alto saxophonist Lee Konitz, tenor sax men Herbie Steward, Al Cohn, Allen Eager, Gene Ammons, Stan Getz and Wardell Gray, guitarist Billy Bauer, and baritone saxophonist Gerry Mulligan. Of them all, Miles Davis is recognized as the most influential and experimental musician, both as an instrumentalist and as a composer.

With Davis the trumpet almost comes full cycle. In addition to his dedicated reverence for the "President," you can find in his playing touches of Dizzy and the Bird—so transmuted, it is true, that they are barely recognizable. More recently, he has begun utilizing electronics, devising unique tonal colorings to go with his rock-tinged groups. But, surprisingly, Davis has also gone back two generations and adapted to his use one of the greatest jazz traditions of them all. Listen to him on almost any standard tune and you can hear faint echoes of Louis Armstrong. The horn of one of today's most sophisticated musicians still pays homage to Satchmo, echoing some of his joyful drive and gusty exuberance.

In this March, 1959, study of Davis, jazz critic Nat Hentoff analyzed the musicianship of a great contemporary jazzman.

Miles Davis, a small, deceptively fragile-looking man, resembles a choirboy who has been reading Vladimir Nabokov on the side and patronizing an expensive Italian tailor. Also not quite fitting the resplendent youthful candor of his features is a voice that was left much hoarser than Louis Armstrong's after an operation a few years ago to remove nodes from his vocal chords. When Miles decides to speak in what is now his characteristic rough whisper, usually punctuated by a coughed chuckle, the choirboy turns into a mocking deflator of pomposity who will usually become serious about music only.

The youthful international jazz figure, who has been ruefully described by one of his several former women friends as possessing "a kind of elegance with a note of arrogance," is bluntly candid when he talks about music, including his own. "Miles is a leader in jazz," says his long-time friend, arranger Gil Evans, "because he has definite confidence in what he likes and he is not *afraid* of what he likes. A lot of other musicians are constantly looking around to hear what the next person is doing and worry about whether they themselves are in style. Miles has confidence in his own taste, and he goes his own way."

Miles Davis has become in the past few years the most influential modern jazz trumpet player since Dizzy Gillespie. The Davis trumpet has been described as the most lyrical in modern jazz, with one British writer, Michael James, going beneath the lyricism to state: "It is no exaggeration to say that never before in jazz has the phenomenon of loneliness been examined in so intransigent a manner." The bristling, spare introspectiveness of Miles' playing and his brooding, intensely personal tone have led to a frequent misconception among most critics and even some listeners that Miles' music is delicately cool with only glints of the fire that marks more extrovertish hornmen like Dizzy and swing-era trumpet players like Roy Eldridge. In fact, the most quoted and least accurate description of Miles' playing compares him to a man walking on eggshells. If Miles walked on an eggshell, he'd grind it into the ground.

The essence of Miles can be determined by listening to the men he surrounds himself with on his regular jobs. (*Cookin' with the Miles Davis Quintet*) There is his favorite drummer, for example, Philly Joe Jones (not to be confused with Basie alumnus Joe Jones). Philly Joe is a fearsomely aggressive, polyrhythmically swinging existentialist who often uses his sticks as if he were a knife-thrower. Philly Joe's excitability propels him at times to play louder than would be necessary for a military band, but Miles was undismayed when Philly was with his band, because the excitement Joe generates is more important to Miles than any volume problems.

"Look," Miles said a few months ago, before Philly Joe left the band temporarily, "I wouldn't care if he came up on the bandstand in his B.V.D.'s and with one arm, just so long as he was there. He's got the fire I want. There's nothing more terrible than playing with a dull rhythm section. Jazz has got to have *that thing*. No," Miles croaked in exasperation, "I don't know how you get that thing. You have to be born with it. You can't even buy it. If you could buy it, they'd have it at the next Newport Festival."

"You must realize," says Gil Evans, "that underneath his lyricism, Miles *swings*. He'll take care of the lyricism, but the rest of the band must complement him with an intense drive. And it's not that they supply a drive he himself lacks. Actually, they have to come up to him. There's nothing flabby or matter-of-fact about his rhythm conception. As subtle as he is in his time and his phrasing and his courage to wait, to use space, he's very forceful. There is a feeling of unhurriedness in his work and yet there's intensity underneath and through it all."

When he's not playing, Miles also will not be hurried and also is inflammable. Unlike most jazzmen with a reputation as established as his, Miles will not take all the dates he can get, however well they pay. "I never work steady. I work enough to do what I want to do. I play music more for pleasure than for work." And he will not yield to any of the intersecting pressures in the music business. When a powerful entrepreneur once asked Miles to let a protégé sit in with his combo while Miles was working at his club, Miles refused. The potentate, paternalistically amiable only so long as his demands are being met, threatened Davis: "You want to work here?"

Miles said with literally obscene gusto that he didn't care and told the man he was going home. The club owner tried to smooth over the hassle, and asked Miles to return to the stand. Later in the night, however, the protégé nonetheless was sent up to the band. Miles and his men simply walked off.

Miles, in fact, says it was one of his frequent arguments with this particular force in the jazz world that prevented his throat from healing properly after an operation. "I wasn't supposed to talk for ten days. The second day I was out of the hospital, I ran into him and he tried to convince me to go into a deal that I didn't want." In the course of the debate, to make himself clear, Miles yelled himself into what may be permanent hoarseness.

Miles Davis' albums sell in sizable figures for jazz sets. Most former skeptics concerning his talent—like John S. Wilson of The New York *Times*—are being converted. Wilson recently recalled he had found Davis' playing for the past decade to have been characterized by "limp whimpering and fumbling uncertainty," but now feels Miles' newest recordings are examples of "hitherto diffused talent" suddenly taking a turn that brings it sharply into focus.

Miles is unimpressed by what little he reads about himself, favorable or not, having small respect for any American critics except Ralph J. Gleason of the San Francisco *Chronicle*. Miles does allow that his playing has come somewhat closer to his own exacting criteria in the past few years.

"Do you find," a jazz expert, George Avakian, asked Miles recently, "there are many things you do now that a few years ago you wouldn't have dared to do?"

Miles laughed. "A few years ago I used to do them anyway. Now maybe I use better taste than then."

Some observers feel that Miles' "comeback," after several years during which his career seemed to be on a treadmill that was slowing down, dates from his appearance at the 1955 Newport Festival where all the reviews underlined the ardor and freshness of Miles' brief contribution. Miles who, like many jazzmen, is contemptuous of the way the Newport supermarket is stocked and serviced, does not agree: "What are they talking about? I just played the way I always play."

Actually, the renaissance of interest in Miles coincided with the fact that by 1955 he had matured emotionally to the point he could handle the multiple pressures of keeping a combo together; and more than that, he wanted to. He has since led a unit which musicians throughout the country consider to be one of the most stimulating and influential forces in present-day jazz. Miles' rejuvenation enabled him to finally establish a consistency in his playing and to develop from night to night in the company of musicians who challenged him and whom he in turn fused into a coherent unit. There have been some personnel changes, but the unmistakably unifying voice has always been Miles'.

Miles is now booked—at the highest prices of his career—in the major American jazz rooms, occasionally spends playing time in Europe, and recently ad libbed the score for a French film, *L'Ascenseur pour L'Echafaud* (in the U.S. it will be called *Elevator to the Hangman*). Among younger American jazzmen, his intransigent musical integrity and intensely personal "conception" (as a man's style is described in the jazz idiom) make him part of the consistory of modern jazz along with Dizzy, Thelonious Monk, the pervasive memory of Charlie Parker and a few others, including a protégé of Miles', tenor Sonny Rollins.

Miles' playing is still unpredictable and it may be necessary to sit through two sets or two nights of an engagement before Miles indicates fully what all the hosannas have been about. "All of us," says one of his sidemen, "are affected in our playing at night by what's happened to us during the day, but of all those in the band, Miles is the most easily influenced by outside events. He reflects everything he feels in his playing immediately."

Despite Miles' contention that he doesn't particularly care what people think of him, he naturally enjoys his position among the jazz nobility. He's been working toward Olympus since grade school in East St. Louis, Illinois, across the river from St. Louis. Miles Dewey Davis was born May 25, 1926, in Alton, Illinois and the family moved to East St. Louis two years later. Miles' father is a dentist who also performs dental surgery. In recent years, the elder Davis has also been breeding about $200,000 worth of cows and hogs on 200 acres near East St. Louis. Miles' mother, since divorced from Dr. Davis, was conscious of the family's place in local society and tried to uphold it. She didn't discourage Miles' early interest in music, but wasn't fervently in favor of his making it a career.

"I didn't know until after I'd gone back there for a visit a few years ago," says Miles, "that my mother even knew one note of piano. But she sat down one day and played some funky blues. Turned out my grandmother used to teach organ. I was surprised my mother could play because she always used to look as if she'd hit me every time I played my horn. She also plays violin, by the way."

When Miles was about thirteen, his mother wanted to get him a violin for his birthday, "but my father gave me a trumpet." Miles' first instruction was at school. "A guy used to come around and have all the kids hold one note every Wednesday. A doctor friend of my father's taught me to play the chromatic scale right away so I wouldn't have to sit there and hold that one note all the time. The next day in school I was the belle of the ball."

Miles also benefited from a local instructor who had been with Andy Kirk. The instructor's favorite trumpet players were Bobby Hackett and Harold Baker (of the Ellington band) and he was opposed to the pronounced vibrato with which many of the traditional and swing-era jazzmen play. He warned Miles, "You're gonna get old anyway and start shaking." "So," adds Miles, "thats how I tried to play. Fast and light—and no vibrato."

Miles soon began to work week ends with drums, piano and an alto "who sounded like Guy Lombardo's first alto." He was also part of a high-school band that rehearsed twice a week and sounded, they hoped, like Count Basie. A local professional trumpet player who especially impressed Miles was Clark Terry, now with Duke Ellington. Miles listened to Clark and other local musicians in all-night jam sessions. Miles has always loved to jam and, during infrequent visits home, sits in for a night in a drab neighborhood club with the resident rock-and-roll band. "It's a funky place," he says happily, "with everybody talking and drinking and no time limits on the sets."

"Miles," says a Paris friend, Boris Vian, a writer and trumpet player, "could play a hundred hours in a row."

Miles had been moved by Charlie Parker's early records with Jay McShann and by what little could be heard of Dizzy Gillespie on the Billy Eckstine band records. Finally, the Eckstine orchestra with Parker and Gillespie arrived in St. Louis. "A friend and I went down to see them. I had my horn with me; we'd just left rehearsal. As soon as I walked in, this guy runs up to me and says, 'Do you have a union card?' It was Dizzy. I didn't even know him. I said, 'Yeah, I have a union card.' 'We need a trumpet player. Come on.' I wanted to hear him; I could always read, so I got on the bandstand and started playing. I couldn't even read the music at first from listening to Dizzy and Bird. The third trumpet man was sick; I knew the book because I loved the music so much, so I played with the Eckstine band around St. Louis for about three weeks. After that I knew I had to go to New York."

After high school, Miles' mother wanted him to go to Fisk University. "You know how women are. She said they had a good music department and the Fisk Jubilee Singers. But I was looking in *Esquire's Jazz Book* and seeing what was happening in jazz in New York, and that's where I wanted to go. I got hold of my father, and got permission to go to New York where I enrolled at Juilliard."

For a week, Miles looked for Charlie Parker, spending his allowance in the search. He found him and moved in with Bird. "I used to follow him around, down to 52nd Street. 'Don't be afraid,' he used to tell me. 'Go ahead and play.' Every night on matchbox covers I'd write down chords I heard. Everybody helped me. Next day I'd play those chords all day in the practice room at Juilliard, instead of going to classes. Monk would write out chords for me, Tadd Dameron, and Dizzy, who advised me to study piano, which I started to. I had some background in understanding progressions from a book I'd bought in St. Louis, *Georgia Gibbs Chord Analysis*. I finally left Juilliard. I realized I wasn't going to get in any symphony orchestra. And I had to go down to the street at night to play with Bird or Coleman Hawkins, so I decided to go that way—all the way."

Miles' close association with Bird was vital to him musically. He learned by listening to Bird play, almost never by hearing him discourse on theory. "He never did talk about music. I always even had to show Duke Jordan, the pianist in the band, the chords. The only time I ever heard Bird talk about music was an argument he had with a classical musician friend of mine about the naming of chords. That was the night Bird said you could do anything with chords. And I disagreed. 'You can't play D natural in the fifth bar of a B flat blues.' 'You, you can,' said Bird. Well, one night in Birdland, I heard Lester Young do it, and it sounded good. But he bent it.

"Bird used to play forty different styles," Miles told a *Down Beat* interviewer. "He was never content to remain the same. I remember how at times he used to turn the rhythm section around. Like we'd be playing the blues, and Bird would start on the 11th bar, and as the rhythm sections stayed where they were and Bird played where he was, it sounded as if the rhythm section was on one and three instead of two and four. Every time that would happen, Max Roach used to scream at Duke Jordan not to follow Bird, but to stay where he was. Then, eventually, it came around as Bird had planned and we were together again. Bird used to make me play. He used to lead me up on the bandstand. I used to quit every night. The tempos were so fast; the challenge so great. I used to ask, 'What do you need me for?'"

Another musician who impressed Miles in his first years in New York was the late Freddie Webster. "I used to love what he did to a note. He didn't play a lot of notes; he didn't waste any. I used to try to get his sound. He had a great big tone, like Billy Butterfield, but without a vibrato. Freddie was my best friend. I wanted to play like him. I used to teach him chords, whatever I learned at Juilliard. He didn't have the money to go. And in return, I'd try to get his tone."

Miles' career progressed through work with Parker, Benny Carter, the Eckstine band, and finally combos of his own. In the early Fifties, Miles worked infrequently. When he did play he was rawly inconsistent. His personality difficulties had become intensified; and, to avoid the mounting pressures, he tried not to care about anything.

During the bleak years, Miles supported himself mostly by recordings and by transcribing music from records for lead sheets. A good deal of what Miles recorded in those years he regards as inferior, and he's angry at his former record company for later releasing some of that material. "I didn't care then. I do now."

It was after several months of exile in Detroit, an attempt at analysis and experiencing the nadir of self-contempt that Miles began to re-establish his career. He has consolidated his style in the past three years, honing it to its present quality of probing lyricism.

When he had arrived in New York in 1945, Miles' tone and technique had been tentative; and he had been intimidated further by the weighty presence of Parker and the fact that Dizzy Gillespie was the prevailing influence on modern jazz trumpet at that time. Most of the acolytes tried to emulate Dizzy's fiercely careening, multi-noted flights that usually reached their climax in the higher register of the horn. Miles, however, had never been able to play very high. When he was thirteen, he'd tried to play *Flight of the Bumble Bee* in the Harry James manner and found he couldn't. "I felt like I was breaking my head. Years later, I asked Dizzy, 'Why can't I play high like you?' 'Because you don't hear up there,' he said. 'You hear in the middle register.' And that's true. There are times when I can't even tell what chords Dizzy is working on when he's up high; and yet he'll tell me what he's playing is just an octave above what I do."

"Miles," notes a French musician, "doesn't take you by storm like Dizzy. He's more insidious, more like somebody calling you from the other shore." Herbie Mann, a flute player, has explained that Miles, rather than any other flutist, was his primary inspiration when he started trying to make the flute a jazz instrument. "The attraction of Miles to me as a flutist was that he could be masculine, could communicate strong feeling with his horn and still be subtle and rarely sound beyond the volume level of the flute. He proved you don't have to yell and scream on your instrument to project feeling."

According to Gil Evans, "A big part of Miles' creative gift is in the creation of sound. First of all, he has his own basic sound which any player must develop. But many players then keep this sound more or less constant. Any variation in their work comes in the actual selection of notes, their harmonic patterns and their rhythmic usages. Miles, however, is aware of his complete surroundings and takes advantage of the wide range of sound possibilities that exist even in one's basic sound. He can, in other words, create a particular sound for the existing context. The quality of a certain chord, its tension or lack of tension, can cause him to create a sound appropriate to it. He can put his own substance, his own flesh on a note and then put that note exactly where it belongs." (Superior examples of Evans' point are Davis' playing in sections of *Music for Brass,* and *Miles Ahead,* for which Evans did the arrangements, evidence of both men's admiration for Duke Ellington.)

It was with Evans as the dominating influence and young writer-players Gerry Mulligan, John Lewis and others assisting

that Miles assembled an epochal nine-piece unit for a series of recordings in 1949-50 (now available in *Birth of the Cool*). These recordings, more than any other single event, shaped the growingly active movement in modern jazz toward carefully integrated "chamber" groups. These Davis sessions helped establish in the consciousness of many modern jazzmen, here and abroad, an unprecedentedly awakening realization of the subtle possibilities of group dynamics and group expression as a whole in which the solos are a flowing part of the entire texture and structure of the work. The records indicated further how much more colorfully challenging the background textures for jazz improvising could become. The instrumentation that included French horn and tuba led to the fact that, in the early Fifties, as Gil Evans observes drily, "it got to be traditional awfully fast to do a date with French horn and tuba."

A lonely man, Miles suffers if he's alone, and his West-Side apartment in New York is usually populated by friends, sidemen and a blaring TV set. "One of my biggest hobbies," he chuckles, "is cursing TV. When I get through cursing all I see on TV, I'm all calmed down." Other hobbies of various degrees of therapeutic aid are sports cars, camera equipment and boxing. He also is fond of fine clothes and expensive furniture. "I love wood. That's why I hang up those *Down Beat* plaques I win. Otherwise, winning a poll doesn't mean anything to me. Look at who some of the other poll winners are."

"He will not make concessions," wrote André Hodeir, reviewing a concert by Miles in Paris some time ago. "When Miles cuts short the applause and moves efficiently from number to number, it's not from contempt of the public. On the contrary, he restores to the public its dignity by refusing it any concession in terms of choice of program or 'showmanship' on the part of himself and his musicians."

Yet Miles does not believe in being as formal in concert work (to which, in any case, he prefers the ease of a night club) as the Modern Jazz Quartet. "I'm a John Lewis fan, and I like all of them, but I don't go with this bringing 'dignity' to jazz. The way they bring 'dignity' to jazz in their formal clothes and the way they bow is like Ray Robinson bringing dignity to boxing by fighting in a tuxedo."

Miles is less annoyed than many other jazzmen by noisy night-club audiences. "I figure if they're missing what Philly Joe Jones is doing, it's their tough luck. I wouldn't like to sit up there and play without anybody liking it, but I just mainly enjoy playing with my own rhythm section and listening to them. The night clubs are all the same to me. All you do is go and play and go home. I never do know what people mean when they talk about acoustics. All I try to do is get my sound—full and round. It's a challenge to play in different clubs, to learn how to regulate your blowing to the club."

"Miles has changed much in the past few years," says an old European friend. "He has become more master of himself. He knows what he wants to express, and he expresses it well, with control."

"I'll tell you," says Miles with a grin, "if I can play good for eight bars, it's enough for me. It's satisfaction. The only thing is," he puts his finger on his nose, "I don't tell anybody which eight bars are the good ones. That's my secret."

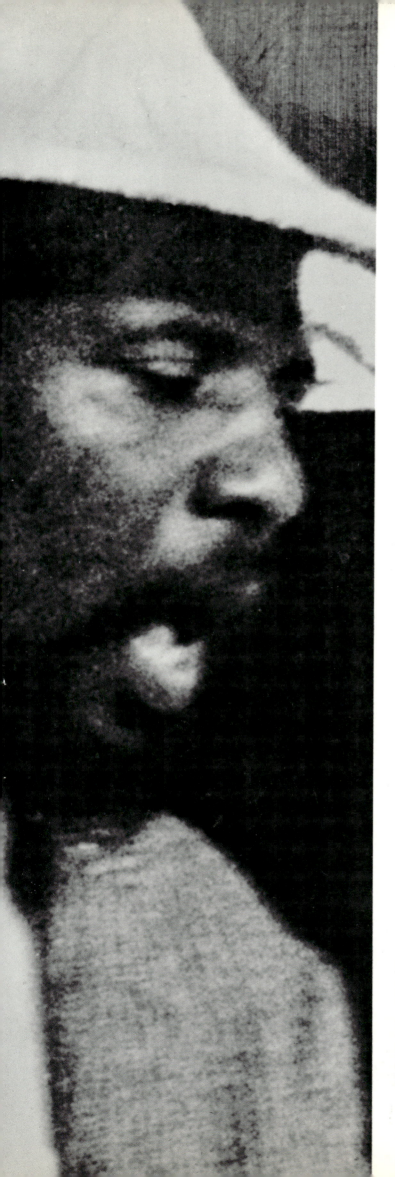

The private world of Thelonious Monk

Another musician with secrets is Thelonious Monk. Once he was readily identifiable as the pianistic ringleader of the bop revolt but, with time, he has become a complete musical maverick. As a pianist, he no longer fits into any school or movement. As the first major jazz composer since Duke Ellington, there are no other compositions being written with which his can be readily compared. Consequently, it's been said of him that he defies classification.

Monk's musicianship is incredible. He is a virtuoso of time, metre, accent, space, all of the basic components of jazz. And he brings to them a wholly original talent, one that is both strikingly expressive and extraordinarily inventive. As critic Martin Williams noted some years ago, "Monk is what no jazzman before him has ever been; after more than fifteen years,

still an innovator and legitimate experimenter . . . still a man who is looked to by young jazzmen for hints about what to do next."

In just what direction Monk will go next cannot be predicted. But whatever his new direction, it is a reasonably safe bet that he will continue to be followed zealously by such outstanding jazz modernists and/or experimentalists as trumpeters Art Farmer and Donald Byrd, altoist Julian "Cannonball" Adderley, drummers Art Blakey and Max Roach, tenor saxist Sonny Rollins, composer-arranger Gigi Gryce, and many others. And they can be sure they won't be led astray. For if past performance means anything, whatever course Monk's music takes it will never lose its fire, its bite, its flowing rhythmic propulsion, its easy ever-swinging beat. In his hands, it seems, jazz can't go wrong. So in one sense Monk *can* be classified. He is one of the giants of jazz. He may even be, as Nat Hentoff suggested in this April, 1960, study of the man and his work, a giant among giants.

"It has become inescapably hip," Hentoff writes, "to accept Thelonious Sphere Monk as one of the reigning council—and perhaps *the* lama—of modern jazz. He has been elevated from a cartoon to an icon, but in the process the man himself has remained as opaque and unpredictable as in his barren years."

Monk's arrival at acceptance seemed to occur, in a way, without his active participation. The music, of course, was there to be argued about, mocked and praised, but there were no interviews (until recently), no friendships (slight or otherwise) with the critics, no letters to the trade-press editors or ghosted articles. There was no personal advocacy at all—except the playing and the writing. The music formed a recognizable entity, although a controversial one; behind it was mostly vapor in dark glasses and a goatee.

Monk's ascent was more asymmetrical than most. He waited a good deal longer—more than twenty years—than is usual if a jazzman is to be called at all.

Although there were always a few musicians who at least partially understood and approved of what Monk was playing and writing, he did not—until the past two or three years—derive much moral support from most modern jazzmen. Some felt his fiercely percussive, unpredictable piano difficult to play with. His penchant for leaving large spaces in his playing left unseasoned sidemen with the sensation, in the middle of a chorus, of having stepped into an abandoned elevator shaft.

Others simply did not understand his music, and since many jazzmen are as conformist as they tell themselves the day people are, they did not try to pierce the veil for fear of being considered too unorthodox by their colleagues. There were those who agreed with most of the critics that while Monk had written a few intriguing tunes ('*Round Midnight* was the only one that had any real currency), he was a limited pianist who was more eccentric than creative, more an historical relic of the Minton's dawn of bop than a lasting influence. And since he was unable to get steady work, he couldn't keep together and thus develop in a unit those few of the younger musicians who were not intimidated by him.

About five years ago, the inside line began to change. In 1957, Monk was hired at the Five Spot Café on New York's lower East Side, and for the first time in years he could be heard six nights a week. The musicians began to come, began to understand, and started to spread the word. In a few months, the first question a New York musician in Los Angeles or London was likely to be asked by the resident faithful was, "Have you heard Monk lately? What's he doing?" At the same time he was being recorded by a company that had come to realize he was developing into its most important property. It promoted his records accordingly, and made new ones available at regular intervals.

The recognition gathered intensity and momentum until Monk's records began to receive nearly unanimous and almost automatic imprimaturs by the critics, and he won more and more polls here and abroad. His compositions are beginning to be played by other groups, and he has become a major formative influence on jazzmen—not only pianists and writers, but players on all the instruments.

Now, on the few occasions when he can be persuaded to leave New York, Monk commands between $1,700 to $2,000 a week for his combo, something more than $1,000 for a single night's work. As late as three years ago, he was being hired—usually as a single—for $350, and might have been able to get $800 a week for a group.

Two of the most qualified critics in jazz pay him tribute usually held for the dead. To Martin Williams, he is "a major composer—the first . . . since Ellington—and one whose work drastically extends the concept of composition in the idiom." The flinty, sternly unsentimental André Hodeir talks of Monk's "urgent beauty" and says it's quite possible that future generations will regard Monk as *the* jazzman of our epoch.

Although he is, of course, aware of the change in the way he is regarded by others, Monk himself has not altered appreciably either in the pungent, angular force of his playing nor in the implacably intuitive way he conducts his personal life. He has, however, begun to worry, an affliction he seldom experienced in his bleaker days. "I wonder," he occasionally says to his wife, Nellie, or to Harry Colomby, his gentle manager who teaches English and history at Far Rockaway High School, "I wonder if it'll last."

The answer lies more with Monk than with external circumstances like changing public taste. Although recognition dawdled cruelly in arriving, Monk's achievements have by now been so solidly accepted that he is assured of sizable listener support as long as he wants to appear in public. "Monk," says his agent, Bert Block, of Joe Glaser's huge and aggressive Associated Booking Corporation, "can be a big piece of property. It's all according to how he acts."

Monk acts according to how he feels, and no one is ever quite sure how he'll feel at any given time, nor even what he feels. He may often stay up two or three days, and he does not eat by clock since his periods of hunger do not always fall into regular rhythms.

In describing the musical experience of playing with Monk, tenor saxophonist John Coltrane also provides insight into Monk in any situation: "You have to be awake all the time. You never know exactly what's going to happen. Rhythmically, for example, Monk creates such tension that it makes horn players *think* instead of falling into regular patterns. He may start a phrase from somewhere you don't expect, and you have to know what to do. And harmonically, he'll go different ways than you'd

Julian "Cannonball" Adderly plays "hard," Progressive jazz.

anticipate. One thing above all that Monk has taught me is not to be afraid to try anything so long as I feel it."

The spontaneous acting out of his feelings—some of them anyway—also characterizes Monk off the stand. On a visit, if he feels like napping, he does. There are times, in his home or outside, when he doesn't feel like talking, and he may not for several hours. This latter condition usually occurs when he's worried, and if he's sufficiently disturbed, he'll answer no one, not even his wife, to whom he's very close, except to say that nothing at all is bothering him.

He is often witty, particularly in his music. Jazz pianist Dick Katz has summarized the abrasive humor of Monk's music:

"He has a beautifully developed sense of sarcasm together with a kind of left-handed veneration for things of the past (he can express respect for stride piano on several of his recordings while making some fun of it too). He has no patience with maudlin sentimentality, but unlike many of the young modernists who approach the sentimental balefully, he can spoof it gently while expressing positive feelings, as Fats Waller did."

In conversation, Monk is of a literal turn of mind. "Would you," a lecturer in jazz at Columbia University directed rather than asked him, "play some of your weird chords for the class?" Monk was affronted. "What do you mean weird? They're perfectly logical chords." Another time, a musician began portentously, "Well, everybody says...." "What do *you* say?" Monk stopped him. He is impatient with interviewers, especially when they ask speculative questions like the future of jazz. "I don't know where it's going," he told Frank London Brown in *Down Beat*. "Maybe it's going to hell. You can't make anything go anywhere. It just happens."

Monk is easily bored, and he will not long bear a situation he finds dull. He may suggest a walk to whoever is with him, or just leave. Walking is a favorite avocation, as is riding around New York in his car. Monk has a great love for the city in which he was raised. When he does get into trouble, it's almost always on the road.

Twice he has become involved in difficulties on the road, and both times were due in part to his losing his ability to communicate. Even close associates know times when Monk simply disconnects and will not be reached.

"Part of that disconnecting," Hall Overton thinks, "has to do with what seems to be a deep distrust at times of his own capacity to communicate what he feels and of others' ability to understand. He may figure at those times that he won't be understood, so why try?" "Or," says another musician, "he may just be escaping from reality."

In any case, in the Fall of 1958, he, tenor-saxophonist Charlie Rouse and the Baroness Koenigswarter, a good friend, were driving to what was to be a week's engagement for Monk at the Comedy Club in Baltimore. They stopped at a motel in Delaware and Monk went in to ask for a glass of water. Monk is an imposing figure. Slightly more than six feet tall and weighing around two hundred pounds, he is physically impressive more by the forceful solidity with which he stands and moves and the intensity of his look than by his mass itself. The motel owner was shocked at this sudden presence, reacted in a way Monk felt to be rude, and Monk, silent all the time was slow in leaving.

The owner, growing more frightened, called the police. Cops tried to pull Monk out of the car to which he had returned, but he held onto the steering wheel, claiming he hadn't done anything to warrant their attention. About half a mile up the road, more police cars appeared, Monk was dragged from the car, thrown to the floor of the police vehicle, pummeled and hit on hands as the baroness tried to tell the officers that Monk was a pianist.

Later, marijuana was found in a can in the trunk of the car. Charges of possession that were filed against Monk were dismissed, since no connection could be proved between him and the marijuana. He was fined for disturbing the peace. He also lost his New York police identity card without which no musician can work in any New York place where liquor is served. His manager, charging race prejudice was involved in the Delaware arrest, asked for a hearing before the New York State Liquor Authority, which must also pass on applicants for a card. Monk, though nervous, was thoroughly articulate and co-operative at the hearing. An incident underlined his concern for absolute candor. "Didn't one of those people at the motel call you 'nigger'?" asked his manager. "No," said Monk. "I didn't hear that. But they were acting weird." He had felt prejudice, he later said, but he would not say what had not actually happened.

In the Spring of 1959, he was booked for a week at Boston's Storyville. He had been up for some three days and nights without sleep. When he arrived, he came to the desk of the Copley Square Hotel, where Storyville is located, with a glass of liquor in his hand after having flitted around the lobby rather disconcertingly, examining the walls. He was refused a room, and at first also declined to accompany his sidemen to the Hotel Bostonian where they were staying. At about ten o'clock, he finally went on stand. The room was nearly full of expectant but patient people. He played two numbers, and came off. At 11:30, he played the same two numbers, sat motionless at the piano for what seemed like half an hour. His bewildered sidemen had left the stand after about eight minutes.

Monk began wandering around the club, obviously disturbed at not having a hotel room. He finally registered at the Bostonian, didn't like the room, and left. He tried the Statler, was refused there, and took a cab to the airport with the idea of going home, collecting his wife, Nellie, and taking a room with her for the rest of the week. Planes, however, were no longer running, and he was picked up by a state trooper to whom he would not or could not communicate. He later did reveal who he was, but it was too late, and he was taken to Grafton State Hospital near Worcester for observation.

He was lost there for a week. No one knew what had happened to him. The local Boston police were checked, but no one thought of trying the state police. A letter the hospital claims it sent to Nellie Monk never arrived. By accident, an acquaintance in Boston heard mention of Monk's whereabouts on a local TV show. Nellie rushed to Massachusetts and secured his release. There had been no grounds on which he could be held. "It was the combination," a friend later speculated, "of exhaustion after several days without sleep, the fact that he discon-

The Color of Jazz

By Robert Andrew Parker

nected at first, and the fact that he was away from New York and Nellie."

Yet much of the time Monk is dependable and concerned with fulfilling his responsibilities. Lapses do occur, but they happen less and less. A recording date was scheduled three days before the CBS-TV Sound of Jazz program in December, 1957. Monk never showed up, and the late Billie Holiday's accompanist, Mal Waldron, hastily substituted a solo for the record. Yet during the rehearsals and the subsequent program, Monk was on time, wholly co-operative, and one of the most stimulating parts of the program. He had stayed up for a couple of days, it was later learned, because he had been so anxious to do well on the show.

A few months before, after a rocky plane ride, Monk spent most of an opening night in Detroit playing with his elbows. "I'm sorry," said a musician who has enormous admiration for Monk's work, "but he or anybody else, genius or not, owes it to an audience to give the best he can." Monk increasingly realizes his responsibilities to an audience, and his troubles on the road may be over. After a recent stay in San Francisco, the owner of the Black Hawk avowed: "Mr. Monk can play my club any time. He's a gentleman. I don't know what they're talking about. This guy was straight with me." Monk, in fact, was often early for the night's work, was on time for every set and even signed autographs.

Monk, in short, remains self-absorbed, but is growing up in the way he relates to an audience. In 1949, Paul Bacon, one of the very few writers on jazz who understood Monk in the Forties, wrote in the French monthly, *Jazz-Hot*, that Monk was very egocentric and that the fact that he considered the world revolved around him gave him a remarkably direct vision of things, very much like that of a child. "To become an adult," wrote Bacon, "it's necessary to make a lot of concessions."

Monk has stubbornly avoided concessions musically and otherwise—as much as he has been able to since boyhood. Drummer Denzil Best first began to play jobs with Monk when the latter was fifteen and is firm on the point that although Monk has certainly developed since then, his approach at the beginning was essentially what it is now. "People," says Denzil, who was then a trumpeter, "would call his changes (chord progressions) wrong to his face. If he hadn't been so strong in his mind, he might easily have become discouraged, but he always went his own way and wouldn't change for anything."

Thelonious (a family name which his father bore and his son now carries) was born October 10, 1920, in North Carolina, but was brought up in New York's San Juan Hill section in the West Sixties close to the Hudson River.

The neighborhood, as it was when Monk was a child, is largely underprivileged. There were scholarships available for children of musical capacity; but from the beginning, Monk's playing was too unorthodox to qualify him despite the fact that his mother had three children to support on a minute income and the boy was obviously deeply involved with music. His mother, a former civil-service worker, is said to have been a strict disciplinarian and there were rigid demands on Thelonious to be neat, obedient, polite.

When he was about six, Monk began tentatively to trace melodies on the piano by ear. He had some formal lessons when he was about eleven, but he's essentially an autodidact as pianist and composer. While quite young, he listened to all the jazz pianists he could find—Earl Hines, Art Tatum, Teddy Wilson and James P. Johnson, among them—partly as an antidote to the two years he played organ in a church. He had soon wearied of the predictable plush chords of the religious music and he found the Dixieland and much of the swing music of the time too limiting. "I never picked no special musicians to follow. Of course, you have to go through certain stages to learn how to play the piano, but that doesn't necessarily mean you're copying somebody's style. I've learned from numerous pianists."

One of the most accurate descriptions of how Monk plays was written by Paul Bacon in the *Record Changer* in 1948: "...he can make a rhythm seem almost separate, so what he does is inside it, or outside it. He may play for a space in nothing but smooth phrases and then suddenly jump on a part and repeat it with an intensity beyond description. His left hand is not constant—it wanders shrewdly around, sometimes playing only a couple of notes, sometimes powerfully on the beat, usually increasing it in variety and occasionally silent.... And Monk has a beat like the ocean waves—no matter how sudden, spasmodic, or obscure his little inventions, he rocks irresistibly on. ...Monk is really making use of all the unused space around jazz, and he makes you feel that there are plenty of unopened doors."

"Where many pianists less original than Monk," Gunther Schuller noted recently in *The Jazz Review*, "are exclusively concerned with playing *the* 'right' (or acceptable) notes, Monk, at his most inspired, thinks of *over-all* shapes and designs or ideas...and, because he is a man of great talent, or perhaps even genius, he does play the *right* notes, almost as a matter of course."

Monk began playing in local bands when he was about thirteen, learning how to read orchestrations at a local community center. Some four years later, he traveled the country as part of a unit accompanying a rocking evangelist. "Rock and roll or rhythm blues," Monk said of this experience, "that's what we were doing. She preached and healed and we played. And then the congregation would sing."

One of the cities the healer visited was Kansas City, and Mary Lou Williams, the perennial modernist, heard Monk there for the first time. "He was playing the same style, to a large extent, that he is now. He told me that he was sick of hearing musicians play the same thing the same way all the time."

Back in New York, Monk began twenty years of scuffling to find steady work. "I worked all over town. Non-union jobs; $20 a week, seven nights a week; and then the boss might fire you at any time and you never got your money. I've been on every kind of job you can think of" said Monk, remembering dance halls and bars, all over New York. "I really found out how to get around this city. There are a lot of things you can't remember—except the heckling." The work was infrequent, the heckling recurrent, because Monk's style was unexpected, and he would not change.

In the late 1930's, Monk began playing occasionally in Harlem with a few musicians with whom he felt some degree of rapport

—the late Charlie Christian, Dizzy Gillespie, Idrees Sulieman, Charlie Parker and drummer Kenny Clarke with whom Monk wrote *Epistrophy*, one of the first modern jazz standards.

Monk recalls of the Minton's era: "I was just playing a gig, trying to play music. While I was at Minton's anybody sat in if he could play. I never bothered anybody. I had no particular feeling that anything new was being built. It's true modern jazz probably began to get popular there, but some of these histories and articles put what happened over the course of ten years into one year. They put people all together in one time in one place. I've seen practically everybody at Minton's, but they were just there playing. They weren't giving any lectures."

But while Monk wasn't lecturing either, he did become a valuable example. "He opened people's ears," says Mary Lou Williams. "If I hadn't met Monk shortly after I first came to New York around 1945," adds Miles Davis, "I wouldn't have advanced as quickly as some say I did. He showed me voicings and progressions, and I remember Charlie Parker would take me down to listen to Monk all the time and make me sit in with him."

Monk was the earliest champion of Bud Powell whose influence on modern jazz piano became as pervasive—until the Monk renaissance of a couple of years ago—as Charlie Parker's on all instruments. It was Monk who insisted Bud sit in at Minton's when Kenny Clarke, Dizzy and others were eager to expel him from the stand. Bud, strongly influenced by Monk musically, a few years later helped convince Cootie Williams to record Monk's *'Round About Midnight,* a wounding melody that Monk wrote when he was nineteen. As has often happened with jazz writers, in return for the first recording of the tune, Monk found Cootie Williams listed with him as co-author. (Among other Monk jazz "standards" are *Ruby, My Dear: Well, You Needn't; Off Minor; In Walked Bud* and *I Mean You.*)

The Forties was a harsh time for Monk, as it was for most of the younger modernists whose music took a number of years to be accepted by even the basic jazz audience. Since Monk, however, was even more uncategorizable than the others, his jobs were fewer. There were quick stands like a week or so at the Savoy with Lucky Millinder in 1942 and a 1944 date with Coleman Hawkins on 52nd Street. Hawkins, unlike many jazzmen of his generation, was intrigued by and encouraged the modernists. Monk's first record date was with Hawkins on four 78 r.p.m. sides made in 1944. Thirteen years later, Hawkins played as a sideman on a Monk album.

Monk made his first records under his own name for Blue Note, beginning in 1947. The company is consistently exploratory, and its artistic integrity—it has never, for example, issued "jazz" version of a Broadway show—has sometimes led it to the brink of economic suicide. The main difficulty with recording Monk, recalls Alfred Lion, the label's recording director, was finding musicians who could play with him, since what he was writing and playing was not in the conventional "bop" vein. He didn't then," remembers Lion, "write much of anything own. The musicians had to learn what he was doing by ear. And even if he had written it all down, he might have changed his mind fifteen times between the time a musician had learned is part and the final take. You really had to have ears to play

with him."

The first Blue Note singles received some attention in Harlem and in the Negro sections of a few other large cities, but it took several years before white jazz listeners began to buy Monk. "They thought," Lion reminisces sadly, "he lacked technique."

Lion managed to get Monk jobs from time to time, often uptown, but underlines that "in those days, Monk was completely isolated. He rarely worked with the boppers—when they did get a little work—because he was going his own way; and so, in all those years into the Forties and Fifties, I doubt if he ever had a job that lasted more than two weeks at a time. Yet the audiences that did come to hear him were usually fascinated and were held by the fact that he always had a beat going."

What scattered night-club work Monk had been getting in and around New York was cut off completely in 1951. Monk and a friend were arrested on a narcotics charge. The consensus of opinion among relatively disinterested observers at the time was that Monk, innocent, took a rap rather than risk being regarded—by himself—as a "drag" for putting full blame on his co-defendant. Monk served sixty days, a particularly nightmarish penalty for someone who abhors restraint as he does. "He kept his dignity though," said a friend. "He never grovels, no matter how bad things get."

Worse than the jail sentence was the loss of his police card. He was sustained by a few record dates, mostly for Prestige to which label he had switched in 1952; very infrequent engagements out of the city; and mostly by his intensely devoted wife, Nellie, who worked during most of Monk's nearly silent years. When he did finally get steady work at the Five Spot in 1957, Nellie would leave their children with a baby sitter for part of most nights so that she could be with her husband. If she didn't arrive, Monk would usually become restless and would eventually call her at home.

Nellie is tall, thin, nervous, and singularly attractive in the way that many people with oversize strength of spirit often are. "Thelonious had trouble getting work even before he lost the card," she looks back. "Therefore, it wasn't a sudden total calamity. People had told so many stories about his being unreliable and eccentric that it had always been hard. But during the worst years we didn't feel the struggle as much as other people might have because we were very close, we felt each of us was doing the best he could, and we didn't suffer for things we couldn't have. In fact, nobody talked about them. If it was a matter of clothes, for instance, I felt it more important that he have them since he's before the public.

"During those long stretches when he wasn't working," she continues, "it was torture for him not to be able to play. But you'd never know it from looking at him, and he didn't get bitter. Anybody with less strength would have snapped. And he was continually omitted from things—records, concerts, and the like. We'd listen to the all-night Birdland radio show, and maybe once in two months they'd play a record of his. There was no money; no place to go. A complete blank. He wasn't even included in benefits. He even had to pay to get into Birdland."

In 1957, with the help of a lawyer retained by Baroness Nica Koenigswarter, Monk regained his police card. The baroness, who is becoming somewhat of a misty legend on the New York

scene, has befriended other jazzmen. She has helped Monk financially in the past, and Monk has occasionally found her home a good place in which to concentrate on composing. In fact, a few times the whole Monk family has lived there.

Monk's ability to concentrate, however, can be formidable, no matter what the environment. Monk does not, however, work on a daily schedule. When he feels "right" he will compose. He won't force himself. When he does work, as Dick Katz observes, "he works very hard, very intensely. He has a lot of fragments in his mind that he'll keep coming back to in the process of composition, and he's always especially concerned with getting the right bridge (the 'inside,' he calls it) for his songs. The inside, he insists, has to make you appreciate the outside."

When Nellie was in the hospital and quite sick, Monk began to release some of his worry in music, and worked doggedly at *Crepuscule with Nellie,* one of his most tender compositions. It took him a month before he worked out the "inside" he felt was right.

"Everything fits so well," adds John Coltrane, "once you get to see the inside." Another musician discovered that "When you learn one of his pieces, you can't learn just the melody and chord symbols. You have to remember the inner voicings and rhythms exactly. Everything is so carefully inter-related; his works are *compositions* in the sense that relatively few jazz 'originals' are."

When rehearsing musicians in his works, Monk will take a long time to make sure they understand exactly what he wants. A few months ago, he was showing an orchestra how his piece, *Little Rootie Tootie,* went. Until they had absorbed his instructions, he had them take the number at a slow tempo, a tempo they assumed was the one he wanted. After he felt satisfied with their grasp of its inner workings he took it at considerably faster tempo. He hadn't wanted them to be any more flustered at first than they needed to be.

During the same run of rehearsals, a young trumpet player persisted in taking conventional "bop" solos on Monk's *Friday the Thirteenth.* The musician based his fluent improvisations on the chord changes of the tune with little concern for the rest of its parts. "If you know the melody," Monk stopped him, "you can make a better solo." "Do you want me to *play* the melody?" the musician asked. "If you know the melody," Monk repeated, "you can make a better solo, and you won't sound as if you're just running changes."

"A good part of the success of what Monk does," Dick Katz goes further in analyzing his music, "depends on the particular sounds, the tone qualities he gets out of the piano. He taught me one of his compositions note for note, but I couldn't make it *sound* the way it was supposed to. The sound of the entire piece is important in his work, not just the melody alone. Of how many jazz composers besides Duke Ellington can one say that?"

"Even the sounds of the horns become different in his work," says altoist-composer Gigi Gryce, "and you have to get exactly those sounds that he wants out of your instrument somehow if you want to keep working with him. He wrote a part for me once that was impossible. I was playing melody and at the same time was playing harmony to his part. In addition, the intervals between the notes were very wide. I told him I couldn't do it.

'You have an instrument, don't you?' he said. 'Either play it or throw it away.' And he left me. Finally, I was able to play it."

Monk's intentness on securing precisely what he wants occasionally results in his suddenly leaving the piano at a club or recording session, standing in front of the musicians and lunging into a dance. Onlookers usually regard Monk's flailing steps as just another badge of his "eccentricity." He dances, however, for a specific reason. "It's as if he were conducting," says Gryce. "It's the way he gets what he wants. At one record date, some of the musicians were laughing as he danced without realizing that meanwhile, by following his rhythmic pulse, they were moving into the rhythm he wanted." "Sometimes, when we're deciding which take to issue for an album," says his recording director, Orrin Keepnews, "he'll do his dance. It's his way of being sure the number is swinging right." "When you're swinging," Monk once told his men, "swing some more!"

Even when seated at the piano, Monk's feet slash into space like the climax of a switch-blade duel. Although physically in repose unto seeming torpor a fair amount of time off the stand, Monk at the piano becomes possessed by immense kinetic energy and plays, in fact, with all his body.

"Monk is all music," says Dick Katz, "not part piano, part music. A lot of what some fine pianists play is, by virtue of their considerable technique, more piano than music. They'll do things of a mechanical, however fluent, nature that are related to the music only intellectually. Actually, Monk does many technical things other pianists would have difficulty with—long, unorthodoxly-fingered whole tone runs, for instance. They may sound slightly crude, but try to do them yourself. Or he'll play a fast succession of chords built on fourths with every note clear as a bell. He gets into areas where the normal pianists wouldn't go. It's like what happened in early jazz history when self-taught musicians would extend the range and capacity of their instruments because they had no instruction books to tell them what they couldn't or shouldn't do."

Thelonious can be challenging in other ways than music. "I used to have a phobia," says Nellie, "about pictures or anything on a wall hanging just a little bit crooked. Thelonious cured me. He nailed a clock to the wall at a very slight angle, just enough to make me furious. We argued about it for two hours, but he wouldn't let me change it. Finally, I got used to it. Now anything can hang at any angle, and it doesn't bother me at all."

Monk challenges his friends as well as his wife. "When Monk found out I was going back to Juilliard to study," said Sahib Shihab with a grin, "he said, 'Well, I hope you don't come out any worse than you sound now.' I knew what he meant. He wasn't putting down the way I was playing. He was referring to what has happened to several jazz musicians who go to school and then, when they get out, are scared to play certain things that don't fit with what they've been taught. They lose that urgency of personal discovery that's jazz."

It's that "urgency of personal discovery" that motivates Monk. "He needs very few things in life," Hall Overton points out. "He's got his one girl, Nellie, and the kids and the music. And I think to him the music is the most important of all. And the dearest."

Sonny Rollins; a neo-bopster with a special feel for the Blues.

126

The fabulous Gypsy

Among the giants who peopled the jazz scene during the first decades of its history only one foreigner can be found—the French gypsy, Django Reinhardt. In a way this is surprising. It is easy to argue that jazz, being indigenous to the United States, can only be played with authenticity and authority by Americans, and that it is only to be expected that they would occupy all the seats in jazz's Hall of Fame. But jazz ceased being indigenous to America many, many years ago. It became the music of the world three decades back.

In fact, jazz was first recognized as a genuine art form in France, around 1928, when it was still considered a mere musical novelty by the general public in the U.S. Even as early as the mid-Thirties, the marked contrast between the limited acclaim they received at home and the overwhelming receptions accorded them wherever they appeared abroad was dumbfounding American jazzmen. They were startled, too, to discover how many foreign musicians were turning to jazz, finding in it the language for self-expression they had long been seeking.

Now, of course, jazz is acknowledged to be the one commodity exported from this country that is greeted with wild enthusiasm wherever it is shipped. Yet, curiously, we seldom find any to import in return. We know it is being produced, in considerable quantity, on every continent. But for some inexplicable reason, although there are countless foreign jazz musicians none of them except Django Reinhardt has ever grown to truly gigantic proportions. As Leonard Feather says of Django, "Beyond dispute, he was the first overseas musician ever to influence his jazz contemporaries in America."

Django was not only musically unique, he also stood alone as a personality. The following dossier, compiled by Gilbert S. McKean shortly before Reinhardt's death in 1953, portrays a man who was as colorful and explosive as his music.

The last time I saw Django, his heart was warm and gay; the last time in London, that is. His costume looked as if it had been picked out of Esquire—one piece per issue over a period of years. From under a wide-brimmed, grey felt hat long strands of jet-black hair were visible—hair so long that it made the average American musicians look as if they had just been crew-cropped for Cornell. Around his neck was loosely knotted a multicolored silk scarf, looking not unlike an Air Force escape map. The suit he was wearing could not have had a more suave, conservative cut had it been styled on Lenox Avenue. His feet were shod in bulky, rugged ski boots.

As he walked down Piccadilly toward the Circus, he caused such consternation that he disrupted two ration queues and it was reported in fairly unreliable circles that a Bond Street tailor was stricken with apoplexy at the sight. The amazing part about the whole thing was that the unconcerned gypsy air with which he wore the outfit made it look *right!* You almost wondered why everybody else was dressed so stupidly.

This sartorial apparition is considered by many to be one of the greatest of all jazz virtuosi, certainly the greatest creative soloist ever to develop outside the United States.

Django was a character, the genuine article—a character with a capital "C," in neon lights. He was unreliable, unreasonable and inordinately vain; at the same time he was sincere, generous, lovable. The appellation "genius" is being flung about considerably these parlous days and there is no valid reason for ignoring the fabulous gypsy. He was a genius. There.

Django's life is as incredible as his music, the latter being described as a sort of flat-foot-floogie with the frou-frou. It's a long way by gypsy caravan from the shantytown at the gates of Paris where he spent his childhood to Carnegie Hall and Café Society, but our hero made it. He always knew he would. The

Django Reinhardt, The Three-Fingered Gypsy by Henry Markowitz.

word *django* is doubtless the French equivalent of the American infinitive *to horatio alger.*

America had always been the good earth, the land of dreams to Reinhardt. As a child he used to slip into the neighborhood movie theatres where he could commune with the daring cowboys and insidious redskins racing across our cinematogaphic wild and woolly West. Later on this land of action attracted him as the only country cut to his own heroic size, a place where an artist would be properly recognized, where palms grew calloused not from manual labor but from being constantly crossed with silver.

For Django was a mercenary soul. He knew that the fiddler must be paid but he was primarily interested in a guitarist. Not that he was a miser in any sense of the word; he was generous and loved spending money even more than making it. And he was supremely contemptuous of the pittances doled out by many French entrepreneurs. Rather than accept a sum he considered beneath his artistry, he would decline offers that would make many another French musician gasp. He chucked the whole show, took to his gypsy train and strummed his costly chords gratis to the four winds.

When the impresarios agreed to pay Django his enormous demands, the money lasted only a few days. He fancied himself the *grand seigneur,* the 18th-century French equivalent of the big operator, and yearned to be considered King of the Gypsies. The Reinhardt table usually groaned with succulent cheeses, tasty sausages, French bread and plenty of good *vin rouge;* at any hour of day or night, "The Man" was surrounded by dozens of his gypsy "cousins" who came to break bread and to gossip.

Gambling was his chief extravagance. He would say *blanc* is *noir* if the odds were decent and had been known to leave Monte Carlo several hundred thousand francs light after a few evenings' differences of opinion with the croupiers. No matter how much money he made with his music, he was always forced to borrow from his old friends. They endeavored to reason with him to be prudent even to the extent of citing the parable of the grasshopper and the ant.

"*Eh, mon vieux,*" they told him. "It is not necessary that you support the casinos as if they are your own private charity. Let them look elsewhere for their rent!"

But Django was incorrigible. He was still a gypsy at heart— a rather willful gypsy, too. His youth was that of a caravan nomadic—until he was twenty he had never worn a suit nor lived in a house. But out of a welter of backward gypsy tribes with many almost medieval customs, the illiterate floating slum of the wagon train, came this guitarist of gigantic creative stature—an instrumentalist to set the "peasants" (which is the gypsies' derisive term for all outsiders) on their ears. For years he had been idolized by jazz fans, first in France and then all over the world.

Django was literally born to the sound of applause. His mother, billed as La belle Laurence, was the star of a group of itinerant gypsy players touring France and Belgium. While the rest of the troupe was giving its show in the little Belgian town of Liverchies on the night of January 23, 1910, she was giving a more important performance in the trailer outside. The baby was baptized Jean, but they called him Django from the first.

By the time the boy was fifteen he was a widely traveled man —all over France, Italy, and Belgium and he saw action with the Algerian Dead End kids in the Casbah. But the charms of music began to soothe his savage breast about the age of ten. His hardboiled playmates eyed him somewhat askance when they saw his preference for the music of gypsy guitars, violins and mandolins—instead of pursuing the manly art of raiding pushcarts and vineyards. At the tender age of thirteen his guitar had been heard in professional appearances in various Apache hangouts in the slums of Paris. La belle Laurence called for him each night to collect his pay lest he wager it away.

By 1928 his good fortune and talent had given him a place in the European limelight. Lady Luck not only smiled at him, she gave him the key to her apartment. But all the good things went up in smoke early one November morning that year.

Returning home Django found his gypsy trailer full of artificial flowers to be sold at the cemetery next day. There was a rustling noise under the flowers.

"*Nom d'un nom!* Those accursed rats again!" He raised the candle sleepily. It was almost burned through and crumbled in his hand, the burning wick falling on the celluloid flowers below. There was an immediate explosion and the place became an inferno.

With stunning rapidity he was almost surrounded by flames. In desperation he clutched a blanket in his left hand to use for a shield as he fought his way out. His life was miraculously saved, but as he ruefully contemplated his injuries he wondered if it was worth saving.

"*Regardez donc!* My left hand!" It was a shapeless mass of seared flesh. And the surgeon recommended amputating his right leg. It developed that the leg stayed on, but it was a year and a half before he learned to walk again. And the hand? Well, nobody expected him ever to play again.

By sheer will power Django trained himself to use first one finger, then another. Not only did he regain his skill but he capitalized on his disability to become an even greater guitarist. Compensating for the paralysis of his fourth and fifth fingers, he developed a new method of chording which made his style completely new and distinctive.

Following his recovery the old wanderlust hit Django. He and his brother traveled through the south of France, earning their way by passing the hat after playing guitar duets in sidewalk cafes.

Credit for "discovering" Django, or rather rediscovering him, should go to Emile Savitry, one of the typical *avant-garde* artists of prewar Montparnasse. While he was spending a few days in Toulon, he ran into two wandering minstrels. One of the motley duet played surpassingly fine guitar, so the intrigued Emile invited them to his apartment for a record bash. On tap were classical records, Hawaiian selections and finally *le jazz hot.* In this little furnished room in the port area of Toulon, Django first heard the orchestra of Duke Ellington, the great artist who was to feature him at Carnegie Hall some fifteen years later. He was so overwhelmed by the torrents of *hot* pouring from the phonograph that he burst into tears. This jazz evoked a profound response in the gypsy. From now on he got his kicks from Louis Armstrong and the Duke, not from the

To get to his Paris gig, and to keep his shoes clean, Django's wife piggy-backed him through the muddy gypsy campsite.

waltzes, tangos and popular French ditties which had previously formed his repertory.

It was only a question of a few months before Savitry had got Django enough jobs to get him up the ladder to Paris. There he impressed Jean Sablon, who was singing in a swank night club, and wanted Django for his personal accompanist. This was agreeable, but the guitarist with typical Gallic insouciance neglected to show up for work half the time. Swallowing his pride, Sablon sent his car to the outskirts of Paris each evening to get the musician out of bed and to work on time.

Before this door-to-door delivery system went into effect, the ever-practical Django had another means of transportation. In the gypsy camp where he lived, just outside the Paris wall, a sector known as the *Zone*, there were no streets. It was unthinkable for his shoes and clothes to become soiled on his way to work. The problem was solved each evening with a most engaging expedient.

"*Attention,* my little cabbage," he would exclaim to his wife. "My sweet, it is time for me to go to the job of music."

"*C'est bien.* I am ready, my love," she would reply. Then she would bend forward, Django would mount her shoulders and off they would go through the mucky ways. When the pavement was reached he would tax her strength no longer, gallantly dismounting to walk the rest of the way toward Montmartre.

The next important step in Django's development was the formation of the Quintet of the Hot Club of France. This club was an organization of French lovers of American jazz music which got together at first to enjoy records, but soon was running concerts of its own featuring the best French musicians and such visiting American stars as Coleman Hawkins and Benny Carter.

By 1934 the HCF had reached the point where it was looking for a band to uphold the banner of France in the jazz world. They found what they wanted in a group drawn mostly from Louis Vola's band which, in the past, used to jam between sets in a back room at the Claridge. Personnel consisted of Stephane Grappelly (violin); Django Reinhardt, Joseph Reinhardt, Roger Chaput (guitars); and Louis Vola (bass).

With their first concerts the Quintet became the rave of Paris and their records enabled the world to share this music. American fans were delighted to hear a European band catch the spirit of jazz music, yet remain unique; many who found blaring trumpets, bleating saxes and obtrusive drums a bit strenuous on the ears were captivated by the delicate improvisations of this ensemble.

Few in this country who avidly followed their record releases realized what a volatile little package this combination was. In the two stars, Grappelly and Reinhardt, there was enough explosive temperament to supply the Metropolitan Opera and a ballet company for a complete season, including matinees. This petty rivalry constantly threatened to split the combination; not only were they bickering over top billing, but they were personally antipathetic toward each other. Grappelly, elegant though penny-pinching and somewhat superficial, was Django's opposite in nature, although they were perfect complements musically. Some of the trouble arose because their records were variously issued for contractual reasons, as Django Reinhardt

and the Quintet of the Hot Club of France or Stephane Grappelly and his Hot Four.

The situation came to a head during the Quintet's first broadcast to the United States in 1937. On their bandstand in the Big Apple cabaret on *Rue Pigalle* (known as Pig Alley since the 1944 American invasion) the musicians grew tense as the time approached. The seconds ticked away and at the "On the Air" signal, the American announcer went confidently into his introduction. . . .

"From Paris we now bring you the music of Stephane Grappelly and his Hot Four."

Django turned white with rage, jumped to his feet and began to stalk out of the studio. Only the humblest of apologies and a promise to correct the error before the end of the program induced him to return. He has not forgiven Grappelly to this day, but the fault was not the violinist's.

The group was playing in England when war broke out in 1939. Stephane chose to remain in England as he is part Italian and was technically a nonbelligerent. All the others returned to France where Django formed a considerably successful big band. After the lull of the phony war, the Germans unleashed their blitzkrieg and Django took to the road with countless thousands of panic-stricken Parisians. On the run his gypsy experience served him well and he fared much better than the hapless city dwellers.

After the Pétain maneuver, things returned to "normal" and Django returned to Paris and greater fame than ever. The rebellious youth of France subtly expressed their hostility toward the Nazis in this fad for American music. A new Quintet was formed with Hubert Rostaing replacing the missing Grappelly. For once Reinhardt's extravagant salary demands were useful; every time the Germans wanted him to play he would ask for an impossible figure.

Among his engagements during this period was a two-week stint in North Africa in 1942. Lady Luck looked the other way when he sailed back to France on November 6. Two days later the Allies invaded Africa, missing a terrific USO recruit by a matter of forty-eight hours.

The next year, tiring of Nazi-occupied France, Django attempted to escape to Switzerland. A German patrol happened upon the café where he was to rendezvous with the guide. A search of his person revealed a letter from a Swiss impresario and a membership card from the British equivalent of ASCAP —the Performing Rights Society. Arrested immediately for espionage, he was taken for interrogation before a German major. The officer took one look, as the story has it, and said, "Reinhardt, old chap! What are you doing here?" It seems the major was an old German jazz fan who collected the Quintet's records before the war. Probably one of the more esthetic Nazis who wouldn't think of handling a record without first washing the blood off his hands.

It will be a surprise for many to learn that, while he could read no music, Django had done considerable writing for the symphony orchestra. His *Boléro* was performed on the same program as the more famous Ravel composition and did not suffer by comparison. An organ Mass composed by him especially for the gypsies to play during their annual pilgrimage to Sainte-

Marie-de-la-Mer prompted the organist of Sacré Cœur Cathedral to remark that he had never heard a better conceived Mass, original yet fully respecting the traditions and harmonies. He even attempted a symphony, but it is so daringly modern that no orchestra has yet programmed it. He dictated his serious work to Gerard Leveque, a young musician who lived in an apartment next to him. Whenever inspiration seized Django, he would bang on the wall until Leveque came rushing in with his paper and pencil.

The war years in France were about the same for Django as for the other Frenchmen, with the exception that he fared better than many because he earned good pay in the night clubs of Paris.

When the Allies swarmed into the barricade-ridden "City of Light," they liberated jazz and Django, incidentally, along with the *mademoiselles, vin ordinaire* with exotic and expensive labels, nonvintage champagne, and immature *Calvados.* He was very popular with the Yanks from the first, making several appearances with Special Services. Any jazz *aficiandos* who were lucky enough to make Paris spent much of their time searching the night clubs of Montmartre for the guitarist.

In the latter part of 1945, he came to London for a reunion with Grappelly. Call it sentiment, call it patriotism—at any rate, when the two first sat down to improvise a bit, there was something of a psychic cue from somewhere. The first selection played was the *Marseillaise*—once through in a slow and noble march tempo and then swung joyously. It was so superb that it was included in the first recording session at His Master's Voice studios where the Quintet needled wax for the first time since the war.

When Django returned to France, he amazed everyone by coolly disregarding all offers and played a return engagement of his famous disappearing act. He mounted his sturdy trailer, joined his gypsy caravan and vanished into the French countryside. Several American booking agents who had been negotiating for an American appearance promptly began growing another ulcer. Finally a letter and a contract from Duke Ellington caught up with him—it sounded *formidable* so he boarded a plane for the promised land.

On tour with the Duke, Django enjoyed considerable success despite the fact that someone had the brilliant idea of giving him an unfamiliar, electrically amplified guitar. He had always played a guitar without amplification. At his Carnegie Hall appearance with Ellington, he also suffered from the world's most ineptly balanced sound system, but managed to play more inventive jazz than any other soloist on the program.

In 1946, a few days before Christmas, New York jazz devotees received an early Yuletide gift in Django's appearance at Café Society's Uptown Branch. Lionel Hampton, Paul Whiteman, King Cole and many others came, saw and went sent. His admirers were delighted. But, for him, they had also hoped that Django would never become as popular as, say Frank Sinatra. Reinhardt, almost illiterate, could sign his name only with great difficulty. If he ever were cornered by a hundred autograph hounds, it would take him a week to sign his way out of the trap."

Looking back on Armstrong, Bix, Tatum, Ellington, Django, Parker, Eldridge, Gillespie, Young, Davis, Monk, and all the other giants, past and present, to whom jazz has given birth, who can worry about the future? A music healthy and fecund enough to produce such titans, generation after generation, will surely go on and on and never cease growing.

Harlem's "Big Maybelle"

By Tom Keough

Part Four

Women
in
Jazz

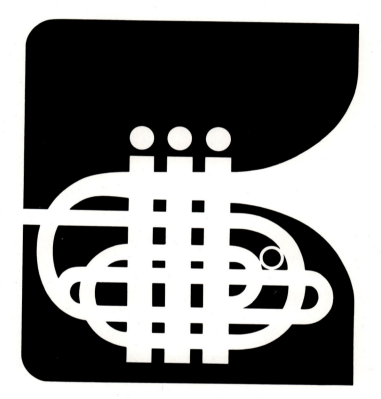

Why so few women succeed in jazz is a question that has never been satisfactorily answered. Some say it is because they haven't got the stamina to follow the tough life of a modern band. Others attribute it simply to the fact that women don't seem to have the same enthusiasm for jazz that men do, due, at least in part, because they regard a career as just an interim before the more sedate profession of a home and a family.

One of the rare women to achieve authentic jazz greatness, the incomparable pianist Mary Lou Williams, thinks still another factor must be taken into account. She says, "Most instruments demand too much physically of the average woman. Furthermore, women don't like to have their faces changed as instruments change faces . . . the lips jutting out a little more . . . the muscles around the nose and mouth hardening . . . that sort of thing.

"Actually, I've known only three or four women musicians who were good enough to take the place of men. As a matter of fact, once I tried to organize an all-girl band and I just couldn't find enough talent. Maybe, though, I've been playing with male musicians for so many years that I've developed a superiority complex."

In contrast to Mary Lou, the distinguished jazz pianist Mary Osborne refuses to admit that women are at all inferior to men when it comes to playing jazz. The equally distinguished Marian McPartland expands on the subject:

You've come a long way, baby

One of my first reviews as a new jazz pianist opening at the Hickory House in 1952 was by Leonard Feather in *Down Beat.* "Marian McPartland has three strikes against her; she's English, white and a woman." Somehow this seemed like an accolade! It made me realize that I was doing something unusual and special. But more than twenty years later, thanks to what has been happening to women in jazz, I look at my role much differently. I don't feel I have any strikes against me—in fact, life for me is really a ball!

Of course, the joy and feeling of freedom in playing jazz might never have materialized were it not for the many accomplishments of women in the jazz field who inspired me: Mary Lou Williams, Hazel Scott, Lil Hardin Armstrong, and Cleo Brown, to name a few. These were my heroines—I heard them on records long before I ever dreamed of coming to the United States. Lil Hardin with Louis Armstrong's Hot Five! What fabulous music, and what a dynamic force this woman was all her life, first to Louis, and then to other people she worked with, and taught. From Hazel Scott I got my first introduction to an exciting way of swinging the classics by listening to her jazz arrangements of Chopin waltzes. I heard Mary Lou Williams with the Andy Kirk Band, and then with various small groups of her own. She had a strong percussive touch, and whatever she played swung as she produced exciting rhythmic figures and patterns. And as for the somewhat lesser-known Cleo Brown, who, Dave Brubeck once told me, was one of his biggest influences, she impressed me with her powerful, rumbling, swinging attack, colored by full, dark chords.

There were also one or two English women players who were outstanding—Rae Da Costa, a brilliant technician, and Winifred Atwill, who played ragtime. My father liked Winifred's playing a lot, and he'd say, "Why don't you get a style like Winifred Atwill? I can understand the melody when SHE plays." This made me furious.

My very first and main influence was not a woman, but a man—a very great man named Duke Ellington. I'll always be grateful to a boyfriend who brought Duke's and other jazz recordings over to our house and made me really listen; he made me aware of the Ellington band's unique orchestral sounds—the quality and tone color of each soloist—Duke as a pianist—his way of voicing chords—the strong, exciting rhythms of the band. I absorbed it all—and from then on I was hooked!

I had played piano by ear from the age of three. Oddly enough, Mary Lou Williams and I had the same sort of beginning—listening to our mothers play and then trying to emulate them; but what each of them played was a world apart. My mother played Chopin on the piano; Mary's mother played spirituals and hymns on the organ. From an early age Mary was surrounded by jazz musicians, and she grew up in this atmosphere; whereas I went from Chopin to nursery rhymes in kindergarten, to the songs we learned in high school and popular music of the day (Bing Crosby singing *Please*) plus everything else on the BBC. When I was seventeen years old, I was accepted at The Guildhall School of Music, where, in addition to piano, I studied composition, harmony, singing, and even the violin. But all the time I kept dreaming about being a jazz player instead of a concert artist.

In between lessons at The Guildhall, I sneaked off and auditioned for one of the "popular" pianists of the day, Billy Mayerl. He immediately offered me a job playing in a four-piano *act* that he was putting together. When I told my parents I wanted to leave The Guildhall and go on the road playing in vaudeville theaters with Mayerl, they were horrified. But I kept insisting, and they finally gave in. Even though the music we played was not really jazz, it was thrilling to be out on my own, a performer!

When the four-piano group finally broke up, I drifted through a variety of jobs, none of them jazz-oriented. I accompanied singers and acts, played in vaudeville and solo piano dates on the BBC, and finally, in World War II, I joined the English equivalent of USO Camp Shows—ENSA. Eventually, I switched from ENSA to USO and went to France in 1944 with the first show to be sent there after the invasion, and sat in with the GI jazz musicians. In St. Vith, Belgium, there was a big army band stationed nearby, and musicians were talking about Jimmy McPartland who, they said, was coming to join the Special Service Company in the area in which USO personnel were billeted. I had listened to Bud Freeman, Muggsy Spanier, Sidney Bechet, and Bix Beiderbecke in England on records, but somehow I had missed hearing and knowing about Jimmy McPartland. Then suddenly one day there he was, a good-looking, smiling man in his thirties, just released from combat in the front lines, and anxious to play. It's ancient history now,

Mary Lou Williams

Marian McPartland

went to see them. This was the first woman vibes player I had ever heard, and she was impressive, showing great technical skill; and she played with a beautiful swinging feeling. Later Jimmy and I worked at the Hi-Note on Clark Street opposite Jeri Southern, a most sensitive singer and a very tasteful pianist. Jeri had a great influence on me. It was the first time I had heard that particular kind of delicate but strong playing, as she accompanied herself without a rhythm section, using her own lush chords.

We came back to New York in 1949 to live, so I was able to meet, and listen to, many of the women musicians in town. Fifty-second Street was still swinging—Mary Osborne, the guitarist, and her trio were at the Hickory House (which later became my home base for so many years); Dardanelle, vibra-harpist, and her group held forth at another club down the street; Barbara Carroll was playing at the Downbeat Club opposite Dizzy Gillespie's big band.

With big ears and eyes we visited every club whenever we could. Jimmy and I went to The Embers, which had become THE place in town, featuring Joe Bushkin and his group. It was an intimate, yet noisy room, and I was eager to play there, so Jimmy talked to Ralph Watkins, the owner, about bringing me in. He agreed. I opened with Eddie Safranski on bass and Don Lamond on drums, my first trio engagement. I was nervous and at the same time thrilled to be playing in a top room in New York with two of the town's best musicians. In addition, the job called for us to accompany Coleman Hawkins and Roy Eldridge! These two musicians were my idols for years, and I never dreamed I would actually be required to play for them. It was almost too much for someone new on the scene, but by this time, from my experience with Jimmy, I knew more about accompanying horn players, and now my apprenticeship in other areas really started—learning how to handle new situations; how to play in different styles; finding out the kind of accompaniment different musicians liked to hear behind them; learning how to relate to an audience, and how to treat the sidemen.

In those first months, I was eager to do well, and though I didn't realize it at the time, I was very competitive. I liked it when someone would say, "You play just like a man," and I appreciated compliments from other musicians. I even liked it when someone would say, "You play good for a girl," or "You're the best WOMAN player I've ever heard." I was so busy trying to play as well as I could that I didn't think about it too much. But finally I asked someone who said "You play just like a man" what he meant. He stammered a bit and said, "Oh, well, you know, I've never heard a *woman* play so STRONG." Once a man stood at the bar watching me intently, and when the set was finished he came over and said with a smile, "You know, you *can't* be a respectable woman the way you play piano." For some reason or other, this struck me as a great compliment.

These were typical observations expressing the prevailing point of view at that time, and there were many variations. It was thought that women who played strongly in a direct, forthright way were "playing like men." Women were supposed to be tentative or frilly in their playing, yet I've heard *men* who

but when he first saw me at the jam session with the G.I. musicians and found out *I* wanted to play, too, his first thought (as he tells it) was "Oh, God, a WOMAN piano player! And she's going to sit in—I know she's going to be lousy." It so happens he was right! In those days I hadn't learned how to back up a jazz soloist. I didn't really keep steady time, or listen enough to the other players. I was so eager to prove myself that I just went barging in with lots of enthusiasm and not too much expertise.

At any rate, Jimmy liked my harmonic ideas (my saving grace), because the army put us together as part of a small group that went out every day at the crack of dawn to play for GIs in the front lines. At last I was starting to get the musical knowledge and experience I so badly needed, learning more tunes, how to play more simply behind solos, and how to keep better time myself. Suddenly jazz records sounded more meaningful. I was able to *hear* more, and to get some ideas from what I heard and put them into my own playing. Jimmy and I got married in Aachen, Germany, on February 4, 1946, and a couple of months later, we left for the U.S. to visit Jimmy's family in Chicago.

I listened avidly to all the local musicians and to groups coming in from out of town. George Shearing and his quintet with Margie Hyams on vibes came through, and of course I

play delicately, with tenderness and a soft touch, who have never been thought to be unmasculine.

As time went on, it became easy to deal with questions from the audience with humor and frankness. Question: "How do you like working with men?" Answer: "*I love* it!" Question: "Does sex enter into your playing at all?" Answer: "You're darn right—especially if you're going with the drummer!" Question: "Why don't you have any girls in your group?" Answer: "One woman is enough, maybe too much." Question: "How can you tell male musicians how you want them to play?" Answer: "I hardly ever do, they usually tell *me*."

The guys had their share of it, too. Bill Crow, who later joined my trio on bass, was asked: "How does it feel to work with a woman?" Bill, with a sly grin: "Well, I've always liked the company of ladies." Around the same time, a drummer said to Joe Morello: "Man, are you still working with that chick?" (When Joe left to join Dave Brubeck, that very drummer was the first to apply for his job!)

During our long runs at the Hickory House, we spent most of our breaks at Birdland, which was only half a block away, listening to the great bands—Duke Ellington, Kenton, Basie, Woody Herman; fabulous singers, Ella Fitzgerald, Sarah Vaughan, Dinah Washington, and June Christy; and small groups such as Dizzie Gillespie or Stan Getz. I played many Monday nights (the off-night) there myself; in fact the first time I ever played Birdland was with a group of black musicians (trumpet, sax, bass, drums) I had never met. Before the first set we all congregated on the bandstand, and I suddenly realized they were extremely displeased at having me, a white unknown woman player, there on the bandstand with them. It was an unforgettable experience. The tunes would be discussed among them and the tempo kicked off, but I was ignored! Luckily I knew all the be-bop "standards," so I just played along, trying to look and feel unconcerned and to get into the music. But it was hard! I'm not sure to this day who I played with that evening—how could I be? Nobody even said hello! And their backs were turned to me the whole time.

In these busy years, the 1950's, I began to meet other women musicians who came to New York to make names for themselves. The Hickory House seemed to have been a proving ground for all of us at one time or another. I certainly can't accuse the owner, John Popkin, of being unfair to women. When I was on the road, he hired the young German pianist Jutta Hipp, with a trio. On another occasion when I was at the Composer Room on Fifty-eighth Street, working opposite Mary Lou Williams, he brought in a vibrant, hard-driving Japanese pianist, Toshiko Akyoshi, fresh from the Berklee College of Music in Boston. Another talented player who acquired a big following at the Hickory House was a young Indiana girl, Pat Moran. It was interesting to hear these women, each with her own trio, and observe their influences, their backgrounds, and their particular styles. Every one was different in her own special way, and each used excellent local sidemen (all men!). One point worth noting: There has never been any difference in the union scale whether the musician was male or female! The music business is one in which there has been no discrimina-

tion between the sexes in this regard. The amount of one's salary depends on drawing power and "name" value, not one's sex.

In those years, girls were not relegated only to trios. Terry Gibb's big band featured Terry Pollard on piano and vibes. This girl was simply great—she was pretty, and she had a fast musical mind. On the four-mallet exchanges with Gibbs on the vibes, she was brilliant, playing with taste, humor, and boundless ideas. Later, Alice McCloud replaced her, playing in a strong, straight-ahead, no-nonsense style, on both piano and vibes. She had a loose, easy, driving beat. Later she married John Coltrane and, since his death, has made many beautiful, intricate-sounding recordings on the harp, with her own group.

Many of these musicians influenced me. And so did the girl singers, who can offer a great source of inspiration to musicians, especially by the way some of them have treated certain songs. For example, I could never enjoy playing *If You Could See Me Now* as much as I do if I hadn't heard Sarah Vaughan's beautiful rendition—one of her first big records. *Here's That Rainy Day* made a lasting impression on me when I heard Peggy Lee's poignant treatment of it at Basin Street East. Years ago I started listening to Ella Fitzgerald, and I was especially fascinated by her singing of Gershwin songs backed by Ellis Larkins. What a way to learn these lovely tunes! And how could one begin to play *Easy Livin'* or *God Bless the Child* without a silent thank you to Billie Holiday? The list is endless. I was eager to learn *While We're Young* after hearing Mildred Bailey sing it. I followed the intricacies woven into *Sweet Georgia Brown* by Anita O'Day when I accompanied her at the Hi Note in Chicago. Working with her gave me special insight into her way with many songs, which undoubtedly has influenced my playing of them. For any musician, knowing the *lyrics* to a song is important—how can one put feeling and understanding into a piece without knowing the words? For this alone all of us appreciate and admire the many great song stylists—Bessie Smith, Ivy Anderson, Ethel Waters, Carmen McRae, Lee Wiley, and one very underrated singer whom I've always loved—Helen Merrill. And now fresh new singers are bursting on the scene to inspire us—Roberta Flack, Aretha Franklin, Dee Dee Bridgewater, Jean Carn, Esther Satterfield. And there are more and more young women jazz singers on the way up.

The same holds true for female musicians. Many people know of Hazel Scott, Mary Lou Williams, and Barbara Carroll, but they've probably never heard of Norma Carson, one of the finest players I know! Years ago, she came and sat in with me at the Hickory House, and I was amazed to hear this slim, pretty woman play trumpet in a style close to that of Miles Davis the way he played in the 1950's.

Guitarist Mary Osborn is another underrated musician. For years she was on the Jack Sterling Show on CBS in New York with Tyree Glenn and a small band, and during her long stay there, she performed consistently in clubs and on records. Mary and her family are now living in Bakersfield, California, where she continues to keep a group together, playing in local clubs.

Mary and many other women musicians have also turned to teaching, and since I am involved in it myself, I can well understand the pleasure they get from it. Vi Redd, the extremely talented alto sax player and singer, lives in Los Angeles and works with retarded children, as well as playing occasional gigs close to home. She was on tour for years, first with Earl Hines and his band, later with Count Basie, but she finally had to quit. "My sons made me get off the road," she says with a rueful laugh. "They said they wanted their mother at home and not flying all over the country. I know you have to travel to really make money, but I felt I should consider the kids, so I quit, and now I love the work I'm doing in the schools."

Melba Liston, the trombonist and arranger, has also begun teaching, and she lives and works in Jamaica. She has been an inspiration to many young players, and to one in particular, Janice Robinson, an up-and-coming trombonist from Pittsburgh. Janice is now 20, and has embarked on a promising career. Fresh out of the Eastman School of Music in 1972, she has been featured with Clark Terry's Big Band, the Thad Jones and Mel Lewis Orchestra, and has played with my groups on several network TV shows.

And what do all these women have in common? All had a musical education. Each has developed her own style, sense of purpose, inner security, flexibility, organization, and knowledge of her instrument. These are the requirements for any musician, male or female—and always have been.

So, how did the misconception start about women players being vague, weak, indecisive, frilly, when it is so obvious that they are not? Mary Lou Williams, who has had to fight this prejudice since her teens, gave me her insight into it: " 'Playing like a man' comes from the days when men were supposed to do all the thinking and decision making and women stayed at home in the kitchen. This was a time when women weren't supposed to think for themselves."

Mary Lou is one person who has entirely transcended the label of "woman musician." In the environment in which she grew up she was steeped in music from early childhood, playing piano with Andy Kirk and His Clouds of Joy while still in her teens, being around great jazz musicians all her life. Earl Hines, Fats Waller, and James P. Johnson were those who helped to instill in her the tremendous creative drive that flows through all her music. These associations gave her strength, encouraged her, and helped to develop her originality. Mary Lou is respected by everybody because she knows her craft so well and everyone *knows* she knows. And it is the reason why she achieved such a high place in the jazz hierarchy so early in life and has continued an an innovator.

Mary Lou once told me: "I used to listen to a man named Jack Howard. He played as if he wanted to break the piano, he would hammer it so, and I thought this was the way to play until I heard James P. and Fats. I've always been around men musicians—that's why I think like a man. But that doesn't mean I'm not feminine."

A long-time admirer of Mary Lou's once said, "She had direct, tough ideas, a sense of organization, of knowing where she was going. But when she walked down the street, she was no *man*!"

Another thing that Mary Lou told me: "When you're playing for people, just be yourself. You must be dedicated to what you're doing. When I'm playing a spirit comes, and I close my eyes and I go away somewhere. You can't be worrying about looking good—when you're playing, get into the music."

This conversation with Mary reminded me of myself at the Hickory House. There was a mirror set up on each end of the bandstand, and as I played I could watch myself playing—and I sometimes did! I guess I must have looked in the mirror once too often—and I know I *was* "worrying about looking good." One night Joe Morello leaned forward and whispered, "Stop looking in the mirror and PLAY!"

I must admit that not only men have shown prejudices against women jazz players. I know of some women who have, too—me for instance! I remember once I was playing a date with Roy Eldridge, and while we were setting up, in came a girl fender bass player! I had an instant feeling of disappointment (how conditioned I was!), but when she started to play, I discovered she really could swing! Later, quite abashed, I told the bassist Carline Rey what I had been thinking. I also said, chauvinistically, that she sounded like a "female Ray Brown." (Today of course I'd say just "Ray Brown.") Carline laughed and thanked me for the compliment, and told me some of the things that had happened to her since she first began playing. "Once I was getting my bass out of the car, and a man standing nearby asked me what I was doing. I told him I was the bassist with the band, and he started to laugh! Later, after he heard me play, he apologized: 'I thought you were kidding,' he said."

Just as I thought there were no accomplished women bassists (after Bonnie Weitzel passed away, that is), I also took it for granted no women played good drums. And so when I heard Dottie Dodgion in the early 1960's, I was amazed at how solid, how swinging, how tasty this woman's playing was!

Dottie and I have not worked together for quite a while, but every time I hear her I marvel at her excellent time sense (at any tempo), and her swinging, hard-driving beat. Dottie is a direct, outspoken woman, with a deep commitment to playing, and her warmth and humor are very much a part of her style. She believes that life is easier now for women musicians, but she is still the victim of ignorance on the part of the average listener.

A customer at a club asked her, after she played her first set, "Do you do this professionally?" And her husband, Jerry Dodgion, the well-known alto sax player, relates with glee his conversation with a fan. Jerry to fan: "You know my wife is a drummer?" Fan: "Really? Well, this guy I was telling you about, he's a *real* drummer, plays good time, and swings . . ."

Dottie is forthright in her views on women players. She says: "Playing strong doesn't mean FORCE, it means solidness. Years ago women weren't supposed to think, and that's what some people mean when they say 'you play like a man.' But most men aren't thinking that! They may secretly be shocked by it, or in awe of it, or threatened by it. But the secure guys can be amazed by it or interested, but *not daunted*."

It is hard to name all the other women players who are on the scene at the present time, but I'd like to try and at the same time ask forgiveness of those I may have inadvertently left out.

Some are playing, some are teaching, some are doing both, and writing and raising families too! All of them are making their unique personal contribution to music:

Dorothy Ashby	Harp
Vera Auer	Vibes
Carla Bley	Composer-Arranger
Bess Bonnier	Piano
Joanne Brackeen	Piano
Patti Brown	Piano
Jessie Cary	Trombone
Gloria Coleman	Organ
Joyce Collins	Piano
Sue Evans	Percussion
Mary Fettig	Sax
Ellie Frankel	Piano
Jane Getz	Piano
Adele Girard	Harp
Corky Hale	Harp
Jean Hoffman	Keyboards
Bobbi Humphrey	Flute
Sarah McLawler	Organ
Flora Purim	Flute
Clora Roberts	Trumpet
Judy Roberts	Keyboards
Muriel Roberts	Piano
Pola Roberts	Drums
Janice Robinson	Trombone
Nina Sheldon	Piano
Mary Taylor	Sax
Patty Wicks	Piano

* * * * *

Having been such an unlikely candidate for a jazz career myself and having surmounted so many intangible obstacles, makes me realize that ANYTHING is possible if one has drive, motivation, and is willing to take trouble—to get involved—to be ready to give unlimited time, to learn by trial and error.

Jazz is American music created by the American Negro, not the Africans (although more and more elements of African music are seeping into it and adding new dimensions to it). And all of us—whether we are black, white, male, female, European or American—have added OUR particular contributions to the music. Each of us is an individual—unique, different—and thus we draw musical ideas from our own personal environment. The kind of life we have lived comes out in our music. Women can, and do, play with "soul"; play "funky"; swing, and improvise "free" music—why not? We are all members of the same race—the human race—and we must all dig into our own heritage and bring forth the creative gift that is within each one of us.

This is what makes jazz the beautiful work of art it is—so many cultures are a part of it, so many different musical forms, different points of view have been woven into it, only to be changed around, re-woven, re-threaded; adding new textures, given different directions—always moving on to something new and different—and better.

To the women musicians past and present I'd say, "Yes, you HAVE come a long way, baby—but you've really always been there."

The emergence of women as jazz instrumentalists contrasts vividly with their long-accepted roles as foremost jazz singers. For example, of the first three blues singers deemed worthy of recording, only one was a man, Blind Lemon Jefferson. The other two were Ma Rainey and Mamie Smith. More blues-singing Smiths, sisters in spirit only, soon followed: Clara, Trixie Laura, and the most famous of them all, the inimitable Bessie Smith.

It was Bessie, along with her predecessors, who founded the great dynasty of female jazz vocalists — a dynasty that remains unbroken to this day, and some of whose most gifted members, delineated in the following pages, have given us some of the most swinging and memorable recordings in the entire library of jazz.

Bessie Smith: blues—like a tolling bell

Born into the worst sort of southern Negro poverty in 1894, in Chattanooga, Bessie worked honky tonks, carnivals and traveling tent shows in her teens and early twenties. When she was eventually discovered and elevated as a recording artist, in 1923, her reception was unprecedented. In her first recording year her records sold over two million copies. Yet she died, neglected, in Memphis in 1937, after an automobile accident. The first hospital to which she was taken refused to admit her because she was a negro and she bled to death while being driven to another hospital. It was possibly the kind of death she had anticipated, for Bessie lived as hard as she sang.

Bessie was called *Empress of the Blues* and, in truth, she truly personified the blues. Her powerful voice, mournful as a tolling bell, made her blues eloquent masterpieces of human misery. When this magnificently large woman chanted her plaints, when she voiced her distrust of all men, all saints, her audience felt completely at one with her. It felt the ugliness of a Mississippi flood in her unforgettable *Backwater Blues* ("When it rain five days and the skies turn dark at night"). And it shared the ache and erotic longing of her *Empty Bed Blues*, which shall forever remain a classic among classics.

Bessie Smith was an artist whose voice, though harsh, had an irresistible natural beauty, and she left behind her a testament of song unequalled in our music. As critic John Hammond says, "She was one of those rare beings, a completely integrated artist capable of projecting her whole personality into music."

Blues singer Bessie Smith.

Ella Fitzgerald: the velvet, unfailing beat

In 1934 a friend of drummer Chick Webb dropped in on an amateur night performance at Harlem's Apollo Theatre, and the world of jazz has been the richer ever since. For that was the night the friend told Chick about a young teen-ager named Ella Fitzgerald, who was to stay with the Webb band until Chick's death in 1939, during which time she built up a glowing reputation among musicians for her purity of tone and her rhythmically brilliant style. In 1938, her novelty song *A-Tisket A-Tasket* became a tremendous success with the general public.

After Webb's death, Ella soared to greatness both as a soloist and as a member of Norman Granz's touring Jazz At The Philharmonic unit. By the mid-forties, she was the favorite singer of virtually all of her musical colleagues, possibly of the entire jazz world. And her popularity, if anything, has continued to grow. It has now reached the point where "Standing Room Only" is the order of the day wherever Ella appears, be it in the Hollywood Bowl, Carnegie Hall, or an auditorium in any European or Asian capital.

The reason is simple enough. Ella combines amazing vitality and native musicianship with an unequalled warmth and tonal clarity. In addition, she can match any inflection, even the most tender, to a truly swinging beat. The musicians say it best, "she's the most."

Anita O'Day: phrasing, stylish and offbeat

They knew her first at the Three Deuces, in Chicago, where her hoarsely astringent voice and off-beat sense of phrasing produced a new swinging style that set the whole town talking. Then, in 1941, Gene Krupa heard her, hired her, and took her on tour—and the whole country began talking. In particular, she won a huge following for her expressive recording of *Let Me Off Uptown,* on which she shared billing with Roy Eldridge, and for her scat version of *That's What You Think.* Moving on to Stan Kenton's band in 1944, her recording of *And Her Tears Flowed Like Wine* won her an even larger audience.

Then the turbulence of her personal life interrupted her career and her star waned, only to rise again in the late fifties when she again became active in clubs and on records. In 1958, she was the vocal hit of the Newport Jazz Festival. In '59, she enjoyed a brilliantly successful tour of Europe with the Benny Goodman band.

Although Anita rose to popularity in the swing era, and while faint traces of Ella Fitzgerald can sometimes be heard in her songs, she is a modern jazz vocalist in the truest sense of the term. As such, she has had a powerful influence on other contemporary singers, most notably Chris Connor and June Christy. And with her truly creative recordings—LPs like *Anita Sings, Drummer Man, An Evening With Anita O'Day, Pick Yourself Up, The Lady Is A Tramp*—she has helped shape the listening habits of a new generation of jazz fans.

Billie Holiday: a tragic lady of tragic songs

Lady Day, as her friends knew her, was born to jazz, her father having been a banjoist with Fletcher Henderson in the early thirties. World famous at the height of her career, in the beginning her admirers had to seek her out in dingy after-hours joints in Harlem, then in squalid little clubs downtown in New York.

With her husky, coarse-grained voice, tremendous pitch, and expressive nuances, Billie Holiday has been called the definitive jazz singer, the vocalist after whom most jazz singing styles since swing have been modeled. She began recording with pickup bands, and the long series of recordings she cut with Teddy Wilson's band, beginning in 1935, made her a jazz immortal.

Few singers have ever combined the attractions, the virtues, and the tragic vices of Lady Day, for she was not only a singer with a great and unique style, but a remarkably beautiful woman as well. And, unhappily, a long and hopeless battle with narcotics ruined her health and hastened her untimely death.

The cornerstone of Billie's greatness was her remarkable fidelity, her trueness to the blues. While she sang a pop tune with incredible artistry, shaping a trite phrase so that it rang truer than it ever had before, it was in the blues, in the basic jazz songs, that she shone at her most brilliant. *Fine And Mellow, Billie's Blues,* these were her great songs, along with such standards as *The Man I Love, Body And Soul* and *Embraceable You,* and the hauntingly unforgettable wail of protest against "lynch justice," *Strange Fruit.*

Sarah Vaughan: a limitless, liquid soprano

Her revolutionary contributions to vocal jazz parallel the instrumental innovations wrought by two of the first jazzmen to acclaim her greatness, Dizzy Gillespie and Charlie Parker. Musically literate, an accomplished pianist as well as a singer, she made her debut with Earl Hines' band in 1943, worked with Billy Eckstine in 1944, John Kirby in '45, then embarked on her distinguished career as a soloist.

From the beginning, her fellow musicians recognized and applauded her artistry. And in short order the public, first here, then abroad, began to realize that the Vaughan voice was unique, unlike that of any of her predecessors, with a warmth and a precision and a way of developing a melodic line that was wholly new to jazz.

Her stunning voice has perhaps best been described by Leonard Feather, who says, "She brought to jazz a rich, beautifully controlled tone and vibrato; an ear for the chord structure of songs, enabling her to change or inflect the melody as an instrumentalist might; and a coy, sometimes archly naive quality alternating with a sense of great sophistication."

Today Sarah is a two-faced gal, forced to satisfy a non-jazz public that is as eager to hear her as are her jazz fans. Happily, since she can sing every type of song, since her liquid soprano knows no limitations, she is able to bathe both of her clamoring audiences in the beauty of her limpid voice.

...aughan

Ella Fitzgerald

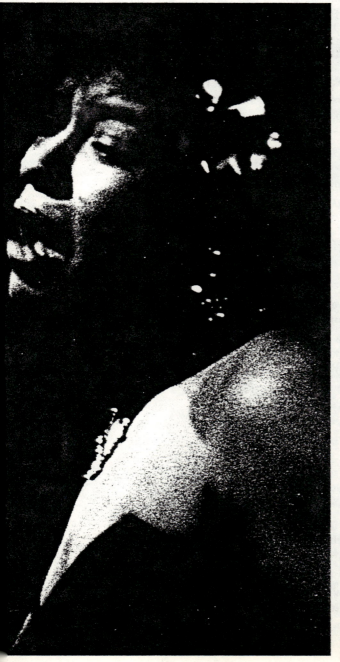

...liday

Anita O'Day

143

Mildred Bailey: the easy rocking chair lady

She rocked her way to fame on a song—Hoagy Carmichael's *Rockin' Chair*. Paul Whiteman found her plugging songs behind a music counter in 1929, in Seattle. And when she made her debut with Whiteman that same year she became, so far as is known, the first white girl band vocalist. Next thing she knew, she was in a recording studio singing a song Hoagy had written especially for her— the first, in fact, he ever wrote with a specific singer in mind. It was called *What Kind Of Man Is You?* Hoagy himself was at the piano. Eddie Lang, Joe Venuti, Frankie Trumbauer and the rest of the Whiteman hot section ad libbed the orchestral accompaniment. It was a memorable record—the first of the many memorable records Mildred cut before her death, in 1951, with her husband, Red Norvo, with Teddy Wilson and John Kirby, and with many of the other jazz greats of her day.

While Mildred was the first non-Negro girl singer to win recognition in jazz, she readily acknowledged that she owed her style primarily to Bessie Smith and Ethel Waters. And traces of Bessie and Ethel can be faintly heard in the two songs most closely identified with Mildred Bailey's name, *Rockin' Chair* and *Lazy Bones*. But Mildred's thin, high-pitched voice had a quality all its own. She had an easy sense of jazz phrasing, a subtle vibrato, and a startling ability to capture the most delicate nuance of a melody. Her vocalizing was jazz at its best. And whenever she sang, the hot men were never far away.

Lee Wiley: warm, husky, erotic

Bing Crosby once claimed her as his favorite vocalist. Fats Waller and Bunny Berigan violated recording contracts to play behind her on obscure recording dates. And George Gershwin said he'd rather hear Lee sing his songs than anybody.

Born in Oklahoma, with a generous strain of Indian blood, Lee Wiley grew up on Ethel Waters' Black Swan releases. When she was only 15, she ran away from home. At 17, she was a featured singer in New York clubs. And before she could vote she was a nationally famous radio and recording star.

On her first records she was supported by such notables as Jack and Charlie Teagarden, Artie Schutt and the Dorseys. She made orchestra leaders out of Joe Bushkin and Max Kaminsky, in her famous Gershwin album. Beginning in 1939, she spent several years as a member of Eddie Condon's Dixieland entourage, then spent the five years she was married to Jess Stacy touring with his band. In the late forties she worked as a single in night clubs, but in the fifties she began to limit herself to an occasional appearance in concerts and on TV and records.

A favorite of many musicians, Lee is limited to no school of jazz, despite her close association with Dixieland. Her most distinctive qualities are her slow, pulsing vibrato, her keen sense of phrase, and the husky eroticism that warms her work.

Ethel Waters: the Bernhardt of the blues

It was a Black Swan record, issued in the early twenties. The band was Fletcher Henderson's, the number was *The Down Home Blues*, and the lyrics were sung by an unknown vocalist named Ethel Waters. It was a "race record," a record you could only find in the shops on the other side of the tracks. But it changed the vocal style of an entire generation of singers.

Today, Ethel Waters is a show business personality, famous for her dramatic roles on the Broadway stage and for her superb movie performances. But once she was a tall, thin youngster singing in a Baltimore dive under the name "Sweet Mama Stringbean." Later, she reached Harlem and the Lincoln Theater, the old stamping ground of Snake Hips Tucker, Butterbeans and Susie, and Louis Armstrong. There she reached out and caught the ear of the New York jazz fraternity. Bix was one of the first to fall in love with her deep, wide-ranging voice, with its rich vibrato and wonderful syncopation, and he brought his friends to hear her.

Inevitably, she sky-rocketed to fame, first as a night club star, then in musical comedies like *Blackbirds*, *Rhapsody in Black*, and *As Thousands Cheer*. In 1939, playing her first dramatic role in *Mamba's Daughter*, she won instant recognition as an actress of tremendous scope and power. Since then she has appeared almost exclusively as a stage and motion picture actress. But among musicians she will always be remembered as one of the universals of all jazz voices.

Dinah Washington: blues with a bible beat

As a youngster Dinah became steeped in religious music, playing piano for and singing with a Chicago church choir. Then she won the inevitable amateur contest, which led her, in turn, to a job at the Garrick Bar. There she was heard by Lionel Hampton, whose band she joined in 1943.

In only three short years of recording with the Hampton sextet, she managed to establish herself as possibly the most important rhythm and blues star of the decade. Leaving Hampton, to work as a single, by applying her distinctive talent to pop and standard tunes she quickly extended her renown far beyond the rhythm and blues field. In the course of spreading her fame she also achieved the seemingly impossible. In her unforgettable recording of *Look To The Rainbow* she proved that it was possible to swing a waltz.

Dinah's gutsy, straightforward blues style carries clearly recognizable overtones of her religious singing background. And because of her curious blend of musical ingredients, her recordings are among the most inimitable and beautiful of our day. Her *After Hours With Miss D*, *Bessie Smith Blues*, *Music For A First Love*, *Best In Blues*, and *What A Difference A Day Makes*, among her many LPs, are enough to guarantee her a niche in the jazz Hall of Fame.

Part Five

Jazzmen Speak for Themselves

The annals of jazz have been written almost exclusively by
its critics, its historians, and its literary-minded devotees
—some of them pompous and didactic, a few remarkable
only for the adjectives and superlatives, many able writers, but
too few well-versed in music. Unfortunately, jazz musicians
themselves seldom, if ever, contribute historical or biographical
major works, and only recently have any of them turned to
criticism.

In a way, this is puzzling and also unfortunate. Talk with
them, and you'll find that they are eager to express themselves.
Their theories are often challenging and provocative, their
observations intriguing and off-beat, and their language colorful and refreshingly inventive. After all, it was the jazz musicians who introduced to the mainstream of American language
words like bug, cool, corny, dig, goof, hip, jive, kicks, pad,
sharp, solid and square.

And yet, apt and inventive though he may be with words
and ideas, the jazzman is seldom interested in putting them on
paper. Ask him why, and he'll usually pat his instrument and
tell you, "Man, I say all I got to say with this." And while this
would seem to be a convincing answer, it isn't always necessarily so. For on several occasions when jazzmen have doubled on
pen, pencil or typewriter, they have come up with some fascinating and expressive pieces. The following examples are not
only cases in point; they are also proof that jazz would be
immeasurably richer if only there were more Boswells in its
performing ranks.

Duke Ellington: "I am a minstrel..."

The eloquence of Duke Ellington's music has been recognized the world over. But there is another quality of Duke's writing with which far fewer people are familiar: his eloquent and poetic use of words.

Much of this has been published in his autobiography, *Music Is My Mistress* (Doubleday), and probably no portion displays more accurately Ellington's poetic bent than these paragraphs that closed a two-part installment of Duke's own writing in the November, 1973, issue of *Esquire*:

I am a minstrel, a pedestrian minstrel, a primitive pedestrian minstrel. Sometimes I imagine I paint, with watercolors or oils, a crystal-clear lake in the sky reflecting the shadows of invisible trees upside down beneath sunkissed, cotton-candy snow. On the fringe, clouds so foamy white—tranquil on top, a raging storm inside. . . . "I'll write it," I think, before returning to that half sleep as the plane roars on to Atlanta . . . or is it Atlantis? Plans, plans, the most impossible of enormous plans, pastel or opaque. Sometimes I'll write a play or plot, drama or comedy, revue or redo. And sometimes I mold a figure, graceful or grotesque, out of whatever material happens to pop into my mind. If it's a chunk of rock or steel, or a trunk of a tree, or maybe just the single petal of a rose, it must be fashioned to the raw, or the ore, according to its dimensions and shape, large or small.

Steel on steel, thousands of miles of steel or tracks, with thousands of round, steel wheels—what a happy marriage! The rhythm of the motion, thirty-nine hours from Chicago to Los Angeles, what a marvel of masculinity, thirty-nine hours, power-stroking all the way. He gave her the high ball in the Loop, stopped in Englewood, and that's all she wrote, grinding up to ninety miles per hour, so hot the steam was bursting out everywhere. She had fine lubrication. You could hear her for miles, whistle-screaming. "Yes, daddy, I'm coming, daddy!" Don't pull that throttle out until you pull into Glendale . . . driving shaft pumping a steady beat . . . long and round, heavin' and strokin' . . . puffin' and smokin' . . . and shovelin' and stokin'. He stopped, let off a little steam. She, out of breath, panted, "Wash up, ready for that red-carpet reception." He got off, glanced over his shoulder at her as she backed out of Union Station, out into the yard, with unraised eyelashes, like the dignified lady she was, she who, between departure and arrival, had given her all to a union laborer, opened her throttle wide, and allowed him his every wish. Truly, a tremendous romance.

Should I write this music with the passion they pumped over the track, or should I maybe start with the wheel, the molten steel, or with those burly black arms behind the thrust that drove the spikes into the railroad ties? There's a grunt with every thrust from the owner of those arms, as though he were rehearsing for the cool of the evening, when he and his woman would be together, when he would drag her out of that hot kitchen. Wringing wet with perspiration, she blushes, but she's been wishing for him all day, to come home and pull her out of that hot place. Now she's hotter than the kitchen stove, on sexually clobbering this cat, until he thinks she's putting everything on him, but . . . do I have to say "the kitchen stove?"

Raw or ore, gold or gook, or indigo, filigree or feathers, carve a breach as deep as desire demands, but don't destroy the maidenhead. Blow Cootie up to the ceiling, make Cat go tooting through the roof, jam Sam into a Charleston beat, let Paul go-go, running through the latticework of brass cacophony, while Jimmy weaves delicate lacework around the edges. Give Harry that "molto profondo," so that Lawrence will cry and wail in the wake of the *après-coup*. Stomp down, those symmetrical after-beats, baby, so that Rab can smelt the melody to smoldering, and over the hush let's hear the broads in the back row whisper, "Tell the story, daddy." Russell's got the kind of wood that Barney had, when Whetsol was playing the unduplicatably dulcet. You can't use Charley Plug or Tricky—one just doesn't anymore. Bubber said it, and he was right *It don't mean a thing if it ain't got that swing*. Mr. Braud's not going to back away from that mike. Like the great Greer used to tell Freddie Guy—"Take it down from the top, pop, and don't stop for the bop. . . ."

"Ole Duke used to have a pretty good left hand after he heard James P., The Lion, and Fats," Greer continues, "but then he heard Fletcher, Redman, Whiteman and Goldkette, and got horn fever . . . *horns, horns, and more horns*. . . . Coppin' out and talkin' 'bout 'the band is my instrument.' What would Doc Perry and Lester Dishman say to that? From six pieces to eleven, twelve, fourteen and fifteen. Then he got up and conducted a symphony of a hundred and ten pieces. After that there was that record album, *The Symphonic Ellington*, with five hundred of the greatest musicians in Europe.

"Will Marion Cook and Henry Grant—they would be pleased. They used to tell Duke to go to the conservatory. Black Bowie used to call him the phony duke, back in Frank Holliday's poolroom. I remember when he was just a yearling, the jive relief piano-plunker. Bill Jones used to be drummin', and he'd catch him out there in those three-four, five-four switches, and scare him stiff. But he'd hang on, and as I said he had a pretty good left hand, and he's hold the solid deuce till Bill let him off the hook. They raised him with discipline and encouragement music-wise. Those East Coast cats were like that. They had the greatest respect for the book. 'If the man didn't want it played that way,' they said, 'he wouldn't have written it that way.' And so Duke listened, and they laid down the laws, and he listened some more, and I guess that's why he calls himself the world's greatest listener today."

Yes, I am the world's greatest listener. Here I am, fifty years later, still getting cats out of bed to come to work, so that I can listen to them and so that they can make a living for their own families. This, however, does not alter the perspective of the pedestrian peddler, who sometimes imagines that he takes a pair of scissors, and some paper or cardboard, and cuts out shapes of paper dolls. He takes them out on the corner and displays them, bending them and plucking them so that they will make a noise. And, of course, the noise is the main thing, because the people hear the noise, and when they like it they say, "Ah, I'll take it. . . ." So I let them have it—the noise, that is. And I collect my dolls and go out the next day to see if I can make other people like the noise. Practically every day I go to a different corner, and sometimes for a change I take my scissors and cut out paper flowers. I wrap them neatly, put them in my pushcart, and take them to the corner. I stand there, plucking them with my third finger to make a noise, hoping it carries an attractive vibration to a passerby's ear. When he shows interest, I'll do an encore, and when he asks, 'How much?" I say: "If you like this little noise, just something in the cup. Don't hurt yourself. Whatever you can stand, and the sound is yours. I can't let you have the flowers. I need them to make more noise. I like to listen myself, you know. I think maybe there's nothing quite like planning and designing at night, and coming out and listening to it next day. I'm impetuous, you know."

There is hardly any money interest in the realm of art, and music will be here when money is gone. After people have destroyed all people everywhere, I see heaping mounds of money strewn over the earth, floating on and sinking into the sea. The animals and fish, who have no use for money, are kicking it out of the way and splattering it with dung. Money and stink, the stink of dung, the stink of money, so foul that in order for the flowers to get a breath of fresh air, the winds will come together and whip the sea into a rage, and blow across the land. Then the green leaves of trees and grass will give up their chlorophyll, so that the sea, the wind, the beasts and the birds will play Nature's old, sweet melody and rhythm. But since you are people, you will not be here to hear it.

Money is becoming too important. So far as the hazards of the big band are concerned, I give musicians the money and I get the kicks. Billy Strayhorn said we were exponents of the aural art. Ours is the responsibility of bringing to the listener and would-be listener—as to those unwilling to be listeners—some agreeable vibration that tickles the fancy of the eardrum. Of course, the connoisseur has a much better appreciation of duet and counter-melody than the average would-be listener. Some people think modern means unattractive, whether it's 1905 or 1975, but consonance is in the imagination of the

hearer. Maybe a sound gives him a nostalgic nudge, back to the one moment to which he has always wanted to return.

Roaming through the jungle, the jungle of "oohs" and "ahs," searching for a more agreeable noise, I live a life of primitivity with the mind of a child and an unquenchable thirst for sharps and flats. The more consonant, the more appetizing and delectable they are. Cacophony is hard to swallow. Living in a cave, I am almost a hermit, but there is a difference, for I have a mistress. Lovers have come and gone, but only my mistress stays. She is beautiful and gentle. She waits on me hand and foot. She is a swinger. She has grace. To hear her speak, you can't believe your ears. She is ten thousand years old. She is as modern as tomorrow, a brand-new woman every day, and as endless as time mathematics. Living with her is a labyrinth of ramifications. I look forward to her every gesture.

Music is my mistress, and she plays second fiddle to no one.

Louis Armstrong scans the history of jazz

In 1956, a Yale freshman named Paul Resnik discovered what a few privileged persons have known firsthand: Louis Armstrong was not only a giant as a musician, but also an exceptionally warm, thoughtful human being. It seems that Resnik wanted a piece from Armstrong for a projected Jazz Supplement in the *Yale Daily News*, and so he went ahead and tried in the most direct way he knew:

"It happened that Armstrong was in New Haven for an evening. I waited for him in the lobby of the Hotel Taft between his appearances across the street. I had about a minute to explain my request. The man was warm, aware of my presence and request, and was receptive to the point of jamming my name and address in his heavy black overcoat.

"The glow of his personality was sufficient to offset the near-certain feeling that the idea would die in his pocket. Yet five days later I received a cable from Toronto: 'Jazz story on way. Hope I am not too late. Regards, Louis Armstrong.' And a week later it arrived with a note saying: 'Hope the article arrived on time.'

"The mere existence of Louis Armstrong's article is evidence of the man's generosity and commitment. He needn't have written it, there was nothing whatsoever to gain for him, and no one else of stature would even talk about contributing an article on my behalf to the *Yale Daily News*."

As it turned out, the student paper's Jazz Supplement *didn't* turn out. But Mr. Resnick held on to the article, and fifteen years later he offered it to *Esquire* for publication in its December, 1971, issue, much of it in Louis' own handwriting:

"Satchmo"   Scanning   ①

The History of Jazz"

The word 'Jazz' as far as I can see
or Can remember, was when I was a
little boy, five years old. The year of
1905. In those days it was Called
Rag Time Music. And when ever
there was a dance or a Lawn Party
the Band (consisted) of six men, would
stand in front of the place on the
Side walk and play a half hour of
Good rag time Music. And us kids
Would stand or dance on the other
side of the street until they went
in side. That was the only way
that we young kids could get the
Chance to hear those Great Musicians
Such as Buddy Bolden — Joe Oliver
CORNET
MY IDOL
over

An original document by Louis Armstrong in his own hand.

Bunk Johnson *CORNET*   2   Freddie Keppard *CORNET*

Henry Allen Sr. *CORNET*   Old Man Moret *CORNET*
+ His - BRASS BAND   AN HIS EXCELSOR

Frankie Ducson *TROMBONE* *KID DRY TROM* BRASS BAND- CORNET
                                    WONDER + LEADER- AT "60"

And A whole lot of the other Players
who will forever live in my mind
As the greatest Musicians that I have
Ever heard since I was big enough
to realize what was happening. Even
to the Brass Bands down in my home
town New Orleans, to witness them
Playing A funeral March, will Make
Something inside of you Just tinkle.
Even to A - b - & - March, they always
expressed themselves, And their very souls
in the music. Joe Oliver (MY Idol) And
                                    CORNET
Emanuel Perez' had A Brass Band
CORNET
by the name of the Onward Brass Band.
                                    ONWARD
And- My 'My' how they could Play in
the street Parades + funerals. Joe Oliver

151

3

"Satchmo"

To me was always a fantastic sort of a
fellow. And the greatest Creator of them all.
One Sunday' All the Hustlers + Pimps
HUSTLERS-GAMBLERS
IN MY NEIGHBORHOOD
Who had a good base ball team. And
Would go all over the City and play
other teams in other Neiborhoods.
One Sunday they went over in Algiers
a little town across the Mississippi
RIVER
to play the team over there. Of course.
Everywhere the'd, go, the neighborhood
Crowd would follow them. Even we kids
Would tag along. They'd, only play for
a large Keg of beer. But it was lots
of fun. And we kids would be thrilled
Just to lick up on a glass of beer.
Well sir— Mc Donald Cemetary was
Just about a mile away from where
the Black Diamonds (MY TEAM) was playing the
Algiers teams. When ever a funeral
from New Orleans, had a body to be
buried in the Mc Donald Cemetary

they would have to cross the Canal Street ferry boat, and march down the same road right near our ball game. Of course when they passed us, playing a slow funeral march, we only paused with the game and tipped our hats as to pay respect. When the last of the funeral passed, we would continue the game. The game was in full force when the Onward band was returning from the cemetery. After they had put the body in the ground, they were swinging *It's A Long Way to Tipperary.* They were swinging so good until Joe Oliver reached up into the high register, beating out those *high notes* in *very fine fashion,* and broke up our ball. Yea, the players commenced to dropping bats an balls, etc., And we all followed them all the way back to the New Orleans side and to their destination.

Of course there were many other greats even before my time, and my days of the wonderful music that every musician were playing in New Orleans. But to me Joe *King* Oliver was the greatest of them all. He certainly didn't get his right place in the mentionings in Jazz history as he so rightfully deserved. He was a Creator, with unlimited Ideas, and had a heart as big as a whale when it came to helping the underdog in music, such as me. I was just a kid, Joe saw I had possibilities and he'd go out of his way to help me or any other ambitious kid who were interested in their instrument as I was. When he played his cornet, there were always happiness. And a certain closeness that he gave out whenever he played and whatever he played. Take Dipper Mouth Stomp, for instance, no one living today could express themselves while playing that tune like Joe Oliver did. When I played second cornet to him at the Lincoln Gardens in Chicago 1922—musicians from all over the world came to hear him. And of course I love the man and his work so very much until we made the most fabulous "cornet team" one ever heard of. No matter where he'd turn while we were playing, whatever note he made I always had a second note to match his *lead.* The musicians who hadn't heard anything like it would go absolutely *wild.* They were some of the top men in the business who came to hear us. Of course there have been many styles in music since those days and in my younger days, such as Bop-Music of tomorrow—"progressive," "cool," etc, But not anyone of them styles have *impressed* me as *Oliver.* And the *good ol* musician played in those days what I am talking about. The *tail gate* those *street parades, funerals, lawn parties,* Balls, they're called *Dances* nowadays. We didn't resort to different styles, etc., we just played good *ragtime music, sweet* when necessary. All these different new styles of this day doesn't do anything for the up & coming youngsters and they leaves not *anything* for the kids to derive on, like the old

timers did for us. Ever since this new stuff has been in port, I myself has been for ever so long—trying to figure out what the *modern* musicians trying to *prove.* And the only solution that I came to is, the majority of them are inferior musicians. Where there would be a real *solid note* to be hit right on the *nose,* they would make a *thousand* notes rather than attempt that *one.* *Screeching* at a *high note* an *praying* to God that they'd *hit* it. The result is a very few musicians are working nowadays. The public itself gotten so tired of hearing so much *modern slop* until they refused to continue paying those big checks. And now if you'll notice it only the *fittest* are *surviving.* No matter *where—who* I play with, I never forget my *first love*—real good music. That's why I am at home, when I am playing *any* kind of music. Most of the fantastic players of today can't even *read music.* They never did want to. All they want to do is *scream.* And if they don't watch out, *I'm gonna scream,* right along with the *public.* Always remember—Louis Armstrong never bother about what the other fellow is playing, etc. A musician's a musician with me. Yea—I am just like the *Sister* in our Church in N.O., my home town. One Sunday our pastor whom we all loved happened to take a Sunday off and sent in another preacher who wasn't near as good. The whole congregation "frowned on him"—except one Sister. She seemed to enjoy the other pastor the same as she did *our* pastor. This arroused the Congregation's curiosity *so much*—until when Church service was over they all rushed over to this *one Sister* and asked her *why* did she enjoy the substitute preacher the *same* as our regular one? She said, Well when *our pastor preach,* I can look right through him and see *Jesus.* And when I hear a preacher who's *not* as good as ours—I just look *over* his *shoulder* and *see Jesus just the same.* That applies to me all through my life in music ever since I left New Orleans. I've been just like that Sister in our Church. I have played with quite a few musicians who weren't so good. But as long as they could hold their instruments *correct,* and display their *willingness* to play as *best* they could, I would look over their shoulders and see Joe Oliver and several other great masters from my home town. So I shall now close and be just like the little boy who sat on a *block* of *ice. My Tale is Told.* Tell all the Fans and *All* musicians, I love *Em Madly.*

Swiss Krissly Yours
Louis Armstrong Satchmo

The spelling is Louis Armstrong's, as are all the remembrances.

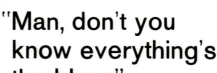

"Man, don't you know everything's the blues"

Drummer George Wettling was one of the finest products of the Chicago era of jazz, a distinguished painter whose works were often exhibited, and one of the few musicians who had ever shown any sustained interest in writing about jazz and the people who make it. His verbal portrait of Wingy Manone brilliantly captures the happy, free-wheeling spirit of this one-armed trumpeter, one of the least-inhibited men who ever blew a horn:

When I got home there was a telegram there for me: *Can you join my band at once? Good band, good salary, good job. Wire me Hotel Roosevelt, Pittsburgh, Pa.*, and it was signed Wingy Manone. Well, that's the way I finally got out of Chicago.

The job Wingy had was working at a nice open air cafe called the Sky Club out alongside of the Pittsburgh airport.

The only trouble was, it seemed to rain every night. The boss got tired of this and fired Wingy and the band. Wingy told us not to worry. He said, "I know a man up in New England that's got a thousand dance halls and we can play a different one every night." He was talking about Charlie Shribman. So we drove to New York where Wingy set a string of one nighters all the way across New England.

I remember one night, up in Shelburne, N.H., I think it was, a girl came up to the bandstand and requested a waltz. Wingy had a quick answer. "Lady," he said, "we haven't played a waltz in twenty years."

There are a number of legends about Wingy's ability to read music. Personally I have always felt that Wingy never found much music worth reading since he could pick up the trumpet and play practically anything he ever heard. One time he told me, "George, I can read 'em, but I can't divide 'em."

I remember when we went back to New York to make records

Wingy Manone, a free wheeling, uninhibited spirit.

for Bluebird after our New England tour, the music publishers all sent a bunch of new tunes around hoping Wingy would record them. One publisher sent a girl piano player along so that she could play one tune for us. The song was orchestrated in G flat. Wingy looked at the signature and then asked the girl what key it was. She told him six flats. Wingy said, "Man, this signature looks like a bunch of grapes to me."

After Wingy made such a hit with his vocal version of *The Isle of Capri*, the recording companies wanted him to do something similar on any other tune possible. In fact, they practically demanded it. On one record date we recorded Jerome Kern's *A Fine Romance*. That was one tune that had Wingy stymied for quite a while. He called a break so he could try to figure out some lyrics. Later on we saw him sitting outside the studio on the running board of somebody's car with a pencil and paper in his hand. He called to us, "Hey, I got it. Get a load of this!" *Our romance, that's fine/Fred Astaire on the line/Yes, yes, yes, I'd like to be up at RKO myself/That fine romance/I'll swing out with Ginger Rogers while I'm there/Oh, romance that's fine/Fred Astaire is really fine/While Hollywood marches on to my time./*

And that's just the way it sounded when we put it on wax. I think that happened the same year that Joe Venuti gave Wingy one cuff link for Christmas.

Another time Wingy sent for me to do a record date with him. It was the time he was determined to do *O Sole Mio* with some very special Wingy lyrics. Here's the way they went: "*O Sole Mio/How do I do-Oh/If I owe you-Oh/I go where you go/A way out wester/With brother Sylvester/O Sole Mio/And so are you-Oh/O Sole Mio/When I'm with you-Oh/I don't feel blue-Oh/My Sole Mio/My I.O.U.-Oh/That I owe you-Oh/To be with you-Oh/O my Sole Mio.*/"

If you don't believe it, listen to the record yourself. Wingy's obstacles were almost insurmountable. Nevertheless you won't find a happier man today than Wingy Manone out in Hollywood. But I remember when things were very tough indeed for him. That was when he was beating around the country from job to job, playing music that most people didn't understand. I remember one time, for example, Wingy got a job playing in a Chinese restaurant. Naturally he was worried about how the Chinese owner of the place would react to his wild little band which included such people as Frank Teschmaker, Bud Freeman and yours truly. After the first set, Wingy went over to the proprietor, who had the usual inscrutable Oriental mien. "How do you like my band?" asked Wingy. The reply was, "Velly good band. Two weeks notice."

Wingy lost his arm when he was riding a bicycle for Western Union and got crushed between two streetcars, back in his New Orleans boyhood. But I'll bet nine out of ten people seeing Wingy in a theater or club haven't any idea he's one-armed. He's so expert in his manipulation of the cork arm that few people ever notice it. Somehow the dexterity of his one hand has increased to such an extent that it almost compensates for the loss of the other. If you're around Wingy don't ever try to help him because he's only got one arm. He doesn't like it. And he doesn't need it. Do you know he ties his bow ties with one hand?

Wingy always has a gang of clothes and I often thought it must be tough for him to get them on. But he will tolerate no help. I thought I had him one evening in his hotel room. The cuff on his good arm was unbuttoned. I didn't see how he could possibly button it. I said, "Wingy, I got you at last. You're going to have to let me button that cuff for you." He said, "Get away from here, boy," and then expertly swung his wrist around and buttoned the cuff with his teeth.

Joe Marsala, the famous Chicago clarinetist, was recently reminiscing about some of his boyhood rambles with Wingy. The band was always in a state of financial panic. Somehow they got to Miami for a job that had been promised, but when they arrived they found the Prohibition agents had put a padlock on the night club. No one had any money, either. So Joe wired home for bus fare and a few eating dollars, which he offered to split with Wingy. But Wingy would only take a five spot. Joe bought his bus ticket and then walked with Wingy to the railroad yards. Wingy found an Army and Navy store nearby, went in, bought a regular railroad man's outfit which he put on over his regular clothes, and then walked with Joe to a hill alongside the railroad track. A few minutes later a fast freight came by. As the hill slowed it down, Wingy expertly clambered up the ladder of one of the freight cars, using his one good arm. And Joe swears that as Wingy vanished he let go for a minute to wave goodbye, catching on again just in time.

Wingy is always a sure cure for the blues. I was in a very bad spot one time when I was working for Wingy at the old Hickory House. It was just at the time of the Hindenburg disaster and big pictures of the flaming dirigible were all over the front pages of the papers. Wingy realized I was very depressed, although he didn't know why. And he came over to me and said, "Boy, you know that Hindenburg story was just a big publicity stunt."

One time Wingy came to New York to play a concert with Eddie Condon at Carnegie Hall. He'd heard a lot of talk about Carnegie Hall, of course, but he'd never been in the auditorium before. When he walked out on stage he looked up and saw the people sitting in the second balcony seats way up near the ceiling. He studied them a minute, then shouted up, "Man, how did you people get way up there?" Then he said, "Never mind that, how are you going to get down!"

In 1939, Wingy was moved to write a song on the war in Europe which had only just begun. As far as I know it was the first song of World War II, and it's still my favorite of all war songs and certainly the most direct. The title was: *Stop That War, Them Cats Is Killing Themselves.*

One important thing about Wingy, he tops anybody beating off a band. And as far as his trumpet playing is concerned, I can only quote what some unknown musician said about that. Wingy and I were touring out someplace and we dropped into a night club in the colored part of some town. A terrific little band was playing on the stand. The leader saw Wingy's instrument and invited us to sit in. Wingy played about eight choruses without stopping. The trumpet player on the job looked at Wingy in pure amazement and this is what he said: "I don't know who yo' is, but yo' sho' *is*."

Jazz Abstract
By George Wettling

Krupa and the symphony

To the uninitiated who know nothing of Gene Krupa and Leonard Bernstein other than, say, what they have seen on television, these two would seem to have had little in common except their unruly shocks of hair. Yet they shared at least one trait that strongly influenced both their professional lives; each had a deep love of the other's type of music. At home, Krupa, the frenetic and inspired swing drummer, would listen almost exclusively to symphonic music—albums by Delius, Ravel, Milhaud, Stravinsky, Debussy. For his personal pleasure, Bernstein, the symphonic conductor and classical composer, listened to the recordings of such as Teddy Wilson, Bix Beiderbecke, Eddie Condon, Pee Wee Russell, Max Kaminsky and Gene Krupa.

Both men, too, had strong opinions. Their friendly controversy began at a private party, when someone innocently raised the question: Has jazz influenced the symphony? Unexpectedly, it was Krupa who said "No," Bernstein who argued "Yes", and the parry and thrust of their polemic duel was so brilliant and provocative that the antagonists were persuaded to continue their debate in print. Both briefs appeared in the February, 1947, issue of *Esquire*. Krupa's was first:

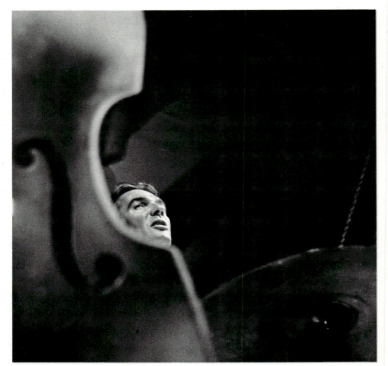

Gene Krupa—poised and in action.

My good friend Leonard Bernstein says that symphonic music, "serious" music written for performance by the full orchestra, has been influenced by jazz. The jazz influence is said by some critics to be especially apparent in Bernstein's own compositions.

I disagree. I have never heard anything genuinely and honestly derivative of jazz in any such music, even, maybe especially, in such works as Igor Stravinsky's *Ebony Suite,* which Woody Herman, with his usual swing instrumentation, brilliantly performed in Carnegie Hall and several other places. I've never heard it in any of the "serious" pieces of George Gershwin, who, anybody will tell you, was pre-eminently "the American jazz composer."

But, then, I've never heard it, as has John Hammond, in the works of Darius Milhaud, for all that during his American visit in the early thirties, Milhaud listened, entranced, to the unsurpassable jazz virtuosity at the hot piano of such great artists as Fats Waller, Earl Hines and Jimmy Johnson. I watched Maurice Ravel, at the old Sunset in Chicago, marvel at Jimmy Noone's transcendent clarinet. Jimmy could fly over a clarinet like no one before him or since—ask Benny Goodman—and it was undoubtedly Noone's technical virtuosity, not the music itself, which obsessed Maurice Ravel. For all his preoccupation with rhythm, I've never heard the least echo of that music, or any music like it, in his compositions.

Leonard Bernstein and others profess to hear traces, echoes, derivations of jazz in Frederick Delius, John Alden Carpenter, Manuel De Falla, Honegger, Prokofieff, even Shostakovich.

The influence of jazz has been found by someone or other, unnecessarily eager to make out a case for jazz that it doesn't need, anxious perhaps to endow it with reflected "respectability" so that he won't need to make excuses to himself and others for liking it, in the works of these composers. But, in my opinion, it isn't there.

Let's pay a little more attention to two of the composers mentioned earlier—Stravinsky and Gershwin. They are reputed to show the most jazz influence. The contention might well stand or fall with them.

Stravinsky did evince preoccupation with jazz music. He talked about it. He wrote a series of compositions with titles referring to "ragtime," but no evidence of that preoccupation appears in the actual music, honestly examined, honestly listened to. That preoccupation was purely verbal. Although apparently able to sense, to feel, the jazz tempo, he has been unable to express it. His tremendous musical vitality did not encompass the peculiar rhythmic, driving, let us say American quality which is the essence of jazz.

Nor is that essence to be found in the more pretentious work of George Gershwin. It exists in the blues feeling of some of his popular songs, particularly when played in the authentic jazz spirit by authentic jazz instrumentalists. But it does not

exist in his *Concerto in F*—even if in some passages he did use derbies to mute the trumpets.

His *Rhapsody in Blue,* which too often had been labeled *The Jazz Symphony,* is much more—as is Gershwin's serious work as a whole—in the tradition of Claude Debussy. I don't believe the opening of *L'Après-midi d'une Faune* is reminiscent of Noone's clarinet work.

Does this mean that I believe that jazz can never and will never form a part of the main stream of America's and of the world's music? To say it can't is to say that America, out of itself, has nothing to contribute musically to the world. Jazz is the United States' own native, original musical idiom.

Jazz can be the basis of great music to be written by an American composer just as much as, say, Czech folk tunes were the basis of the music of Smetana and Dvorak.

But jazz can only make its proper contribution to the whole of music; will only make that contribution when both the composition and performance of the music which is developing out of it are executed by musicians who are completely at home in the idiom. Music must be both conceived and performed, composed and played.

And jazz cannot be approached from outside. It cannot be approached synthetically and artificially. Above all, it cannot be approached unsympathetically.

Too many "good," "pure" and "serious" musicians, and let's admit that, composing and playing in the idiom to which they are accustomed, are *good* musicians—approach the native American idiom, the jazz idiom, with intolerance, even with condescension. They stoop, but not to conquer. And so, they almost invariably make an unholy mess of their attempts. Then, of course, they sneer at jazz. They tell anyone who will listen that the stuff wasn't music in the first place, but naturally. However, the failure was with them, and all the name calling in the world cannot disguise that fact.

Are there in existence musicians who can compose and, equally important, play this music? A generation ago my answer would have had to be no. The traditional "great men" of jazz, Johnny Dodds and Frank Teschemacher on the clarinet, Joe Oliver, Louis Armstrong and others on the trumpet, Earl Hines and James P. Johnson, Jess Stacy and Fats Waller at the piano, Chick Webb and Baby Dodds at percussion, were not such, even if it is almost blasphemy to say so. It wasn't their fault. They were great musicians in spite of it. But they came up the hard way. All of them played for dough, played professionally, many while they were still in short pants. They never had the chance to get highly technical classical training. And, essentially, they were performers, virtuosos, not creators. At most, they were improvisors. They achieved a certain measure of greatness in performance because they'd never been told that this or that was "impossible." They achieved, through very lack of classical training, effects which transcended themselves and their instru-

Woody Herman played Stravinsky at Carnegie Hall.

we have a great composition called *Histoire du Soldat*, which contains a "ragtime" that the average American would dismiss as "corny"; and we have a composition, equally great in another sense, called *Rhapsody in Blue*, which is usually considered formally inept and unintegrated.

By integration I mean that quality in a piece of music which makes it all one homogeneous piece of music. We recognize, for example, that two themes in a Brahms symphony may be Ger-

man in feeling; but what occurs to bind them together is equally German in feeling, formally and stylistically in step with the themes themselves. That this does not obtain in Gershwin's music constitutes its greatest weakness, in spite of the fact that his melodies are among the most wonderful ever invented by man. But how, after all, could this fault have been avoided? Taking jazz intact, as it were, and baking it into a symphony pie, afforded him no opportunity of developing a consistent

stylistic flow; the crust remained crust, the filling, filling. So it is with our *Rhapsody in Blue,* a succession of magnificent and inspired tunes connected in a haphazard way by Lisztian cadenzas, Tchaikovskian sequences, and Debussyan ramblings. And as such it stands today as a great monument to the terrific, but, oh so imperfect, Twenties.

Came the crash. Again, many things stopped happening, and many new things began to happen. Again, a new decade ran itself out, this time at a far slower and wearier pace. Musically, it meant a new conservatism, a new reflectiveness, a reconsideration of traditional values. It was just at this point, that, for the very first time, the moment arrived for the sober absorption of all that had happened, and the consequent opportunity for the development of a real, unconsciously derived, American style. And it is the music of this decade which I feel owes the greatest debt to jazz.

This is the moment which arrives in the writing of any article on an academic subject when one courts the danger of turning it into a baccalaureate thesis. In other words, it is the moment for bringing in and piling up musical examples from music of the Thirties to show what I mean about its debt to jazz. This is obviously inadvisable except in learned journals; and I am confronted by the problem of having to talk about that most ineffable subject—music—without being able to demonstrate what I mean. Furthermore, I have to make assertions without being able to advance tangible proof. Therefore, rather than resort to verbosity to say what a few notes could say so easily, I will try to be as brief as possible; and lacking musical illustrations, you'll just have to take my word for it.

We must first take a strong stand on what we mean by "jazz." Avoiding all the lengthy discussion that usually accompanies attempts to define the word, let us make the simple distinction between the commercial song, as we understand the term on Broadway, and the freely improvised jazz of Negro origin, which we know usually in the few formal variants of the Blues. The "popular song" has had, and can have, no influence whatsoever on serious music. It is created for money, sung for money, and dies when the money stops rolling in. It is imitative, conventional, emotionless. This has nothing to do with the fact that there are many such songs of which I am very fond. I wish I had written *I Get a Kick Out of You;* but I must insist that Mr. Porter has no influence on serious music. I love a Gershwin or a Rodgers tune; but the same truth still holds. There are those who show, for example, the influence of a song like *Fascinatin' Rhythm* on symphonic music. Well and good, but the influence is not original with *Fascinatin' Rhythm.* Those charming, truncated phrases of Gershwin's go back to the improvised jazz, the real source. It is this jazz, then, that we have to take into account.

My old piano teacher, Heinrich Gebhard, used to say that music was divisible into melody, harmony, rhythm, form, counterpoint, and color. To be at all complete I should devote a chapter apiece from here on to considering these six elements. For jazz has influenced our composers on all six counts. But perhaps one will stand for all; a short discussion of *rhythm,* the most important influence, may give you some idea of what I have meant all along by "unconscious."

One invariably associates the word "syncopation" with jazz. Literally it means a shortening, or cutting off. Musically, it means putting an accent on a weak beat, or in an unexpected place; or bringing in a note a little earlier or a little later than would seem indicated. For instance, if we consider a conventional musical bar, of 4/4 meter, we see easily that the strongest beat is always the first, the next strongest the third, then the second and fourth (weak beats). Putting special accents on 2 and 4 (either or both) would amount to a simple syncopation. (This is something they all did over a century ago.)

But that is too simple. Let us go further. If we break this bar up into eighth-notes (eight to the bar), we find we have even weaker beats, and many more of them. For, if 2 is a weak beat in a group of four quarter-notes, how much weaker, then, is the second half of this beat alone in a group of eight eighth-notes! Now put a special accent on this unsuspecting member, 1234' 5678 and you begin to get a suggestion of jazz. It was this innocent act, merely the replacing of an accent, which caused the Charleston, the Rumba, the Conga, and many a bump and grind to happen.

Now let us take the rumba pattern as we know it most simply: 123/456/78. We see at once that these eight eighth-notes now seem to divide themselves into smaller groups of three's and two's. One might rewrite the pattern in the following way: 123/123/12. Thus, a passage of music in 4/4 time which used to run smoothly in this way: 1234/5678/1234/5678 can now become 123/123/12/123/123/12, or if juggled accordingly to the composer's whim: 12/123/12/12/123/123 /12, or any other variation of this pattern. This simple procedure opens up new vistas for the serious composer. In the Twenties, when he borrowed overtly from jazz, he used these rhythms as jazz used them, over a steady and monotonous bass which kept the old reliable quarter-note constantly beating. But now that he does not consciously borrow from jazz, these rhythms crop up in a non-jazzy context, without a meter bass necessarily holding them up, but with a life of their own. They have acquired personal qualities—not always hard and percussive, but sometimes graceful, sometimes singing, sometimes even nostalgic. The whole procedure has unconsciously become common usage among American composers. And the startling thing is that very rarely does this music ever sound like jazz! The scherzo movement of my symphony *Jeremiah* would certainly not bring any connotation of jazz to mind; and yet it could never have been written if jazz were not an integral part of my life.

This abbreviated and sketchy investigation into one aspect of American rhythm is certainly insufficient for instructive purposes; but I am hoping that it may serve, for the purpose of this discussion, to point a new way of thinking about the influence of jazz. The whole subject is extremely subtle, and it is all too easy to make erroneous diagnoses. For something *inner* in jazz has entered into our serious music. In every case it is not the superficial "jazziness" that should be sought, but a more profound influence: the cross relations in melodic writing, the peculiarly American sentimentality of harmonization, the intense freedom of the counterpoint, the glorious instrumental color that derives particularly from Negro wind-playing, the healthy, optimistic percussiveness of youthful gaiety, or the neurotic percussiveness of the American citizen when he is on a spree.

For those of you who are further interested I recommend careful listening to and study of the works of Copland, Harris, Sessions, Schuman, and Barber, to name only a few. For those of you who are not, don't worry about it. Just listen to the best in jazz and the best in serious American music, and enjoy it. For analyses and diagnoses notwithstanding, the great synthesis goes irrevocably on."

The Drummer

By Larry Rivers

"Jazz is too good for Americans"

—Dizzy

Until recently, the jazzman has seldom written critically about his music and the way it is received. This is particularly to be deplored because, after all, no one is in as good a position to pass enlightened judgment on the jazz scene. This also makes the following trenchant essay by Dizzy Gillespie of special interest; it is that rare thing, an example of a jazzman speaking his mind publicly. Paradoxically, Dizzy didn't risk incurring the ill-will of the American jazz public until after he'd proved himself a remarkably able ambassador of goodwill abroad, on his tours of the Middle East and South America for our State Department. As he

Harlem assemblage of jazz greats. (Identifications on following page.)

points out, it was the reception he got abroad which opened his eyes to the problems the jazzman faces at home and inspired these comments:

Using the two common standards of artistic success—making some money and having a chance for self-expression—I should feel pretty satisfied I suppose.

But I don't. At least not completely.

I say this because jazz, the music I play most often, has never really been accepted as an art form by the people of my own country.

The people of the United States, the people who gave birth to this wonderful music, have never fully acknowledged it as an important part of culture.

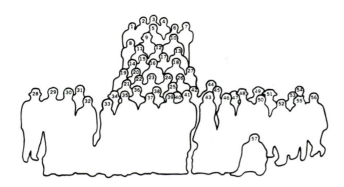

The jazz greats in the historic photograph on the preceding pages are numbered above for your ready reference: 1. Hilton Jefferson; 2. Benny Golson; 3. Art Farmer; 4. Wilbur Ware; 5. Art Blakey; 6. Chubby Jackson; 7. Johnny Griffin; 8. Dickie Wells; 9. Buck Clayton; 10. Taft Jordan; 11. Zutty Singleton; 12. Red Allen; 13. Tyree Glenn; 14. Miff Mole; 15. Sonny Greer; 16. Jay C. Higginbotham; 17. Jimmy Jones; 18. Charles Mingus; 19. Jo Jones; 20. Gene Krupa; 21. Max Kaminsky; 22. George Wettling; 23. Bud Freeman; 24. Pee Wee Russell; 25. Ernie Wilkins; 26. Buster Bailey; 27. Osie Johnson; 28. Gigi Gryce; 29. Hank Jones; 30. Eddie Locke; 31. Horace Silver; 32. Luckey Roberts; 33. Maxine Sullivan; 34. Jimmy Rushing; 35. Joe Thomas; 36. Scoville Browne; 37. Stuff Smith; 38. Bill Crump; 39. Coleman Hawkins; 40. Rudy Powell; 41. Oscar Pettiford; 42. Sahib Shihab; 43. Marian McPartland; 44. Sonny Rollins; 45. Lawrence Brown; 46. Mary Lou Williams; 47. Emmett Berry; 48. Thelonious Monk; 49. Vic Dickenson; 50. Milt Hinton; 51. Lester Young; 52. Rex Stewart; 53. J. C. Heard; 54. Gerry Mulligan; 55. Roy Eldridge; 56. Dizzy Gillespie; 57. Count Basie.

Sure, a great number of intellectuals—particularly younger intellectuals—recognize jazz as art. And I'm told that the number of intellectuals listening to jazz is increasing all the time.

But I believe that the great mass of the American people still consider jazz as lowbrow music. They believe, as John Philip Sousa said, that "People hear jazz through their feet, not their brains." To them, jazz is music for kids and dope addicts. Music to get high to. Music to take a fling to. Music to rub bodies to. Not "serious" music. Not concert-hall material. Not music to listen to. Not music to study. Not music to enjoy purely for its listening kicks.

Like most other jazz musicians, I've been uncomfortable about this attitude ever since I started playing jazz. But when my band toured Asia, the Middle East, the Balkans and South America last year, I became more and more concerned with the problem.

In far-off countries where the people have not had quite so many years to become accustomed to the novelty of jazz and where the sound and instrumentation of jazz is almost completely alien to their ears, I've found that the people have a healthier attitude toward jazz than we do.

They don't make a moral issue out of it, as we sometimes do. It's of no moment to them that jazz was first played in the whore houses of New Orleans, that it was heard in Prohibition speakeasies. Nor do they make a racial issue out of jazz. There is no significant amount of anti-Negro prejudice in their countries for them to hold out against this music.

They are interested in jazz for jazz sake. They listen to it for its musical message, not its sociological implications.

And their response to the jazz they have heard in recent years is tremendous—far greater than most Americans know.

I don't think I shall ever forget the tremendous reception my band and I got in Ankara and Istanbul, for example, where the only way to put a stop to hour after hour of screaming by the audience for "More!...More!...More!" was to play the Turkish national anthem and then close the curtain while the audience was still standing up.

Nor will I forget Athens, where we played to a seething audience of anti-American students who in a pro-Cyprus demonstration the day before, had stoned and nearly destroyed the United States Information Agency office. They loved us so much that when we finished playing they tossed their jackets into the air and carried me on their shoulders through the streets of the city. The local English newspaper ran a headline the next day: STUDENTS DROP ROCKS AND ROLL WITH DIZZY.

To be sure my band hasn't been the only band to tour overseas with great success in recent months. Far from it.

Ever since 1950 there has been a steadily growing exodus of our U.S. jazzmen to tour abroad. This exodus has probably become the most important jazz development of the post-World War II era.

It has included such American musicians as Benny Goodman, Charlie Ventura, Chet Baker and Gene Krupa, who've played the Far East; Louis Armstrong, who played Africa and the Continent (and who now wants to play Russia); Roy Eldridge, Lester Young, Miles Davis, Bud Powell, James Moody, Ella Fitzgerald, Red Norvo, Lionel Hampton, Woody Herman, Duke Ellington, Kid Ory, Lucky Thompson, Count Basie, Lena Horne, The Modern Jazz Quartet, Lee Konitz, Herbie Mann, Mel Torme, Gerry Mulligan, Stan Kenton and Billy Eckstine, all of whom have performed in Europe. And I'm sure I've overlooked many, many others.

Everywhere the reception given these American jazzmen has been fantastic.

As you might guess, this lionizing of American jazzmen overseas has had a great effect upon our morale. It has caused many of my closest friends to compare foreign audiences with those at home.

Lionel Hampton, who now plays Europe so often he regards his trips to the United States as mere visits, says, "We live on the enthusiasm in Europe. That's what's most rewarding. Jazz means not only them enjoying us; it's also us enjoying them."

Impresario Norman Granz, who has taken jazz troupes abroad for many years, compares European to American audiences this

Such fine U.S. jazz stars as Pee Wee Russell (far left) Joe Williams (top) and Zoot Sims have performed to exhaustion for American audiences. "In Europe," says Dizzy Gillespie, "they are far better appreciated."

way: "The Europeans are far more attentive as audiences than the Americans. This stems from the fact that Europeans have a healthier attitude not only toward jazz, but toward all the arts."

Jazz flutist Herbie Mann backs this up even further. Writing for *Down Beat* Magazine about a successful tour of Scandinavia, he points out that jazz in Europe never serves just as background music for drinking, as often happens here. In fact, jazz purists there have seen to it that most jazz clubs serve nothing more than soft drinks and weak beer.

Because of this respect for jazz, it has reached a point where most of the jazz musicians I know always leap at the chance to make a trip abroad.

A number of American jazzmen who went overseas for just a short stay were so impressed and well received by European fans that they stayed over there permanently.

The two best-known men, of course, are Don Byas, who lives in Amsterdam, and the late Sidney Bechet, who made his home in Paris. But there have been many others, too, including drummers Kansas Fields and Kenny Clarke, and ex-Charlie Barnet trumpeter, Peanuts Holland.

In addition to the personal experiences of jazzmen who've played overseas, I can give you many other examples of the flash fire of jazz enthusiasm abroad.

Just about every publicity man I know will tell you that press coverage for jazz in Europe is infinitely greater than it is in America.

Government-operated radio networks abroad are broadcasting so much jazz that the average overseas listener has a much greater selection of good jazz than the average American.

In almost every European country I've visited, children are studying jazz instruments as they never have here. And the national jazz clubs and academies of all Western Europe—which, ironically, have no counterparts here in the United States—are more active than ever, with new ones springing up almost monthly in Asia, Africa and South America.

Several governments not only actively encourage jazz concerts at home, but The Netherlands, for example, is also sending troupes of jazzmen to its colonies so that Dutchmen everywhere may enjoy the music.

Even behind the Iron Curtain, I have learned from the State Department and other sources, the former ban against "dzhaz" has been lifted. Where Communists used to denounce it as "poison for the workingman's mind" and "the wild wailing, hissing and moaning of madmen and sex maniacs," it is now permitted on all satellite radio networks, in Moscow night clubs and at an annual jazz festival in Poland. One American newsman even reported hearing it before the sacrosanct Stalin-Lenin mausoleum in Red Square.

Now, as a musician, I am not bothered that foreign countries have taken our music and adopted it as their own. In fact, I'm flattered.

But as an American, I'm deeply sorry that they have beat us to the punch in exploiting so fully a music we originally created.

Most of all—and this is really the great irony—I'm disappointed that the enormous upswing of jazz enthusiasm abroad has been accompanied by a decline in several major areas of jazz interest here at home.

This statement may come as a great surprise to many people outside the music business, so let me be specific.

Let's take the broadcasting industry first.

Remember all the great bands that had their own regular programs back in the late Thirties and early Forties? There was Harry James, Raymond Scott, Glenn Miller, Duke Ellington, Benny Goodman and a host of others. Also, almost any night of the week, following these regular network programs, you could tune to remote pickups and take your choice of big bands and jazz groups playing one-nighters all around the country. Then, around midnight or thereafter, almost every major city had two or three all-night disc jockeys who played pure jazz.

I had the feeling in those days that jazz was well on its way to becoming the real folk music of America.

But now almost all that's gone. The folk music of America today is a mongrel made up of strains of Presley, Liberace, Tennessee Ernie, Lombardo, and Mack the Knife!

Of all network radio, only one program continues to feature live jazz of merit on any consistent basis—Bandstand, U.S.A., on Mutual Radio, Saturday nights. But even it has no sponsor and may well be off the air by the time you read this. Its gross listenership is 250,000, as compared with 35,000,000 for Lawrence Welk—with his zany hats, cuckoo clocks, tramp costumes and other gimmicks that have absolutely nothing to do with good music. They're on at the very same time, incidentally, with Bandstand on radio, Welk on TV.

And speaking of television, man, what a disappointment that's been for jazz fans!

TV has been big time now for about 15 years. Yet in all that time only one honest-to-goodness network jazz program has been presented. That was Stan Kenton's Music '55, a low-budget filler thrown into some unsold summer time a few years ago. Despite some schmaltzing up with novelty acts to bring the show in line with the taste of the masses, the public just didn't go for it. Ratings fell, no sponsor appeared and of course the show was dropped.

Elsewhere in the music business it's the same depressing story for jazz.

In juke boxes, according to Bob Austin of *Cash Box* Magazine, only about 10 per cent of the country's 575,000 machines now carry jazz, and this percentage is made up mainly of the two or three records included among the 300-or-so selections in the biggest jukes.

Record sales are the one exception to the general jazz decline, with jazz albums moving now as never before. However, it's my private theory that their hot sale is due strictly to the fact that fans are unable to find good jazz on the airwaves.

On 52nd Street in New York, once the mecca of the jazz world, every one of the many jazz clubs has been closed down or turned into a strip joint. Would you have thought this possible ten years ago?

In the publishing field, America's biggest jazz magazine, *Down Beat,* operates as a trade periodical with 60,000 circulation, never having succeeded in becoming a mass magazine, while *Melody Maker,* its counterpart in England, has skyrocketed to a circulation nearly twice that size. Elsewhere

W. C. Handy is admired throughout the world as the father of the Blues.

abroad 110 jazz magazines have sprung up and they are known to be flourishing in such remote places as Reykjavik (Iceland), Batavia (Java), Sastre (Argentina) and Tokyo, where Benny Goodman reports seeing five or six of them on the newsstands.

Perhaps the most tragic part of this over-all decline of jazz here at home is the increasing inability to find work by a surprising number of seasoned musicians. I won't embarrass them by naming them, but Roy Eldridge has made public statements to this effect. He told jazz writer Nat Hentoff in a pathetic interview not long ago, "There just are no places for people who play like we do to jam any more."

Placing domestic unemployment in perspective against the continual requests of such European booking agents as Benoit-Levi of France for more jazzmen to come play overseas, I am not surprised that many musicians, in bitter moments, are saying that jazz is too good for Americans.

I know that I have not painted a pleasant picture of jazz in America today. And, frankly, I'd much rather play jazz than talk about it any time, especially in this pessimistic way.

But except for a handful of bands like my own, the jazz picture is a dismal one. And the sooner everyone recognizes it, the better for jazz fans, the better for musicians, the better for America.

I remember reading that years ago both Sinclair Lewis and F. Scott Fitzgerald were critical of America's permitting Europe to steal our thunder in discovering and exploiting American writing talent. And I'm sure American literature has benefited because they voiced their criticisms.

In the same way, I hope, these criticisms of mine will help America to a healthier appreciation of its own music.

What I ask is that jazz be recognized as a real and impressive part of American culture. The continuous commercial success of jazz will then be assured, I feel.

Coming down to particulars, what I ask is that jazz be taught to school children at all levels of their education.

From the very first day in their very first Music Appreciation class, let the children be made aware that no class distinction should exist between jazz and the classics. Let them be told that jazz is, in effect, free speech in music, that it's America's music.

Let them be taught jazz traditions and what elements to listen for when they come into contact with jazz in their daily lives. Then, as adults with the power of selection, they will be less likely to accept bad music and reject the good, which is largely the present state of affairs.

Let organizations such as the National Congress of Parents and Teachers and the National Education Association give serious consideration to such a jazz-education program and I am sure that in the long run they will do considerably less worrying about periodic flare-ups like the rock-and-roll craze. The courage to teach new things eliminates old evils, as I think the Bible has said, and I am sure this would hold true of jazz education as well.

On the Federal level, I would like to see the United States Government set up a national collection of all the working materials and archives of jazz. Believe it or not, there is no central public agency anywhere in our country which keeps copies of all jazz records made, as there is with books, for example, in the Copyright Office.

Congressman Frank Thompson, Jr., of New Jersey, who has expressed eagerness to "give jazz the veneration it deserves," is interested in investigating the possibility of starting such a National Jazz Collection, possibly as part of the Library of Congress.

In it, the music, books, periodicals and recordings of jazz would be assembled under one roof. Biographical material on jazz pioneers and taped interviews with them (while many of them are still alive) would also be included. This collection would become an invaluable reference source for musicologists, folklorists, semanticists and sociologists.

Finally, I'd like to appeal to the disc jockeys of the nation to cease and desist the drone-drone-droning out of the so-called "Top Ten" or "Top Twenty" most popular tunes of the day.

What happens is that some awful novelty tune starts off at the bottom of a list of questionable accuracy. It stands out because it is so wacky. The disc jockey, eager to cater to what he thinks is the public taste, plays it on his Top Ten scoreboard. Before long, the self-promoting features of the Top Ten merry-go-round have shoved the tune to the top of the heap and it stays there, for weeks on end. People buy and play the record, not because it is great music, but because it is a great gag.

Now I don't think the 15,000 disc jockeys of this country realize that, as the single most important block of musical tastemakers in America, they owe the public more than entertainment. I feel they also owe it an educational responsibility. If they realized this, I'm sure they would have done a better job in recent years.

I say this knowing full well that nobody owes the disc jockeys of this land a greater debt of gratitude than I do. Their spinning of my records in past years has been responsible, more than any other single factor, for any success or reputation I enjoy today.

Nevertheless, the sorry fact remains that nowadays an American traveling overseas can get better jazz from the disc jockeys of any country in the western world than he can from the deejays in the U.S.A.

There's no logical reason for this. Our deejays certainly have the ear to select records that are musically good. They can sift, as well as anyone, the records that seem to have staying power from those that will be forgotten next year.

In short, all I'm asking of the disc jockeys is that they exercise a bit more taste and discretion in the records they select for the public. I feel that this would automatically increase the amount of good jazz listening.

If the disc jockeys and other communications and educational forces of this country were to expose the American public to greater amounts of jazz, I am convinced that the public would soon recognize—and demand—the superior vitality and honesty of jazz.

Thus jazz would attain the cultural stature at home that it has been given abroad. People like Senator Ellender of Louisiana would no longer come out publicly and say of jazz, "I never heard so much pure noise in my life." And we would see the end of the day when some people in this country think, as I have often found to be the case, that the name of Louis Armstrong has something to do with a rubber company."

The joy of jazz is expressed best by its deepest devotees, musicians such as pianist, Ahmad Jamal and guitarist, Jean "Toots" Thielemans.

The "Lost Generation" of jazz

In quoting Roy Eldridge to the effect, "There just are no places for people who play like we do to jam any more," Dizzy merely touched in passing on what is unquestionably the most tragic absurdity in jazz today—its blatant artistic discrimination. At present, in sociological terms jazzmen are either in-musicians or out-musicians. Lovers of jazz are hip only if they are modernists. And anyone who admits to an ardent admiration of early jazz is derisively labelled a "mouldy fig."

Herein, of course, is the distressing proof that jazz is still a young, callow, immature art. A Hemingway doesn't lose his entire audience just because a Salinger appears on the scene. Nor do museums remove their primitives from their walls just because a Dali has carried the technique of painting to a level undreamed of by earlier artists. Yet the talents of an important seminal artist like Roy Eldridge, and the other great jazzmen of his generation, go begging.

The waste is not only tragic, it is also an indictment of the intelligence of those responsible for it, as pianist Billy Taylor here points out in his moving plea for jazz honor to be paid where jazz honor is due. And for those hipsters who can read between lines, Taylor's 1958 words harbor a hidden message. It's simply this: if jazz doesn't soon grow up and develop a proper appreciation and respect for its trail-blazers, of whatever generation, today's arrogant modernists will soon be tomorrow's mouldy figs.

"Back in 1937," Taylor writes, "Jelly Roll Morton was part owner of a sleazy night club upstairs from a U Street hamburger stand in Washington, D.C. At the time, I was finishing high school and playing gigs around the city as often as they came my way. I was a good, proud, seventeen years old then, and quite naturally very little remained which I did not know about life and music. I used to hang around with several other young pianists, kids like myself who were starting to study their Hindemith and Bartók and Schönberg and Webern; we also knew our jazz. Of course, *our* jazz began with Art Tatum and Prez, and obviously there was no place in it for old men like Mr. Morton. We had never even bothered to listen to him.

But when we heard that Jelly had this little club in Washington—I think it was called the Jungle Inn—we decided to take a ride down and have a few laughs. Even though it was a Saturday night we had no trouble getting a booth in the place. Somebody recognized us as part of the new crop of jazz pianists; word started to pass around the house that some young hipsters had stopped in to have some fun with old Jelly Roll.

And then Jelly came on. He looked shockingly sick and feeble —old and a little mad. But he wore his old, southern-gentleman's suit with dignity, and when he smiled the diamond in his tooth still glittered hard. He played a new piece of his called *Sweet Substitute,* and then (since the grapevine grows quick in little places like this) he looked straight over at our booth. His eyes had a very personal kind of pride which I had never seen before. His look had the strangely arrogant wisdom of those who know, those who have been there and seen it and at the end realized that nothing very shattering has happened after all. Dying is a slow and shabby business.

Then Jelly spoke only to us: "You punks can't play this."

I forget the tune. What I do remember is a big, full, two-handed piano player—a ragtimer modified and relaxed by way of New Orleans, and *very* swinging. I suppose the tune was corny, now that I look back on it, but it had a charm of its own. There was something extremely personal about it which defied description; and as I listened suddenly I knew. "Golly, he's right. I *can't* play what he's playing. Just purely technically I can't play two hands together and separately the way he does." I looked over at the other confident young men who had come with me; I saw that they knew they couldn't either. Ours was a very quiet booth for the next three hours.

So this sick old man who had been playing good whorehouse piano in New Orleans when Louis Armstrong was two years old, and I had yet twenty years to be born, taught us a lesson that night. It is a lesson I've never forgotten and I think it is one that might be learned today by a lot of jazz buffs and jazz critics and—above all—by young jazz musicians. The lesson is simply this: great men don't only grow old; they grow. They still have things to say to you, and if you ignore them or neglect them or dismiss them without ever having listened, as I had dismissed Jelly Roll Morton before that night in Washington, you are diminishing yourselves. *They* don't diminish. They may go out of fashion, but that's our fault. Great jazz is great jazz whether it is the jazz of Kid Ory or Vic Dickenson or J. J. Johnson. It is a direct and highly personal communication of experience by men who have seen much and lived full lives, and it is therefore timeless.

Anyone who lets other people's opinions becloud what he hears (whether the claims are that jazz died at the breakup of Louis' Hot Five or began in Minton's Playhouse) is cheating himself. Jazz began long before most of us were born. Since then it's traveled far and, contrary to many self-styled authorities, it hasn't gotten lost on the way. It has a continuity, and one of its many great periods was the late Thirties and early Forties.

Pianist, Billy Taylor insists upon paying honor to the true jazz originals.

Anyone, of course, has the right to disagree, but for me that would be like passing by filet mignon because crêpe suzettes taste so good.

What a lot to miss! Coleman Hawkins, Roy Eldridge, Jo Jones, Buck Clayton, Ben Webster, J. C. Higginbotham, Pete Brown, Buster Bailey, Benny Morton, Harry Edison. Stuff Smith, Benny Carter and so many others—you might call it the "lost generation" of jazz. Many of them are now in their fifties; all of them still play wonderfully when given half the chance they deserve. Any legitimate Jazz Hall of Fame would have these names high on the roster, along with its King Olivers and its Modern Jazz Quartets. Yet today too many of these men must scrounge around for weekend dates and hope for occasional recording dates with some independent recording company which still appreciates what they are playing. And they *can* play, right now, with all the power and authority of great musicians, if anyone will bother to listen.

In fact, these are actually the elder wise men of jazz, as wise in their way as O'Casey and Bertrand Russell. And they still have so much to say.

When I call them elder wise men I mean, of course, that they are old in experience. Chronologically most of them are still in late forties or fifties—a time of life at which artists in other fields are very often at the peak of their creativity, as I believe these men are, or at least could be today, given the proper opportunity to express themselves in their chosen medium without interruption. But in today's world of jazz everything happens "right here" and "right now." Here, where styles and human beings are both frighteningly perishable, they are considered —if they are thought of at all—old and feeble and mute, much like knee-weary halfbacks or fence-shy outfielders, whose skills, however well developed and beautiful they once may have been, have deteriorated with the passing of youth. But jazz isn't a game or a weight-lifting contest.

The tragedy is that the creative part of a musician soon becomes outdated at a time when his "interpretive half" has reached a plateau of excellence. You would hardly expect a present-day composer to be unfamiliar with Bach and Beethoven and Mozart, and of course he isn't. If he is concerned now mainly with contemporaries, it is because he has served a long apprenticeship. After years of study, he has learned all that Schutz and Monteverdi, Handel, Haydn, Berlioz and Wagner can teach him. Yet I know jazz musicians who admire Miles' style to the point of adulation, while the mention of Bix Beiderbecke barely stirs their memory. He is someone infinitely remote who played old-hat trumpet in an old hat (or was it cornet?) way back in the Twenties. (Or was it the Thirties?) They had vaguely heard of him, but they certainly never heard his music …all of this in spite of real affinities between the styles of Miles and Bix, affinities like delicacy and harmonic awareness. Wouldn't their musical background and comprehension be more complete if they could relate what is going on today to what preceded it? This is what is done in the other arts. When the serious jazz musician listens exclusively to Bird and his chicks he imposes unnecessary limitations upon himself and his art.

Jazz, like any other musical form, has a continuity; it doesn't begin with John Lewis, and it didn't end with John Dodds.

Musicians are constantly learning from each other. When I first came to New York, I was more or less Art Tatum's protégé. One day I heard Art using something I had played. Of course it was so altered that it had become Art's and he was having fun with me, but nonetheless I was extremely flattered. In a larger framework the same thing was true with Roy and Diz. Young Gillespie had tried to play like Roy, to outplay him—actually —at Roy's own forte. Naturally he couldn't do it. But Dizzy learned enough to depart gradually from Eldridge and to experiment. Finally he developed a style that was uniquely his own. After a while, Roy was picking up things from Diz. Now the two of them are not nearly so far apart as during the first years. A kind of synthesis evolves from the mutual respect and friendly exchange of ideas.

But today in New York, except occasionally, there's just no opportunity for the old and new, the now-great and the past-great to work things out together. Closing hours are strictly enforced; the union discourages sitting in; most club proprietors are less than friendly toward performances which fail to coincide with what's advertised outside.

I know that one of Roy's main beefs is the need for a place where people like Bean and he could stretch out and jam with anyone who wanted to fall in. As he was quoted in *The Jazz Makers:* "The other guys have the gigs today. And they don't want you to play with them if you don't play their things. They let me, but they don't mean it, and I can feel the draft."

Many of the men of the Thirties who have been bypassed epitomize to me things which jazz should never lose. It has to swing; it has to comunicate feeling; it has to feel spontaneous. The Ben Websters and Jo Joneses and Buck Claytons remain as spontaneous as ever. They swing now more than ever when they have the chance."

Joe Rotis by Bruce Mitchell

Part Six

Jazz—
At
Home
and
Abroad

The World of Jazz has expanded considerably since the publication in 1963 of the original, unrevised, un-updated edition of this book—and in various directions at that—harmonically, rhythmically, electronically, even emotionally. Some of its best players, weary of the music's self-imposed restrictions, have been experimenting, often very boldly, incorporating other forms of music, including rock, into their jazz evolutions. And, at the same time, rock artists have begun incorporating elements of jazz into their music.

The result has been both fusion and confusion. Many jazz purists have abhorred the excessive wattage utilized by the jazz experimenters, some insisting that these players have forsaken their art purely for the recognition of the younger generation and, not too incidentally, for the millions of dollars it spends on recordings and concert appearances.

But, these jazz artists and their followers point out, jazz cannot and should not stand still, or it will wither and die. So they have continued to move ahead in various directions, and often very dramatically so. Dan Morgenstern, who edited *Down Beat* during part of this period, and who has been recognized as one of the music's most respected and respectful chroniclers, has been right there in the midst of all this fusion and confusion. Herewith, he brings us up to date on what has been happening in the World of Jazz during the last dozen years:

Jazz today

The most striking feature of the jazz scene as it unfolds today is diversity. Far from being best defined in terms of its most recent or most radical stylistic manifestation—as simplistic theories of successively more "advanced" styles would have it—the music now includes, in a vital and creative sense, elements of all its many periods and styles, from ragtime to electronic jazz.

Once deemed a passing fad, jazz is today the object of serious study from musicological, sociological, historical and aesthetic vantage points. When Jelly Roll Morton sang about "Doctor Jazz," he didn't have in mind the jazz Ph.D's who, for better and sometimes worse, are beginning to populate the academic landscape.

Once pretty much the domain of American musicians exclusively, jazz has become the first global music, and though American musicians continue to set the creative pace, it is no longer possible to dismiss the "foreigners" as mere imitators: think of Jean-Luc Ponty, Miroslav Vitous, Albert Mangelsdorff, Niels Henning Orsted-Pedersen, Jan Hammer, etc.

Much has happened in jazz during the past twelve years—a period both turbulent and fertile. Let's look at some of the major events and try to identify significant trends, keeping in mind that our subject is a living art, and thus in constant flux.

From new thing to free jazz

The social and political upheavals of the 1960's did not go unreflected in jazz. This was a decade of extremes. By 1962, the major figures in what was then still most often referred to as "avant-garde" jazz or "the new thing" were firmly established: John Coltrane, Ornette Coleman and Cecil Taylor.

Of these, Coltrane, who might initially have appeared to be the most conservative, was to emerge as by far the most influential. Equally accomplished on tenor and soprano saxophones, and helped especially by his extraordinary drummer, Elvin Jones, Coltrane made music of a restless, searching nature that extended the harmonic, rhythmic and temporal boundaries of jazz well beyond anything that had gone before.

In the realm of intensity, in particular, Coltrane went as far as it seemed possible to go. Deeply influenced by non-Western music (especially Indian and Arabic), his extended improvisations sometimes seemed the work of a man possessed, though he was also capable of achieving moments of serenity.

Coltrane's post-1965 work took on an increasingly spiritual connotation, reinforced by poetry, chanting, and such titles as *A Love Supreme* and *Ascension*. His influence was not only musical but also personal (he considered it his duty to aid and further young players who had proclaimed themselves his followers), and his sudden death at 40 in July 1967 produced a shock to the avant-grade movement from which it never quite recovered. In any event, Coltrane's late work seemed to have gone about as far in the direction of extended, ecstatic improvisation as possible.

Coltrane's direct followers include Pharaoh Sanders, who had worked in his group and tried to continue the spiritual aspect of the music, but with relatively banal results. Another self-proclaimed disciple, Archie Shepp, is a musical eclectic who by the mid-70's had turned increasingly to teaching. But almost every saxophonist was influenced by Coltrane, who was also responsible for the rise of the soprano saxophone, a once arcane instrument, to a footing almost equal to that of alto and tenor.

An interesting offshoot of the Coltrane branch was tenor saxophonist Albert Ayler, whose reputation, like those of several avant-garde musicians, was first made in Europe. A musical primitive, who made dramatic use of the instrument's potential for overblowing and producing eccentric sounds, his music had a basically cheerful character, often reminiscent of circus, marching or village brass band sounds. In the two years preceding his death at 34 in 1970, he seemed to be moving back to his musical roots: the rhythm-and-blues tradition.

Meanwhile, Ornette Coleman, the Texas iconoclast whose initial New York appearance in 1959 had created unprecedented controversy in jazz circles, announced in late 1962 that he would retire temporarily from public music-making to study and compose. He returned in 1965, playing trumpet and violin as well as alto sax. Despite these new ingredients, and the new musicians with whom he appeared, Coleman's music—its essential unorthodoxy notwithstanding—now seemed almost conventional compared to other developments.

Coleman continued to go his own way. He composed a string quartet, a piece for woodwind quintet, and a large-scale work for full symphony orchestra and jazz quartet, *The Skies of America*, which was recorded in England in 1972 and performed at the Newport–New York festival in 1973. In addition, he continued to work strictly within a jazz context for some

Thad Jones

years with such near-ideal partners as tenor saxist Dewey Redman and bassist Charlie Haden.

Cecil Taylor has yet to be embraced by a wider audience, though he has received such recognition as visiting professorships at Antioch College and the University of Wisconsin, and commands a hard-core following that includes many young musicians taught by him. First and foremost an incredible pianist with ferocious energy, endurance and dexterity, he has also created interesting ensemble music, such as the 1966 *Unit Structures*. As a pianist, he has had considerable influence on Don Pullen and Keith Jarrett, among others.

The trumpeter in the quartet that introduced Ornette Coleman's music to New York was Don Cherry, whose ability to play unison passages with Coleman was then considered near miraculous. After stints with Sonny Rollins and Albert Ayler, he settled in Europe. Such Cherry recordings as *Complete Communion* (1965), *Symphony for Improvisers* (1966) and *Relativity Suite* (1973) remain among the high points of free jazz. More recently, Cherry seems to have been diffusing his talent through forays into mysticism and multi-instrumentalism.

The essential characteristics of what has fittingly come to be known as free jazz are a rhythmic conception that breaks decisively with the tradition of the steady pulse and includes the disintegration of meter, beat and symmetry; the use of non-Western musical elements, including modes, scales and improvisatory practices derived from Indian and Arabic music, and, concomitantly, the incorporation of atonal and aleatory elements adopted from contemporary "serious" music; extension of the concept of musical sound toward the inclusion of

what earlier might have been regarded as noise (i.e., overblowing; screeching, singing or hollering while playing; using instrumental sound to imitate the human voice or animal cries, etc.).

Some of these aspects, of course, harken back to the earliest known jazz practices (such as the barnyard imitations of the Original Dixieland Jazz Band and the use of "freak" and "talking" effects by King Oliver and other brass men), and can be seen as a reaction to the emphasis on the technical and harmonic "correctness" and purity of sound ideal stressed by the bebop and cool schools.

In any event, by the end of the 60's, free jazz in its most extreme forms was on the wane. What always seems to happen in jazz is that the most vital elements of a new style become part of the mainstream, while unessential characteristics are discarded. Furthermore, total freedom after a while was felt to be just another limitation on creative music-making. The work of Miles Davis, certainly one of the fountainheads of modern jazz, points up these conclusions.

Mercurial miles

It was Miles Davis's 1955-60 groups that launched John Coltrane to fame and popularized the concept of modal (i.e., based on scales rather than chord sequences) improvisation. After Coltrane left to go out on his own, Davis retained the trumpet–tenor saxophone–rhythm section format, and an essentially neo-bop (though increasingly modal) structure. Though he made unflattering comments about some of the leading avant-garde figures during this period, he consistently hired

Charlie Mingus

gifted young modernists (all of whom eventually blossomed into major jazz artists) and gave them invaluable schooling. These included pianist-composers Herbie Hancock and Chick Corea; tenor and soprano saxophonist-composer Wayne Shorter; bassist Ron Carter, and the brilliant drummer Tony Williams who was not yet 18 when hired by Miles in 1963.

In 1968, however, the appearance of a new phase in Davis's development was heralded by the LP *In A Silent Way* and became even more evident with the next album, *Bitches Brew*. This made use of many free jazz practices and utilized the new electronic instruments popularized by rock as well as some of its rhythms. The album became perhaps the biggest-selling jazz LP in history; it sold more than 300,000 copies.

For this venture, Davis had added to the nucleus of his group a number of other musicians, among them extra percussion and keyboard players. Included were Austrian pianist Joe Zawinul, who'd come to the U.S. in 1958, had been Dinah Washington's accompanist, and for nearly a decade was with Cannonball Adderley's successful group; British guitarist John McLaughlin; and organist Larry Young (a.k.a. Khalid Yasin), all of whom also became important figures in the jazz of the early 70's.

Meanwhile, Miles himself moved further in the directions implied by *Bitches Brew*. He adapted a wa-wa pedal to his hitherto pure-toned trumpet, regularly employed exotic percus-

sion (for a while, an Indian tabla drummer and the Brazilian percussion wizard Airto Moreira, performing on an arsenal of devices ranging from folk instruments to sound-producing objects of his own devising), and electric piano and organ (in 1973, he began to play organ himself). Most significantly, perhaps, he incorporated into his increasingly percussive and aharmonic music the rhythms of contemporary rock (or rather, of "soul," its black counterpart). And for the first time since Miles's 1949 "Birth of the Cool" achievement, he disillusioned many jazz players and fans, who felt that he was deserting what *they* considered to be jazz.

Rock jazz and jazz rock

When rock and roll (as it was first called) burst upon the music scene, it was greeted with scorn and hostility by most of the jazz community. But as this once primitive and clumsy music began to show signs of growth and maturity (and, incidentally, no signs of diminished commercial potential), some jazz musicians began to change their attitude; not unexpectedly, the younger, less tradition-bound ones in particular.

Some had already begun to make use of rock elements before Miles Davis. Such "soul jazz" hits as Cannonball Adderley's *Mercy, Mercy* combined a gospel feeling with a modified rock rhythm. The gifted vibraharpist Gary Burton's collaborations with guitarist Larry Coryell made clever use of rock. As the 60's moved into the 70's, the use of at least a few electronic devices (electric bass had become ubiquitous) became common practice in jazz groups with a contemporary orientation.

First came the relatively simple electric pianos and combo organs (each make with its own tonal characteristics), and the electric guitar (introduced into jazz by Charlie Christian but now extended far beyond simple amplification by means of pedal and fuzz attachments and a variety of new body designs, including double necks), and such accessories as phase shifters, ring modulators, echo-, reverb- and feedback-units, etc. Varitones and multividers (for octave duplication and automatic harmonization of melodic lines) were used by horn players, Gene Ammons and Lee Konitz among them. And then came the Moog and ARP synthesizers and their variants: true electronic instruments capable of producing a facsimile of almost any sound known to man, plus quite a few hitherto unheard.

Since jazz has always held individuality in the highest esteem (a player's sound is his proudest possession, and he wants it to be his and his alone), it was with some trepidation that players began to make use of these new and seemingly impersonal devices. But jazz also is a music that has proven its capacity for assimilating anything it finds useful. Thus, such musicians as trumpeter Davis and saxophonist Sonny Stitt; Herbie Hancock, Chick Corea, Joe Zawinul, and a host of other keyboard players; violinist Jean-Luc Ponty; bassist Miroslav Vitous; guitarists John McLaughlin, Larry Coryell et al.; arranger Gil Evans, etc., have made use of the electronic potential far surpassing most rock attempts at creative adaptation of technology. (An exception: The brilliant composer, instigator, satirist and leader of the Mothers of Invention, Frank Zappa, who not coincidentally is very much aware of jazz and of Stockhausen and other contemporary "serious" experimenters.)

Rock rhythms, as noted, had also made inroads, and by 1974, Hancock, Corea, and Joe Zawinul and Wayne Shorter's Weather Report were enjoying considerable record sales and audience appeal with a brand of music that in some ways veered toward that made by such "soul" artists as the very gifted Stevie Wonder, and Sly and the Family Stone, albeit without lyrics or excessive amplification. Donald Byrd, the erstwhile hard bop trumpeter who'd established a jazz department at Howard University, coached some of his most gifted students and launched them as The Blackbyrds with considerable success among youthful black audiences. His own album, *Black Byrd*, was a 1973 hit.

These have been examples of rock (and soul) influences on jazz players. The other side of the coin is jazz rock, the story of which is perhaps best circumscribed by the rise and fall of Blood, Sweat & Tears. Formed in 1968, this group, though made up mainly of musicians with a background in rock, employed a horn section (eventually two trumpets, trombone and alto sax) and utilized big bandlike riff patterns. This led many jazz followers to rejoice (prematurely) and predict that rock was coming 'round. Euphoria was reinforced by the appearance of Chicago, a group that similarly employed horns and jazz-laced arrangements.

However, while BS&T produced some quite acceptable and certainly influential jazz-flavored music (Chicago never realized the *jazz* promise of its first album, though it went on to rock success), the group declined sharply in popularity when it temporarily lost its lead singer, David Clayton-Thomas, went through other personnel changes, and attempted to feature more jazz.

The promise of Chase, a group organized by former Woody Herman lead trumpeter Bill Chase, which after some years of searching seemed to have found an exciting and viable combination of jazz and rock, was snuffed out when Bill Chase and several of his sidemen were killed in a tragic plane crash in 1974.

The short tale of Dreams, potentially the musically most interesting jazz-rock group, indicates the problems of this movement. With a nucleus of two really gifted jazz improvisers (the brothers Randy and Mike Brecker, on trumpet and saxophones respectively, both products of the college jazz movement) and the spectacular jazz and rock drummer Billy Cobham, plus a Columbia recording contract, the group attempted to mix jazz and rock creatively. It avoided the riff emphasis of BS&T, focusing on the freedom to improvise so necessary to good jazz, yet retaining the rock conventions of lead singer, electrified sounds, and triplet rhythms. But the mixture failed to satisfy either camp, and Dreams soon evaporated.

Cobham subsequently became a key figure in the Mahavishnu Orchestra, a quartet led by guitarist John McLaughlin, who after his stint with Miles Davis had joined drummer Tony Williams and organist Larry Young in Williams Lifetime, another attempt to blend jazz and rock that failed. With Czech jazz keyboard man Jan Hammer, the rock-and-classically ori-

ented violinist Jerry Goodman, Cobham on his two-bass drum setup, and himself on double-barreled twelve-string guitar, McLaughlin achieved what others had failed to accomplish: He attracted a mass audience with a music that featured a considerable amount of jazz-like improvisation, if within a sonic and rhythmic context far removed from jazz conventions.

Apparently, the time was ripe for the rock audience to accept more extended and demanding improvisation, but when Mahavishnu appeared at jazz festivals, that public found the group's level of amplification painfully loud. McLaughlin disbanded at the peak of success in 1974, following up with a new Mahavishnu Orchestra even further removed from jazz basics, while Cobham formed a much more jazz-flavored band including the Brecker Brothers.

Though rock sounds and rhythms have made an impact on jazz, and jazz has had some influence on rock (both, after all, have firm roots in the blues tradition), the hoped-for or dreaded merger has failed to take place. Even after the catastrophes that befell it in 1970 (the deaths of Janis Joplin and Jimi Hendrix, the breakup of The Beatles, the tragedy at Altamont), rock has refused to go away. It is unlikely that the needs for entertainment, the "philosophies" of life and dance music that rock fulfills can or should be supplied by jazz. But rock has undergone its own process of diversification, and by the mid-70's, gifted young musicians seemed increasingly able to deal with both jazz and rock on their own terms.

Jazz in school

The collegiate jazz movement has grown and prospered greatly since 1962. Beginning in the 50's as the "stage band" phenomenon (jazz was still a taboo word with many school administrators), it now boasts hundreds of bands (there are thousands more in high schools), dozens of annual festivals and competitions, and some very respectable musical accomplishments.

Outstanding jazz programs at the Berklee College of Music in Boston and at North Texas State University in Denton have between them provided most of the young sidemen employed by band leaders Stan Kenton, Woody Herman and Buddy Rich. Both schools pioneered in a now crowded field. The excellent program at Indiana University headed by David Baker (former George Russell trombonist, jazz cellist and accomplished "classical" composer) also includes substantial attention to jazz history, something rather lacking at the two other institutions.

For many years, the college and high school jazz movement was dominated by Stan Kenton, whose sincere and lengthy dedication to the cause, hard work in the field, and development of effective use of his band in seminar and workshop situations had no or little competition from comparable figures. In recent years, however, more band leaders have seen the light—not to mention the job opportunities. Furthermore, many leading jazz instrumentalists now work regularly in schools as clinicians and judges, enabling the student musician of today to come into direct contact with a variety of artistically inspiring and professionally useful influences.

Ornette Coleman

From a relatively sterile exercise in discipline and polish, the college jazz programs have progressed to a point where their best bands (such as the prize-winning University of Illinois Jazz Band of the late 60's) can compare with top professional outfits, and talented youngsters acquire useful knowledge and skills previously available only through much trial and error, and often years of on-the-road training. Unfortunately, for every band director who knows his jazz, there are still a dozen who cannot convey to their charges an understanding of the principles of jazz improvisation, because they don't know what they are.

Often, as a result of increased cultural pride and awareness among blacks, some jazz programs now exist in most major U.S. cities, frequently under the auspices of community-minded professional musicians, and the time may soon come when every American child will at last be exposed to this most important part of the country's cultural heritage. But much work still needs to be done.

Big bands forever?

The existence of so many big bands in colleges and high schools does not reflect a similar abundance in the outside world. Nevertheless, while big bands may never again be as popular as they were in the 30's and 40's, the form has shown amazing stamina and durability.

Basie, Herman, Kenton and James have hung on. The death in May 1974 of Duke Ellington was a serious blow, for Duke was both a symbol and a creative force, but his son Mercer has pledged to carry on in the Ellington tradition.

Buddy Rich launched a band in the mid-60's that achieved considerable popularity before the volatile drummer disbanded in 1974 for a year to open a jazz nightclub. Maynard Ferguson's compact thirteen-piece band made up of British youngsters has gained a solid foothold in the U.S. during the past few years. Woody Herman, without compromising his musical integrity, was able to keep his band up-to-date and appealing, not least due to the work of the gifted New Zealand-born, Lennie Tristano and Berklee College–trained arranger-composer Alan Broadbent. All three of these bands employed some modicum of electronics and borrowed from the rock and pop repertoire to keep their sounds *au courant*.

Along more traditional lines, the World's Greatest Jazz Band, led by Yank Lawson and Bob Haggart, though not quite up to big band size, revitalized the spirit of the Bob Crosby Band.

Don Ellis, a trumpeter with roots in the avant-garde (he made his first mark as a member of the sextet led by the important composer-pianist George Russell), later studied and experimented with Indian music and created quite a stir with a big band specializing in unorthodox time signatures and the use of tape loops and other electronic devices. While much of Ellis' work was precious and/or pretentious, he did much (along with Dave Brubeck's forays) to help familiarize jazz players with meters far more complex than 4/4 and 3/4.

But it is a band formed in 1965, as a once-a-week rehearsal group, that grew, survived and became a true creative force in a field showing signs of artistic stagnation. This is the band co-led by Thad Jones (former trumpeter-arranger for Count Basie and others) and Mel Lewis (former Stan Kenton and Dizzy Gillespie drummer). Jones does the bulk of the writing, and while he has retained the traditional framework of sections and instrumentation, he has imbued it with new life. The band has toured abroad (including a State Department tour of the Soviet Union), appeared at major festivals, and developed important new solo and lead voices, among them the phenomenal lead trumpeter John Faddis, who joined the band at 18 and at the ripe old age of 20, according to Jones, is the equal of the best veterans. Richard Davis, one of the great virtuosos of the bass, played an important role during the band's early years.

If Jones has reinvested the big band tradition with new vitality, Gil Evans has continued to extend its boundaries. Since late 1969, he has been refining a new tonal palette that includes electronic sounds as well as the deep brass tones he always has liked. The band began to jell in 1972, finally got on record the following year, and in 1974 made an astonishing album of the music of Jimi Hendrix—a rapprochement between jazz and rock that worked. Evans' blend of electric piano, synthesizer, electric guitar, all sorts of percussion, and scaled-down, refined brass and reed sections (from tuba to piccolo) is a big band sound for the electronic age.

While free jazz elements enter into Evans' compound, they protrude as the dominant color in the work of Sun Ra, an enigmatic figure who has built a loyal following since starting a large ensemble in Chicago in the late 50's. Still employing some of his original musicians, his "Solar Arkestra" is based on a communal concept and cryptoreligious teachings about space and time. A typical Sun Ra performance makes use of dance, light projection, films and group singing as well as the instrumental music that is the core of his work.

There have been many occasional and part-time big bands of interest during the last twelve years, among them Gerry Mulligan's, Clark Terry's, Bill Berry's, Louis Bellson's, Pat Williams', Al Porcinos' and Bill Watrous', but in this field the efforts of Charles Mingus must be singled out. A 1963 experiment did not bear fruit, but in 1972 and 1973 there were several worthwhile appearances and two brilliant LPs by Mingus-led big bands, one of them recorded in concert at New York's Philharmonic Hall and bringing together such seemingly diverse figures as Gene Ammons, Lee Konitz, John Faddis and Gerry Mulligan.

Mingus also led excellent combos—especially the one that included pianist Jaki Byard, altoist Charles McPherson, and trumpeter Lonnie Hillyer, and another that reunited him with Eric Dolphy just prior to the gifted reedman's death in 1964.

The durable ones

But Mingus wasn't the only established figure to continue to make important contributions.

Especially rewarding was the return to full visibility of Earl Hines. Upon being rediscovered by the critics after a 1963 concert in New York produced by this writer, the veteran musician finally embarked on a phase of his long career that focused on his genius as a pianist (rather than bandleader-showman-organizer). And there were Roy Eldridge, who wouldn't allow the accumulation of years to interfere with his enthusiasm for playing; Bobby Hackett, who went on making lovely music (often in partnership with trombonist Vic Dickenson, whose wit remains timeless); Clark Terry, unique, warm, witty and wise; Dizzy Gillespie, who needs only a more stimulating context than his usual groups provide to prove that he is still far ahead of any trumpeter following in his wake; Ella Fitzgerald, still the First Lady of song; Sarah Vaughan of the wondrous voice, who made a strong comeback in the 70's; Stan Getz, who never rests on his laurels, and whose great popular and artistic success with that passing fancy, the bossa nova, earned that Brazilian import a permanent niche in jazz annals; Dexter Gordon, who made a strong comeback in the early 60's and hasn't left off since; Sonny Stitt, another ex-bopper with staying power; James Moody and his magic flute and saxophones; Lee Konitz, who after finally freeing himself from the domination of Lennie Tristano has become one of the greatest improvisers the music has known; Zoot Sims, who just kept on swinging until he was rediscovered, and still kept on swinging; Erroll Garner, seemingly immutable, yet subtly aware of change and always remaining fresh within a unique style; Bill Evans, masterful influence on a generation of pianists; super-fiddler Joe Venuti, all but forgotten, coming back to astonish with his vitality and humor; McCoy Tyner, keeping alive the Coltrane tradition in a fresh and inspired manner; and finally, on a list that could be much longer, that symbol of creative renewal, the marvelous Sonny Rollins, whose second comeback, in 1971, returned him to the vanguard of jazz and so far has been one of the key musical events of the seventies.

Ragtime and repertory

While jazz continues to expand its present, it also seems to be rediscovering its past.

Ragtime, long thought of as a cartoon and silent movie joke, suddenly revealed itself as a form of music filled with unsuspected beauties and subtleties, evoking nostalgia rather than giggles.

It was rediscovered not by the jazz sector of the music world but by the classical one. Joshua Rifkin, a young concert pianist in search of repertoire, recorded an album of Scott Joplin rags; it became a 200,000 seller, led to a second volume, and to such happy side effects as the renewed career of nonagenarian pianist-composer Eubie Blake, a vital and direct link with the Age of Ragtime. (It should be noted that such jazz players as Dick Wellstood, among others, had long preached and practiced the gospel of ragtime.)

Not only pianistically was ragtime rediscovered: Gunther Schuller's interpretations, with the New England Conservatory Ensemble, of Joplin arrangements from the famous *Red Back Book of Rags* (it had been Bunk Johnson's musical bible) became a best-selling, 1973 Grammy Award–winning "classical" album. And in its wake, the post-ragtime music of Jelly Roll Morton was also re-created, to the letter by Bob Greene, and more daringly by Dick Hyman.

Meanwhile, a bunch of California saxophonists had got together to transcribe from recordings and perform as a section solos by Charlie Parker. What began as a pastime resounded so well at first public hearings that a name (Supersax), an album (*Supersax Plays Bird*) and a national tour soon followed. And the year before, producer George Wein (whose famed Newport Jazz Festival had survived and prospered after rowdyism had forced evacuation from its home base and a move to New York) had put together, as The Giants of Jazz, a group including Dizzy Gillespie, Kai Winding, Sonny Stitt, Thelonious Monk and Art Blakey—a superbop group that toured the world to great acclaim.

No wonder, then, that in New York, bassist Chuck Israels, now teaching jazz at Brooklyn College, and Wein, independently of each other, hit upon the idea of jazz repertory ensemble. Both groups—Israels' National Jazz Ensemble and Wein's New Jazz Repertory Company—debuted in 1973, and though there were conceptual differences, both converged on the basic idea that the history of jazz offers a vast repository of works no longer performed, but most worthy of being heard.

Occasional re-creations have of course been part and parcel of jazz for decades. But the idea of a company of musicians, plus guest artists, dedicated to the reconstruction of works, most of which had first to be transcribed from recordings, is new. Growing pains notwithstanding, the first season of both ensembles was promising, and the NYJRC's tribute to Louis Armstrong that opened its second season in the fall of 1974 was a labor of love and insight that seemed to redeem that promise.

Such concepts require considerable funding. Happily, the kind of support long routinely extended to the "establishment arts" has at last begun to trickle down to jazz.

When the National Foundation for the Arts and Humanities was established by Lyndon B. Johnson as the first federal agency in the history of the U.S. directly charged with supporting arts and letters, it had a music program of considerable size, but no place within it for jazz.

Slowly, certain friends of the music—chief among them Willis Conover, whose broadcasts for the Voice of America have for so long done so much to spread the jazz message all over the world—managed to gain enough influence to initiate a modest jazz program that by 1973 had grown to a jazz/folk/ethnic program with almost half a million dollars in annual grants. And such private foundations as the John S. Guggenheim have gradually begun to recognize the existence of jazz with fellowship grants to composers Mary Lou Williams, Ornette Coleman, Charlie Haden and others, while the Ford Foundation has supported jazz research and archival work.

It's a beginning.

Honor roll

The deaths of Louis Armstrong in 1971 and Duke Ellington in 1974 symbolize the passing of the first great creative generation in the music's history, but illness, accident, addiction and other scourges also took a heavy toll.

The honor roll includes Red Allen, Gene Ammons, Albert Ayler, Buster Bailey, Denzil Best, Don Byas, Harry Carney, Sonny Clark, Nat Cole, John Coltrane, Eddie Condon, Tadd Dameron, Willie Dennis, Eric Dolphy, Kenny Dorham, Booker Ervin, Tyree Glenn, Paul Gonsalves, Edmond Hall, Bill Harris, Coleman Hawkins, J. C. Higginbotham, Johnny Hodges, Gene Krupa, Gary McFarland, Billy Kyle, Mezz Mezzrow, Wes Montgomery, Lee Morgan, Red Nichols, Kid Ory, Don Redman, Jimmy Rushing, Luis Russell, Pee Wee Russell, Charlie Shavers, Stuff Smith, Willie Smith, Muggsy Spanier, Willie The Lion Smith, Rex Stewart, Billy Strayhorn, Joe Sullivan, Jack Teagarden, Claude Thornhill, George Tucker, Dinah Washington, Ben Webster, George Wettling and Paul Whiteman.

Summing up

Still, the music prevails. One hears recurrent talk about a jazz renaissance or resurgence, but that seems beside the point. Jazz has had ups and downs in terms of popularity, but the music has always been very much here, ever since it first burst out of the South almost sixty years ago.

As I write this, a weekly jazz information sheet for the greater New York area lists eighty clubs featuring jazz, plus seventeen concerts and other events. Some of the greatest names in jazz, as well as up-and-coming youngsters and near forgotten veterans, are involved in this massive outpouring of musical energy. When it comes to record sales and radio play, jazz may lag behind the latest eight-day wonders, but in live music, jazz is out front.

As innovation or repertory, in all its marvelous diversity, jazz is here to stay.

Gil Evans

Joe Zawinul

187

The role and reception of American jazz musicians overseas has often been glamorized. "Europeans appreciate jazz musicians much more than Americans do," many writers have stated, intimating that all of them live wonderfully peaceful and secure lives on the other side of the Atlantic, discovering personal acceptance and job securities that their own land had never provided.

But how true is this picture? Michael Zwerin, author, critic, and a musician of no mean accomplishments himself (he was once a member of the Miles Davis group), visited several of America's best-known jazz expatriates in 1967. His findings, released a year later, indicate that although some American jazz musicians have found greener pastures abroad, for others the green may be less closely related to money than to envy:

Le jazz triste

Everybody is somewhere else. I've been tracking them all summer with little success. Jazz musicians are forever traveling, even in Europe.

So I am pessimistic, asking the man in the post office if he knows where I can find *"M. Clarke, le musicien negre americain."* But he answers quickly, with enthusiasm, *"Oui, Oui. Kenny Clarke, le batterie. Boom boom boom."* He makes drumming gestures and points the way.

The only movable things on the main street are me and a cat. A fountain, shaded by two giant maples, trickles softly in the main square. Tables in front of a café are deserted. Le Tabac is closed for lunch. There are no cars parked. My sandals echo on the cobblestones. Figanières is a strange place to find a drummer born in Pittsburgh, bred on the road and in smoke-filled joints with Louis Armstrong, Charlie Parker, Dizzy Gillespie, The Modern Jazz Quartet and Thelonious Monk.

Klook (his nickname—it is awkward calling him anything else) spends time in Figanières with French friends every August. This year he is more than vacationing. A bulldozer is clearing a road up the hill to his five-and-a-half acres. There are plans for a split-level with a pool.

After a tour we sit on one of his rocks. The valley below is gentle—vineyards and a few red-tile roofs. Klook was very busy in New York in the early Fifties: studios, clubs, concerts. As people discovered he could read music as well as swing, real money came in. But he never saw the sun. Time off was rare. The momentum was greedy. Once he had to hide in a closet in order to get away for a weekend in Vermont. Miles Davis was knocking on the door. "Tell him I'm not home," he said to Carmen McRae, his wife at the time. Miles kept insisting, "I know he's in there."

"When you have to hide from a cat offering you a job, something's wrong;" Klook thought.

The Winter of 1955 he was working at Basin Street East. Michel Legrand, the French arranger and composer, came to town and to the club. They chatted. Klook told him he missed Europe. "Hey, you want a job?" Legrand asked him. Legrand's uncle, Jacques Hélian, was reorganizing his theatre band in Paris. "All you have to do is say yes."

Klook said yes, not really taking it seriously. A month later Hélian mailed a year's contract. Klook signed and returned it, but the idea was still unreal. A month after that he received a one-way first-class ticket on the *Liberté*. "This time I'm going to stay a long time," he told Thelonious Monk, with whom he was recording at the time.

"You're crazy, man," Monk said. "You can't leave New York. There's no scene over there."

Two days out the purser paged him. Hélian had cabled $200 spending money along with regards. And when the boat train pulled into Paris, a band composed of friends serenaded him on the platform. Europe had been waiting a long time for a first-rate drummer.

During the year with Hélian, Klook made future commitments. He was in demand and stayed busy. He made less but felt better and it cost less to live. He was featured on at least one film track—*Elevator to the Gallows*, released in the States as *Frantic*—played many jazz concerts, recorded all the time. For three years he was house drummer at the Blue Note Club, where the policy was importing American jazz names. Klook still played with the best six nights a week.

Now he lives in Montreuil-Sous-Bois, the suburbs. He and his Dutch wife Daisy have a son. (They send him to a Reform synagogue, Daisy's wish.) Klook is home about fifteen days each month, flying to work the rest of the time. He doesn't have to hide in closets. He can choose his life. He is a star. The Premier people provide drums for him wherever he goes—a tour of Spain for Philip Morris cigarettes (*Jazz U.S.A.*), festivals in Molde, Norway or Antibes, France, record dates in Cologne. He can plan a future home in Figanières, an hour or so from Nice airport, three hours from anywhere in Europe.

It turned out that Klook, after all, was able to leave "the scene." He was good enough to make his own.

Everything isn't so idyllic. There are many players scuffling in Europe. They weren't Kenny Clarke when they went over and local musicians' unions make trouble for those who are no better—or better known—than their own best. Brew Moore is like that in Copenhagen.

"You are looking good, Brew." Niels Jorgen Steen joins our table in the Montmartre Club.

"If this is good, what the hell did I look like the last time you saw me?" Brew Moore is drinking a strong beer. His face is very creased, his eyes deep-set, intelligent and bloodshot.

"It was at your wedding. Remember? You were somewhat pale."

"That's right." Brew shakes his head, remembering. "Somewhat pale! Niels had to carry me out—like that." He pantomimes a sack of potatoes over a shoulder.

"I haven't seen you in many months. What have you been doing?"

"That's what I'd like to know. Not much."

The Montmartre is built like a cave and lighted like one. It features live jazz from one in the afternoon till four in the morning. Dexter Gordon usually plays here. Dexter is very pop-

Is the grass really greener for jazz musicians in other parts of the world? For Ben Webster, a resounding "no!"

Kenny Clarke, drums, in his home outside Paris. "You learn to slow down over here—things manage to get done anyway."

George Russell composer, hikes in a Norwegian snowfield. "I figure I'll stay as far north as possible."

ular in Denmark. When he returned last year after trouble with the French police, the authorities refused to renew his working permit. There were demonstrations. Students protested, carrying signs saying, "We want Dexter." The ruling was reversed. There were testimonial dinners, big television spots, front-page treatment. Now Dexter is working in Helsinki for a month and Brew Moore is a filler booking between Yusef Lateef and Jimmy Heath.

Brew moves out again. Three saxophones sitting in are already on the bandstand. "This set, we are featuring an all-American saxophone section," he announces. "Bent on tenor is Swedish, Peter and Jan on alto are Danish—and I'm the all-American."

Brew is not the "all-American" type. He hasn't won any polls. He hasn't made many records. He only knows how to play jazz on the tenor saxophone and somebody like that struggles, even in Copenhagen.

Don Cherry too. Don used to play the pocket trumpet with Ornette Coleman. He is a major figure in the new jazz and his abstract lines are sweet and lyrical. Music is everything to him, comforts unimportant. He grew up in Watts, lived in a bare loft in Brooklyn and managed to find a slum dwelling in Stockholm, where they are rare. He, his Swedish wife and their baby lived without electricity, running water or facilities, and with only a small coal stove. Once a day they took a wooden box downstairs and emptied it into a garbage can. Don is considered something of a saint.

On a rare night last winter, he was working—at the Montmartre. He climbed onto the bandstand well-enough dressed but without shoes. Kenny Drew said from the piano, "Man, why don't you put some shoes on? Your feet stink."

"What's feet got to do with music?" Don replied in a saintly manner.

"Well, your feet smell so bad they make me want to play some funky blues. . . . And that's what we're playing next. *That's* what feet got to do with music."

Kenny almost laughs himself off his couch telling the story. He isn't working now because of a broken bone in his arm. His Danish wife Mariann, a stewardess for SAS, is in Tel Aviv. We have been hanging out in his five-room apartment five flights up all weekend. The place is newly reconditioned and spotless, furnished tastefully in Danish modern. His study is big enough to have a grand piano in a corner. There is a lot of expensive audio hardware around. The kitchen is American style. The Drews' two parakeets sing when music is playing, which is most of the time.

"Any facts you need are in here." Kenny hands me the July 1967 issue of *Jazz Monthly*, a British magazine containing the transcript of a taped interview with him. I scan it: "I came over with the prize-winning play *The Connection*, by Jack Gelber, a good friend of mine from my San Francisco days. . . . I was curious about the European jazz scene and wanted to see what was happening. I packed my bags, but included winter clothing, just in case I liked it and decided to stay. Of course I did stay. . . . Well here in Denmark I've found many things, including myself I guess. . . . My playing has definitely

Don Byas, tenor sax, beside an Amsterdam canal. "I may do that—one more trip in the States. One more grand tour. Then I'll lay down and die."

improved because of the more relaxed mental attitude in this part of the world and also because I'm always playing and working. I've worked with players of all schools when they came to Copenhagen. . . . Although I'll never be satisfied with my playing, I can see I've matured very much. With Niels-Henning I have a weekly duo program of a half hour. . . . The radio has a resident jazz group. I am writing some material for them to perform. . . . Jazz is played every day on radio. . . . The New Jazz Club has been formed for youngsters who can attend for next to nothing. All the musicians playing in and around Denmark play these concerts for the young. . . . There are big concerts in the Concert Hall at least once a month. I've played a number of these. . . . The club owners are generally straight and okay to deal with and pianos are always good, a pianist's dream come true. . . . So you can see it's a very healthy scene all around."

Kenny and I went to high school together. We learned about jazz together. We learned about pot together. Later, while I went my white-Jewish way in my father's business,

Kenny worked with Lester Young, Charlie Parker, Coleman Hawkins, Buddy Rich, almost everybody else—and he continued to experiment with drugs. . . . He is through with drugs now, looks and lives like it. "I'm freer over here in respect to my person and that does have a marked influence on your mental intake."

He's still reminded of home. Once, in Stockholm, the American Embassy threw a party for the jazz tour Kenny was with. At one point, an official referred to him—friendly like, you understand—as "boy." He walked out.

But I think it is true, what Mezz Mezzrow says: "Most of the Negroes who are here aren't here because of the race question. It's just that you can live your own life the way you wish and nobody bothers you—as long as you don't bother no one else. The life here is slow and easy. People treat you as an artist, not the way they treat jazz musicians in the States."

Mezz lives two flights up on Rue Truffaut, near Place Clichy. The double bed in the one and only room is made. He is

Brew Moore: "If this is good, what the hell did I look like the last time you saw me?"

Kenny Drew: "I was curious about the European jazz scene. . . ."

Mezz Mezzrow, clarinet, at the races in Paris. "They got the best racehorses in the world in France."

in his late sixties now, and has taken care of himself. His thin grey hair is combed, his shirt pressed, his tie tasteful. There is a neat, high pile of *Racing Forms* on the radiator beside the well-ordered desk, where he sits and does most of the talking.

"The first time I came over was in '29. I met Hugues Pannassié then. He was interested in jazz but he never knew people like Louis Armstrong existed. I introduced him to the records. That's what actually started the Hot Club of France. I came back every so often after that. In '50 I made a tour all over the Continent. And I've been here ever since. I went back to the States once—in '52—to get some business straight, but I came back and I stayed.

"I'll play music as long as it is physically possible. It's very important to me. I do concerts all over Europe with bands I've never seen or heard before. They write me and ask if I'd like to play with their little jazz band. Recently, in Stockholm, there was a kind of contest. There were bands of kids from twelve-to-fourteen, fourteen-to-sixteen, sixteen-to-eighteen, and so on. I played with three of them. The hall was packed for two concerts the same day. When it was through, I got more flowers than if I was at a wake.

"The last concert I gave was in Frankfurt, Germany. A friend of mine works for the State Department and he started a little jazz band for the American House, one of those social things getting the Americans and Germans together. I played with them. We got wonderful write-ups and I was treated like a real V.I.P. They had a big car meet me at the airport and they rode me around town—anywhere I wanted to go. . . . Hey, are you going to Germany? You can do me a favor in Germany.

I have arthritis, see, and I use this medicine—Polamidon they call it in Germany. They don't make it in France. I need a German prescription. I can get all the prescriptions I want in France but they're no good in Germany. Maybe you could find a doctor there. Tell him . . . you see, it covers two things for me. I've got a second stomach, what they call a diverticulum in the States, on my windpipe. I live with heartburn practically all the time. I carry bicarb in my pocket but sometimes the bicarb don't take it away. And this stuff here—Polamidon—it just kills all the pain. It don't give you no kick or nothing. You don't even know you took it, but you don't feel no pain. Tell the doctor what you want it for."

The room is extremely quiet. Mezz's voice has been soft, hypnotic, a musical voice. When he is silent, writing out the information, I am reluctant to break the spell. He prints very slowly, gripping the pen awkwardly, with pain. I leave him rubbing his hands.

Ben Webster rubs his eyes, which are watering. Ben sits frog-like at Mrs. Hartlooper's linoleum-covered table appearing older than his fifty-nine years. The sun streams through the bay window behind him. The view: a broad, treeless street lined with four-story attached brick buildings.

He is listening to taped vintage Duke Ellington, including his own solos. Mrs. Hartlooper offers coffee. "Ben, do you like some kaw-fee too?"

"Okay. And some cake."

A year and a half ago, Ben figured, "If Don Byas liked it in Amsterdam, it should be good enough for me." When he arrived he couldn't get a hotel room. Finally Byas found Mrs. Hartlooper, who took in roomers. Ben is her only tenant now. He pays her twenty dollars a week, buys his own food and she takes care of him.

She is in the kitchen. "You know what Hartlooper means?" Ben asks me. "Fast runner. And she is too. I can't keep up with her. You know how old she is? Seventy-two. Don't know what I'd do without her. She can cook, too. Man! Look at this." He pats his large stomach.

"Trouble is, about the only exercise I get these days is playing billiards. You play billiards? Last night I played an eighty-two-year-old man in the little pub around the corner. It's a nice neighborhood pub—you know. I go there a lot. Well, this guy was so old he could hardly stand up. Sure could handle a cue though. I never seen anything like it. I was doing okay for a while but then I missed an easy shot and left him a good lay. He ran me right out. That's right."

Mrs. Hartlooper strides in with a tray. She sets the table and starts back to the kitchen.

"Come on Mrs. Hartlooper, sit down with us."

"No, Ben," she says. "I got work."

Two weeks later Ben Webster is in London, Don Byas back home from Belgium. Byas was the first over after the war, more than twenty years ago. He is fifty-five, married to a blonde, jolly Dutch woman. They live with their three girls under five on a wide, luxurious canal in a new district. Byas is small, almost shrunken now. He plays with his children a lot. He speaks English with a Dutch accent.

Just like Kenny Clarke ten years later, Don Byas was on top when he left the States. He won the Esquire poll in 1946 and his recording of *Laura* was something of a hit. He did very well all over Europe. Not now. Ironically, his good friend Ben Webster has been getting some of his gigs. Clubs have been closing and there has been an explosion of the expatriate population in the last decade. Don keeps working but can't put money away anymore. He's been in Europe so long he's not "exotic" anymore.

So he's thinking of the States again. "I may do that. One more trip. One grand tour. I'll make some money, come back and," Don smiles as if kidding, "I'll lay down and die."

George Russell is thinking that way too, in Oslo. "The Norweigians are different from the Swedes, man. They're groovier, more open. I lived in Stockholm for a couple of years and it gets strange after a while. I think Oslo is the most exciting city in Scandinavia right now."

"What about the winters? I don't know about all that cold."

"The cold doesn't bother me. Besides, I have a theory, man. Bad things in this world come from the south. Look at the South of our country. South Vietnam. South Africa. Stalin was born in the south of Russia."

"What about Germany? That's north."

"What part of Germany did Hitler get started in? No, man. I figure I'll stay as far north as possible. Also I like being in a place where the laws are more or less on your side. Scandi-

navia isn't perfect but it's the best I've found so far."

George has been writing his clean, linear, modal music without enough appreciation for a long time. It all started when Miles Davis said, "George, you know what I'm going to do? I'm going to learn all the changes." George figured that if Miles was going to do that, he'd better find something else. He learned all the scales. Later, Miles came to modes and scales himself when chord changes ran dry on him. But while Miles was making it, George worked in Macy's. He was bitter. He wrote nasty letters to *Down Beat*. He could be awfully belligerent. He split and things have been getting better. In Scandinavia, he has respect as well as a living. His book, *The Lydian Chromatic Concept*, is now a text in a number of universities around the world. His music is becoming more controlled, more personal, more ambitious. But, like Gil Evans and Duke Ellington, it doesn't sound right sight-read. It requires repeated attention and empathy between the players. He absolutely must have a working orchestra. This is one thing Scandinavia hasn't provided for him.

George is having personnel problems with his retrospective concert in Oslo. The band has been rehearsing only three days and they aren't completely together. "There are enough good players in Scandinavia—but just enough," he says. He smokes his pipe, calm, very different from three years ago. "If one or two guys are unavailable for some reason, I'm in trouble." He doesn't seem like a man in trouble. His manner reminds me of Klook and Kenny Drew; fulfilled, settled, in control of his life.

"You think I could get together a rehearsal band in New York?" he asks without really wanting to know. "Maybe we could get a Tuesday afternoon at the Five Spot or something."

I tell him he's nuts. In the States his dues, both racial and artistic, would be as heavy as ever. In Sweden he is featured on prime-time television; often. At home he would have lots of trouble finding a decent place to live. In Finland he sat on an arts panel with Buckminster Fuller. In America, his music would be played in saloons, if at all.

In Oslo, the following night, his concert is sponsored by the Norwegian chapter of the International Society for Contemporary Music. The Aula Hall is the best in town. Its walls are covered with heroic murals by Edvard Munch. Norwegian television is taping. The hall is full, the audience attractive and attentive.

However the "17 Manns Interskandinaviske Storband" has intonation and phrasing problems. Balance is far from precise. When "correct" they are stiff. I understand why George may come home—he wants to hear his music properly played. America remains the only place.

The response is enthusiastic though. Minutes of applause continue into a rhythmical pulse of approval. George bows many times, then he claps too, in between, as if on two and four.

Backstage, Gunnar Rugstad, chairman of the concert committee, asks me if Russell is well-known in the States. He doesn't realize how little someone like George counts in the American scheme of things. I cannot explain it to him.

"Yes," I say. "He is important. You are lucky to have him."

Part Seven

The Future
of
Jazz

As with every field of human endeavor, jazz had had its prophets of doom, and no spokesman has been more impassioned than jazz traditionalist Jean P. Le Blanc. Speaking in April, 1962, for those who believed we were witnessing the decline and fall of a once-glorious jazz empire, he gloomily contended that jazz was moribund, sick nigh unto death. The gist of his argument:

What was once, only a few choruses ago, the unspoiled child of the American arts is now a debilitated, pain-wracked adult. Neurotic musicians are serving up nerve-wracking music for nervous critics. With the help of these self-appointed experts, jazz has been manufacturing its own mausoleum.

For twenty years these experts gnashed and grieved at the lack of acceptance for the One True American Art Form. Since that acceptance finally came, they have denounced it at every step, flailing away at the network television shows (musical prostitution), deriding the major jazz festivals (circuses), opposing every new attempt to bring the music into a mass medium.

For twenty years they bemoaned the relegation of jazz to cheap saloons and dance halls. Today, instead of rejoicing at the profusion of national concerts and global tours, they whine that too many acts are crowded into the shows and bemoan the low intellectual level of the audiences and the profit motives of the promoters.

For twenty years they complained that the giants in the field had earned pygmy recognition. Today the top jazzmen have been so glamourized and oversentimentalized by these same experts that a chorus blown by a now-dead artist while under the influence of sesame seeds, taped on a home recorder in the basement of a bordello at 5 a.m., evokes more learned analyses than the most brilliant work of a nationally popular bandleader taped in eight-track stereophonic high fidelity.

Popularity, of course, is the sure road to excommunication among these solemn seekers after a world they wish they had never found. To qualify among the cognoscenti as a jazzman of consequence you need (a) an active rejection of the public's interest, or preferably no public interest at all, (b) a police record, preferably for violation of the narcotics laws, (c) an utter lack of concern for beauty of sound, (d) a death certificate and/or (e) a capacity for solemnity and the conviction that jazz is a deadly serious business.

This narrows the field neatly. In (a) you have Miles Davis, who turns his back on audiences, and Thelonious Monk, who seems unaware that they exist. We won't go into the unhealthy details of (b); the constant newspaper headlines, though slanted, are basically factual.

Chief contenders for (c) are Ornette Coleman, John Col-

trane and Sonny Rollins; in (d) Charlie Parker and Lester Young, in (e) John Lewis, Gunther Schuller and a handful of other Third Stream jazzniks. Adding Gerry Mulligan and a couple more, you find that this minute minority, representing five per cent of the top jazz talent, gathers more than fifty per cent of the national-magazine feature articles on jazz. The rest are too popular, too witty or too alive.

When Bix Beiderbecke flourished, Jelly Roll Morton had his Red Hot Peppers, Venuti and Lang their Blue Four, and Ellington his original Cotton Club band, there were no jazz pundits; the musicians relied on their own knowledge of what they were doing. Today we have a score of Socratic sages who say to them, in effect: "Let me explain to you exactly what was in your mind when you played that last passage. Let me show you, and my readers, its social and racial and aesthetic significance."

Before the critics' day, jazzmen were a happy bunch, content to play their horns, collect their pay and maybe kill a fifth of gin or smoke an occasional stick of pot. Heroin was unknown. Coincidentally, no doubt, after the experts had instilled in them a terrifying sense of responsibility about the validity and significance of their art, a new breed of jazzmen arose, typically a mass of complexes and neuroses, some of which find their outlet in distorted music, some in a variety of antisocial activities.

And with this new breed of jazzmen, too, the uncomplicated, happy spirit that produced the most treasured moments of the Dixieland and swing eras is waning, a victim of musical malnutrition and critical attrition. Slowly but surely, the happy sound is dying."

So goes the argument of the diehards who would cling to the classic jazz of the past, who look at the present and find it not to their Dixieland taste, and who have no eyes for the future because they question its existence. But to most jazz buffs the argument that jazz is dying because the sound is changing is senseless. Painting survived the transition from Rembrandt to Jackson Pollock, classical music the journey from Wagner to Stravinsky, and writing is no less an art form because the sonnet gave way to free verse. In truth, the degree to which an art form changes is the measure of its viability, its vigor. The time to cry out, to view with alarm, is when an art remains static. And with evidence aplenty that now, as never before, the jazz world is astir, there can be no argument about whether or not jazz has a future. The only question is the direction it will take. Where is it going?

The view in the crystal ball

It's been said that knowing whence one came is the first step toward glimpsing whither one may be going. Respecting the adage, John Clellon Holmes in January, 1959, looked at the past and found some significant portents for the future of jazz:

"Future historians may well say that the moment when jazz was transformed, all unknowingly, from a folk music to an art music occurred sometime in the early Forties when a disgruntled group of ex-sidemen (later the leaders of the bop movement) first succeeded in drastically enlarging the materials out of which all previous jazz had been created. The importance of this event is best testified to by the fact that what immediately followed it was perhaps the ugliest and most uncertain period in the history of jazz. Whatever large audience it possessed at that time, it quickly lost: the dance-band business collapsed, throwing hundreds of sidemen out of work; an attempted Dixieland revival never really came off despite massive publicity; and factional bitterness reached a pitch of violence which in itself revealed how deeply the challenge of bop had penetrated into the body of jazz. Critics, musicians and whatever fans remained squared off into two irreconcilable camps, and for a time it looked as if jazz, which had survived Prohibition, Depression, and global war, was about to be destroyed by a flatted-fifth.

Fortunately, the bop men went right on blowing, if mostly for each other. But though their music was often pointlessly eccentric and sometimes destructive, what came out of it (when the curses and the dissonance had died down) was nothing less than an aesthetic revolution which freed jazz forever from the rhythmic, harmonic, and melodic tyrannies under which it had labored until then. The word fell out of use, but the sound remained, to give birth to modern jazz, and to a new sort of dignity in the music, as well as in the musician. For perhaps the most far-reaching result of the disorder and experimentation of bop, and the re-evaluation it precipitated, is that jazz can no longer be understood merely as dance music, like all other music, and should be judged as such. Equally, the contemporary musician need no longer think of himself as a happy minstrel, or a sort of urban Pied Piper, but as the creative artist and performer he actually is. And this is bound to have consequences in the music itself, of which we are as yet scarcely aware.

Perhaps more important, however, is the fact that this aesthetic revolution has opened up vistas which give the present-day jazz scene a diversity and an excitement it has never possessed before. It is a diversity which is best illustrated by the roster of different combos which appear, side by side, at Newport, or Randall's Island, or in the Berkshires every summer: big roaring bands that make the very stage rock; delicate chamber groups capable of hushing an audience of ten thousand; hard-swinging quintets that prove how high the moon can sometimes get; exuberant Dixieland outfits, parading a South Rampart Street that stretches these days all the way from Louisiana to Rhode Island; singers covering the local spectrum from pop to gospel.

The over-all similarity of voicing and instrumentation which characterized jazz from Buddy Bolden to Benny Goodman is now a thing of the past—a matter of choice, rather than necessity; and contemporary jazz musicians have learned, at last, that it is not the specific instrument that swings, but the man who blows it. As a result, flutes and cellos are more common; oboes and French horns not much more unusual; and the day is certainly not far hence when a funky bassoonist will take his thirty-two bars with the rest of the cats. Along with new horns have come new melodies for them to play, for jazz's age-old dependence for its raw material on the produce of Tin Pan Alley or the creations of the folk-tradition has come to an end, and composers today are as much inclined to write fugues as ballads or blues. The ancient rule-of-thumb, which stated that anything that was written down was *not* jazz, has been found to be just as meaningless and restrictive as the idea that only a four-four, or two-four, beat *was;* and most groups today, use just as many complex arrangements as they do tempos that were heretofore considered non-jazz. By the strange paradox that accompanies all periods of transition, the aesthetic revolution of the Forties, that at the time seemed to be so hopelessly anarchic, has led directly to a widening of possibilities and a deepening of potentialities, which jazzmen may not be fully able to exhaust for many years.

Perhaps one of the most striking evidences of this is the fact that bop's major innovators, after the years of relative obscurity that followed the official "demise" of the style, have once again become the prime influences among younger musicians all across the country. Thelonious Monk, as an example, who has been playing in pretty much the same way for fifteen years, but who was almost totally ignored during the "cool" hiatus of the early Fifties, has suddenly emerged as a mover and shaker of the first magnitude, acting as a creative catalyst on almost everyone with whom he works. Equally, it would be difficult to measure the impact of the recent Miles Davis and Max Roach quintets on the most promising of today's new musicians—an impact that is not a little responsible for the great number of fresh talents that are coming up every day, making reputations and records almost overnight. The stream of development, dangerously muddied by all the talk of cool versus hot, is flowing smoothly once more, and it seems inevitable that it will lead to a period of unparalleled creativity in all phases of jazz.

For instance, there are some theorists, questioning whether even improvisation is essential, who insist that it is the destiny of jazz to either absorb, or be absorbed by, classical music. Such men as Gunther Schuller and Charlie Mingus have already taken firm, and sometimes fascinating, steps in this direction. There are others who believe that the most important individual contribution ever made to jazz (a contribution inadequately understood even by many musicians) is Charlie Parker's radical attack upon the bar line, and the untold possibilities for fresh improvisation which are inherent in it—and a whole school of hard-swinging, uncompromising tenors and altos are resolutely pursuing this path. There are even indications that the men-who-blow and the men-who-write will one day be forced into a decisive contest, the outcome of which may very well chart the direction in which all the jazz of tomorrow must inevitably go, for the air is already murmurous with conflicting opinions about such things as "extended form" and "the primacy of the beat." But even if it comes—even if two musicians as influential, say, as John Lewis and Sonny Rollins should find themselves in basic disagreement as to whether jazz is primarily a performer's or a composers' medium, the future (whatever it may turn out to be) is as secure as their respect for each other as musicians, and their devotion to their common art. Indeed, in view of the new possibilities, as well as the new opportunities, the next sixty years are certain to be more incredible than the last."

The eye of the beholder

In contrast to John Clellon **Holmes's** ebullient optimism, jazz critic and historian Nat Hentoff, saw in January, 1960, much that boded ill for the future unless it was quickly remedied. For example, playing conditions that seemed highly "salutary" to Holmes, were, to Hentoff, wholly unsatisfactory. It was his contention that: "the playing conditions for jazzmen have not changed nearly so organically as most of the musicians would like. The once promising summer-festival circuit, while economically more and more important to the musician, is—with the exception of the Monterey, California, event —frustrating to jazzmen. They've discovered that aside from the fresh air, most of the festivals differ not in the least from the crammed package shows of the winter. Programs are poorly balanced; commercial but egregiously unhip 'names' are imported; and there is hardly time to begin to stretch out musically before the next group is due. The audiences besides are becoming boozy and uncontrollable at more and more of these alfresco beer gardens, and clearly a large percentage do not come because they're jazz *aficionados.* Murray Kempton, New York *Post* columnist, started a piece on Miles Davis with the observation that 'it takes only one trip to the Newport Jazz Festival—the gentry in the front row with their Martini shakers, the sailors squatting in the back, their heads between their knees, upchucking their beer—to remember what a weird mixture is Miles Davis' world. Was ever anything in America at once so fashionable and so squalid?' "

The Original Ornette Coleman Band. Bronze sculpture by William King.

The jazz-club scene remains wearisome. Many young jazzmen, upon reflection, no longer see their liberation from night clubs into concert halls as the distinct advantage they once did. They've discovered that the concert atmosphere is usually inhibiting and that in a club there are more chances in the course of a night to express oneself fully and under less pressure than in a setting where the audience, mollified by neither food nor drink, is sitting before them waiting for the musicians to "produce." Most players do feel, however, that night-club owners would not lose clientele—and might well gain some—if they kept a more orderly room so far as working conditions for the musicians are concerned."

Hentoff also doubts that we have witnessed "an aesthetic revolution freeing jazz forever from its rhythmic, harmonic and melodic tyrannies," as Holmes claims. On the contrary, Hentoff believes that what we are witnessing today is an attempt to replace old tyrannies with new ones. For, as he points out, a whole new orthodoxy has arisen among the young as a result of the widespread acceptance of modern jazz. As a consequence, most of the modernists are far more interested in consolidating the achievements of the early "bop" players—Charlie Parker, Dizzy Gillespie, Bud Powell, etc.— than in widening the horizons of jazz by initiative and experimentation.

The growth of conformity has been strengthened in recent years by the growing sanctification of "funky" blues, "soul" music and other synonyms for the earthiest vein of American Negro music that goes back to field hollers and country blues. The admixture of the modern jazz language and the rather self-conscious use of this older loam in many combos has led to a resistance to experimentation among many of the modernists. They are now comfortable with a language in which they grew up, and most of them prefer to concentrate on making that language more malleable for their personal expressive needs and are made uneasy by restless, unsatisfied contemporaries who, like Parker and Gillespie in the late Thirties, feel that jazz has become too predictable and too safe.

Economic pressures also are involved in the desire of the new orthodoxy to maintain current musical usages. Despite the appearances of a jazz boom, the business is still fiercely competitive and all but a few of the more resplendent names have to worry about gaps in the booking schedule. The musicians know all too well that the jazz public—especially the "hippies" who support jazz mainly to be "in" on something the squares are out of—is fickle. The new conservatives grumble at talk of "new sensations" because there is always the fear that the years of learning to play with facility in the accepted modern style may have been wasted economically if the fashion were to change suddenly and a new style were to be required for steady work. No young jazzman with a capacity for observation can ignore the object lesson of the older players, unwanted in most of the clubs and nearly all the concert tours. They see Ben Webster, a major tenor saxophonist who has never played more creatively than in the past five years, scuffling for enough work in order to eat. They know or hear of quite competent swing-era musicians who have either had to abandon jazz entirely or depend on a day job to be sure the rent can be paid.

Philly Joe Jones is one of the most thoroughly respected of contemporary drummers—among musicians, writers, and the jazz public—but he recently said worriedly to a *Down Beat* reporter: "I want to keep time *behind* me and don't want to let it catch up. When time catches up with you, you become passé, so I'm striving to keep time behind me. I don't want time to pass me, and go ahead, and wake up someday and I'm old-fashioned." "I'm already old hat," Gerry Mulligan said half-seriously on a recent TV panel. "There's another generation coming along."

In any case, the new orthodoxy is easily scared. Some of the most venturesome heretics, for that matter, are not immune to worry about fading popularity. The controversial tenor saxophonist Sonny Rollins, at first criticized by writers and the public for his often jarring tone and, to them, difficult thematic improvisations, finally began to win some polls and was booked on fairly lucrative club and festival dates. Then John Coltrane, an even more controversial tenor with an even harsher tone and more complex (this time, harmonically) style, began to upset the firmament. Toward the end of 1959, Sonny disappeared. He may well have had other personal reasons for going into temporary retirement, but he did say, on one of his few nights on the scene in recent months, that he was practicing a yet more challenging advance in his style. "I guess," said another musician, "that John just drove Sonny back into the woodshed."

Yet even in this time of the new orthodoxy there are hopeful portents for the future. For what continues to drive most jazzmen is, as one young player puts it, "the man inside . . . all you can do is to try to satisfy yourself by trusting the man inside." Among the heretics, he is more irascible, more demanding, more insatiable, and that is why the present dissidents are searching fiercely for more form and substance—in improvisation as well as composition. Musician-critic Larry Gushee said of Sonny Rollins (but could have been referring to other jazzmen as well) that "there are too many cultured and sophisticated musicians with great gifts for improvising for jazz to remain something you can tap your foot to. It will be a good thing for our musical culture in general to regain some of the vitality and unity of the past when improvisation and composition went hand in hand. And it will be good for jazz to be faced with the necessity of dealing with form and content."

Meanwhile, more listeners are beginning to realize that the range of content possible in jazz is not nearly so limited as it was once thought to be. "There isn't," says Marc Blitzstein, "a single emotion that jazz cannot encompass. Not only joy and depression, but indignation, anger, and scores of other specific emotions. There is, for another example, the incredibly powerful jazz of fear." Moreover, the intellectual attraction of jazz is growing as more players and writers are meeting the "problems of form and content."

Jazz, even in a period of comparative consolidation, continues to develop and occasionally to burst through another restricting custom. And it has known enough generations by now to have established a pattern of new orthodoxies being replaced by heretics who in turn try to reinforce their legitimacy. But inevitably they in turn will be swept aside by a "new wave." For succession to power in jazz happens more suddenly than in any other art, and a jazz orthodoxy can never be more than a sometime thing.

Coltrane

The Oscar Peterson Trio

By Bruce Mitchell

Basic Jazz Combo

By Robert Andrew Parker

What the performer thinks

Musicians, understandably, approach the question of the future of jazz from a different viewpoint than the critic or the historian. And since the future lies in their province, we asked some outstanding musicians, in the early sixties, to speculate on what they thought lay ahead for jazz.

By Thelonious Monk

I listen to everybody I get a chance to hear, always hoping there's a new movement on the scene. Jazz sort of needs movements. They always remind some people of some things they haven't been paying any attention to, or bring about something new that is real crazy.

The best thing about jazz is that it makes a person appreciate freedom. Jazz and freedom go hand in hand. That's all there is to tell about that. That explains it. Just think about it and *you'll* dig it.

As for a young guy who wants to be a jazz musician in the future, he has to learn the fundamentals of music. In order to speak the language, you learn by reading and writing, don't you? You've got to have experience. So listen to *all* types of music. And listen to *every*body. Just listen to *every*body, that's all.

By Duke Ellington

Tomorrow? I don't know about tomorrow. I don't see how anybody can predict what tomorrow is, because tomorrow is going to be decided by the musician and his acceptance by the audience. If a guy paints a picture and nobody digs it, I mean how long can he hold his independence and that sort of thing? In other words, if a guy plays something and nobody digs it, then he hasn't communicated with his audience. And either he goes somewhere to an audience that does dig him, or else he adjusts what he's doing to the audience that he has.

As far as I'm concerned, jazz is a dangerous word anyway, because nobody seems to know where to draw the line. You know,

the jazz musicians are writing serious—the serious musicians kind of like jazz, you know? And it's very difficult to find the line now, and I don't know where one starts and the other ends. The music of the future, of course, is going to be a real reflection of the people and the times they live in, as projected by the musicians of tomorrow. Now the promise for tomorrow is very, very high, because the American standard of music is pretty high, and the audience is becoming more musically mature. Now everybody is dependent more or less on the audience and we have to recognize the fact that this thing has to be subsidized. I mean, if a man is going to write music, then somebody is going to have to play it. And the guys are going to have to play it the way he wants it played—and this means the best instrumentalists. And the best technicians want a lot of money. This is no longer an art-in-the-garret thing.

I believe that the music for tomorrow will be great big beautiful combinations, which will be constructed for the ear of a much more matured musical audience, and it's going to be a thing that will take in everything—what we call jazz, these things and everything all together, and it's going to be progress, it's going to be wonderful. It will have the best of America in it.

By Gerry Mulligan

For myself, I would like to see if I can't develop sort of a split musical personality. I would like to retain the approach to *jazz* that I've evolved and not let my interest in composing conflict with that side of it. I don't want my band to become an outlet for that because I'll write myself right out of jazz in no time. On the other side, I'd like to become a symphonic composer because the chance at expression is so much greater. Much more satisfying. Much less restricted. Sort of endless possibilities.

There *is* a possibility of improvisation within the symphonic form, the baroque or classical, or forms being much simpler and more concise, more obvious. But even though they don't have a set number of bars necessarily, there are basic over-all patterns that could be used. You run into some problems there, though. The first thing that's got to happen is that we have to be as familiar with those forms as we are with the standard song forms, in order to do anything with them.

Sure, it ceases to be jazz. And whether it actually ceases to be jazz is something the critics will have a good time discussing. And then many musicians can spend their lives arguing whether they are or are not jazz players—it's up to themselves individually, of course, whether they talk themselves into or out of it.

If the question is, where would I like jazz to be, I'd say that I would like to see it become a more homogeneous whole. Jazz *is* a whole, whether we want it to be or not, as far as what the music means, even though the expression is individual. And that's the point. I just get sort of overwhelmed with the possibilities of what could come out of it.

By Sonny Rollins

I don't know what *I'm* going to do next, much less where jazz is going to go. But nothing is new, you know, actually. At the same time there are new things, you know, it's paradoxical. There are good things and bad things, and most of the good things have been done and are still being done, so actually they're not new, but in a way of speaking they are new, and there are people. . . . Monk and Bud Powell, you know, a few people of that sort.

Jazz might be helped if it could be taken out of the night clubs. About three years ago, I was certain that it would have moved out completely. I still hope that it might be, but it's very difficult, because night-club people live on jazz and a lot of people like to come to night clubs to hear jazz. But I would like to see it on a concert stage represented with the same dignity with which classical music is being represented today.

What jazz needs right now, in my opinion, is more emphasis on rhythm and originality. And we need good musicians, guys that try and have a background and have listened to jazz for a long time and try to play something new.

By Dave Brubeck

Jazz seems to be developing in the direction of a listening audience now, and whether that is to be the course of the future remains to be seen. Personally, I prefer to play for an audience in a dance hall more than for any other audience.

As to the music itself, I think that the small forms used by jazz will probably always be used by jazz, and the most exciting jazz will be played within the limitations still of the 32 bars and the 12-bar blues. But I do think as far as composition goes that musicians will use more and more complex forms, although the improvisation is always going to be done within the simplest forms, where the mind is *more* free because the basic form is so simple. As old as jazz gets, all the complexities discovered in music will always be adaptable to the blues form, or the 32-bar popular-song form that we use today. So I don't think jazz in its

improvisational way is going to change much in the type of form used.

I think, too, that jazz is going to develop rhythmically, and so will our so-called classical music, because we've just about run out of harmonic developments that a public can accept.

But I truly believe that the greatest jazz will always be improvised, and I feel somewhat qualified to state this because I have composed jazz and I've written many arrangements, and I've also gone into a studio with nothing prepared and improvised. Improvisation has always been the high light of my own performance, and I think for the audience improvisation is the high light of a performance. Now, contradictory to this, my favorite jazz artist is Duke Ellington, but this gets into a problem in that I consider Duke's great contribution to American music has been composition. And I'd like to state that for myself if it is jazz composition, I leave off the word jazz and call it contemporary composition. In the future, the world of music will realize that all the composition—whether it's done by someone who's learned to notate Indian music or Chinese music or jazz or gypsy music—is primarily composed music. And the world over, folk music will be considered akin to jazz, the improvised music. And that's the way we'll divide the music of the world later on, I believe, into two camps: composed and improvised music; jazz will be a part of the improvised music unless it's written, and then it will be considered composition, without the title "jazz" in it.

By John Lewis

No, I don't think anything like the revolution that took place in the early Forties will ever happen again. It happened one time, it's never happened before, and it won't happen again.

I think the goal is to find some way to escape the 32 bars or escape 16 bars or escape 12 bars, and this has been done before in other music, classical music, by using sectional forms. Instead of the form being determined by this 32 bars, it's determined only by four or eight bars, and after that new material can be introduced and then a new four-bar improvisational section can be introduced this way; and through a very careful hearing of what you're doing, you can make all this music hold together, in a sense. (This is saying all this very quickly.) The style period that we're in now is a much more florid and a virtuoso kind of thing where you don't go from an amateur to a professional as fast as you could in the early Thirties. The young people today are not aware of the limitations in the way that we were, and therefore what they hear they absorb immediately, and they go from that point. So the future will be much broader for them. They won't have to contend with the things we did.

A new sound— or just a bigger noise?

During a symposium on *Whither Jazz?* at the Newport Festival some years ago, Quincy Jones, a band leader and arranger, impatiently rejected the academic speculations of the other panel members. "Hell," he exploded, "nobody knows where jazz is really going to go. There may be a kid right now in Chitling Switch, Georgia, who's going to come along and upset everybody."

As if to prove Jones prophetic, the kid showed up a couple of years later, to upset a jazz world that had for nearly twenty years been dominated by the musical language of Charlie Parker and Dizzy Gillespie. The kid, not from Chitling Switch but from Fort Worth, Texas, is a saxophonist named Ornette Coleman. And he has unquestionably created more angry and confused divisions of opinion among critics and musicians then any jazz figure since Bird.

To his infatuated fans, Coleman is a messiah heralding a radical new departure in jazz variously called "the new thing," "space music," or, more accurately, "atonal jazz." To his angry detractors, he is simply a pretentious fraud. "If that's music," one old jazzman has said, "I've been doing something else all my life."

To the more dispassionate, Coleman is neither messiah nor fraud, but probably the most exciting and radical innovator to appear in recent years. As such, he of course symbolizes the one, single factor that can guarantee jazz a future—the dedicated young musician who is determined to play his own way no matter what the consequences. And if for no other reason, Coleman richly deserves the close inspection Nat Hentoff gave him in March, 1961, during the following profile:

"A few months ago one of England's most intelligent jazz critics, Francis Newton, visited New York's Five Spot to hear the controversial Ornette Coleman, then wrote of him in the *New Statesman:* "The far-out boys do him an injustice by insisting on the revolutionary character of the sounds which, in defiance of all the rules of all musical games, he produces out of his plastic alto-sax. Widening the technical range of an instrument is not enough to make a player more than a freak. The unforgettable thing about this very dark, soft-handed man playing with a vertical fold over his nose is the passion with which he blows. I have heard nothing like it in modern jazz since Parker. He can and does play the chorus of a standard straight—with an intense...lamenting feeling for the blues which lays his critic flat on his back."

Most jazz musicians in New York have not been so ready to be blown down. For months, grimly skeptical jazzmen lined up at the Five Spot's bar. They made fun of Coleman but were naggingly worried that he might, after all, have something to say—and in a new way. They had read of the unprecedented assertion by John Lewis, whose own music is comparatively conservative, that Coleman was the first actual *extension* of the work of Charlie Parker. They had watched with mounting envy the space Coleman was getting in the general as well as the

music press, even including the motley distinction of being asked to write a column for the vacationing Dorothy Kilgallen.

Trumpeter Roy Eldridge, who conscientiously tries to solve any jazz problems that puzzle him, visited the Five Spot several times to examine the plastic phenomenon. "I listened to him all kinds of ways," Eldridge told a friend. "I listened to him high and I listened to him cold sober. I even played with him. I think he's jiving, baby. He's putting everybody on. They start with a nice lead-off figure, but then they go off into outer space. They disregard the chords and they play odd numbers of bars. I can't follow them. I even listened to him with Paul Chambers, Miles Davis' bass player. 'You're younger than me,' I said to him. 'Can you follow Ornette?' Paul said he couldn't either."

Coleman Hawkins, a jazz patriarch, has always been sympathetic to experimenters and gave Thelonious Monk and Dizzy Gillespie work when others of his generation hooted at them. "Now you know," Hawkins says of Ornette Coleman, "that I never like to criticize anyone publicly. Just say I think he needs seasoning. A lot of seasoning." Miles Davis is forthrightly brief. "I like Ornette," says Davis, "because he doesn't play clichés." Pianist-teacher-critic John Mehegan at first was one of the most alarmed of the Coleman opponents. Mehegan has since calmed down somewhat: "Ornette Coleman simply isn't playing jazz. He's an excellent performer and he knows his instrument, but what he plays is something else. There are kids all over Long Island and New Jersey—and I presume elsewhere in the country —trying to imitate Ornette. Their attitude is, 'I'll play anything I want to; you do the same thing; and we'll see what happens.' That's not the way music is made."

Mr. Coleman is more perplexed than perturbed by the brouhaha he has caused. Slight, shy but stubborn, he is a man inordinately patient with his attackers. Coleman has yet to answer his critics with the slightest touch of malice or rancor. Long interested in various forms of redemptive religion, he speaks of "love" in much the same diffuse but incandescent way as a successful cult leader. Some months ago, one musician, a major figure in modern jazz, hit Coleman hard in the mouth as a result of Coleman's reluctance to join a guild of rebel jazzmen which the drummer was helping to organize in an assault against booking offices, club owners, and festival promoters. Coleman did not hit back. "I love him for his art," he later explained, "not his behavior. I couldn't hit a man who plays that well."

For all his faith in his musical mission and his stance as the Gandhi of jazz, Coleman does occasionally become depressed at the naked hostility his music has provoked. Until he came to New York and the Five Spot, he had known exceedingly hard times, but worse than the worry about money was the acutely disheartening experience of seeing musicians walk off the stand when he appeared at jam sessions.

"When I arrived in New York," Coleman says, "I was surprised that most musicians here too treated me the same way as the ones in California where I'd been for several years. I thought they were more serious in New York. The main support I've gotten here has been from John Lewis; J. J. Johnson; George Russell, the jazz composer; and Gunther Schuller, a classical composer who sometimes writes jazz pieces. Marc

Blitzstein, Leonard Bernstein and Aaron Copland have come in and seem to like what I'm doing, and I'm told Virgil Thomson is impressed. But from the jazz musicians, all I got was a wall of hostility. They *had* to listen because what we do automatically catches your ear, but I could feel their anger. I guess it's pretty shocking to hear someone like me come on the scene when they're already comfortable in Charlie Parker's language. They figure that now they may have to learn something else.

"And at least," he notes with satisfaction, "the people seem to like it. We never did have a night at the Five Spot with a cold audience."

It has been a novel experience for Coleman to have had a chance to reach an audience. His stay at the Five Spot was the first extended engagement as a leader he's ever had anywhere except Forth Worth. For that chance, Coleman has had to wait much longer than it normally takes a jazz musician to at least reach the first plateau of acceptance. Despite the widening audience for jazz, the apprentice still does have to "pay dues" for a considerable length of time, but no contemporary of his has had to pay as much dues as Coleman or travel so circuitous and seemingly hopeless a route to his first job.

Coleman was born on March 19, 1930, in Fort Worth. His father died when Ornette was about seven, and his mother did domestic work. An elder sister, Truvenza, became a singer and now heads her own band in Fort Worth. A major influence and goad in Ornette's early attempts at music was a cousin, James Jordan, who played alto and baritone saxophones and had been formally trained. In contrast to the careful Jordan who, as Coleman recalls, "had to know exactly what a thing was all about before he did it," Coleman was self-taught and awkward. "I always wanted to earn respect from Jordan because he went to school, and I didn't."

Coleman was not only self-taught but he was an inaccurate teacher. He misinterpreted an instruction book he'd bought and believed the low C on his horn was the A in the book. Finally, when he joined a church band, the leader said scornfully, 'Look at this boy. Playing the instrument wrong for two years. He'll never be a saxophone player.'"

Coleman had bought his own alto saxophone in 1944, but switched to tenor two years later because more jobs were open for the heavier, more aggressive-sounding horn. "At first, I used to be one of those people like Big Jay McNeeley," Coleman admits with some embarrassment. "I'd lie on the floor and play and do all those other gimmicks." But Coleman was also listening intently to a local musician, Red Connor, an alto saxophonist Coleman claims was more inventive than Charlie Parker. "Red died young. He died of several different things. He lived a jazzman's life, and in the late Thirties and early Forties, that was really a night-time life. It was listening to Red and his group when I was a kid that made me feel ashamed of myself. They were really playing *music*. I was getting all the praise around town, but I wasn't making any contribution."

Connor, according to Coleman, did not influence his style so much as he did his respect for jazz. "No one ever really influenced me fundamentally, although I did listen to many players. I liked Jimmy Dorsey, Peter Brown, Lester Young, Charlie Parker and many others. I've always been able to play

exactly like anyone I've ever liked, but fortunately I found out pretty early that I could also play myself."

In 1949, Coleman went on the road. Two months after the journey began, Ornette was fired in Natchez, Mississippi. He had tried to teach a jazz number to the other tenor in the combo, and the latter complained to the leader that a subversive in the band was trying to make a "bebopper" out of him. Not wanting his men contaminated, the leader cashiered Coleman. While in Natchez, Coleman made a tape for a local record company, but never heard it or found out what had happened to it. "The police department ran me out of town. I told them I was from Texas, but they thought I was from the North. I was just sitting in a place eating one day, and they said I had to leave." So he moved on to New Orleans where a joined a rhythm and blues band that toured the surrounding area.

Ornette stayed in New Orleans for nearly a year, playing occasionally at night and doing yard work and other laboring jobs during the day. Having left his twisted tenor in Baton Rouge, Coleman returned to the alto. He also went back to Fort Worth toward the end of 1950. Coleman then joined Pee Wee Crayton's touring rhythm and blues band but was stranded in Los Angeles because Crayton was appalled by the bearded altoist's sound and style. "We'd worked around ten one-nighters when Crayton told me, 'You don't have to play tonight. I'll pay you anyway.' The next night I left."

In Los Angeles, Coleman became a house boy. "A wonderful middle-aged lady let me rent out the back part of a converted garage. There was no heat, but at least it was a place to stay. I took care of the kids—she ran a little nursery—cleaned the kitchen and did other odd jobs."

Coleman started to go to sessions. Having very little money, he would walk the long distance to the Negro section of Los Angeles. After one such walk, he tried to sit in with tenor saxophonist Dexter Gordon, a musician who at that time was influencing many young players. "He made me stop playing. I had no money left, so I walked all the way home again in the rain. That sort of thing happened a lot. Some musicians would promise me I could play but they'd keep me waiting all night. Then, with the place due to close at two in the morning, they'd put me on at three minutes to two. I was getting discouraged. They said I didn't know the changes and was out of tune, but I knew that wasn't so. But something, I thought, must be wrong. I didn't know what."

During much of his first Los Angeles period, Coleman had to play on a rented horn. His own had collapsed. When the rented alto was taken back, he had no instrument at all. Finally, he decided to go back to Fort Worth and stayed from 1952 to 1954. There at least he had an audience. "I got a horn and formed my own band. We played what the people liked, but I wasn't playing the way I wanted to." Coleman tried Los Angeles again. He worked at Bullock's department store for several years, first as an elevator operator and then as a stock boy.

Coleman continued teaching himself music theory. The only music lesson he'd ever had was given him in New York during a brief visit he made there when he was fifteen. He was staying with an aunt who was married at the time to jazz-trumpeter Doc Cheatham. Cheatham brought the youngster to Walter "Foots"

Thomas, a big-band veteran. "It seemed I made a lot of faces when I played. Thomas had me look into the mirror and play for an hour. That was my lesson."

While he was an elevator operator, Coleman continued his more serious education, bringing several books on music theory to work. "I used to go up to the tenth floor, park there, and read." Automation came to Bullock's, and Coleman lost his study hall. At jam sessions meanwhile Coleman was still welcomed with the degree of warmth Senator James O. Eastland might have received. There was little more encouragement at home. Coleman had married a California girl who was thoroughly oriented in modern jazz and played cello as well. She was not, however, convinced that her husband was leading a new wave of significance. "My wife would start in, 'People say you're crazy,' and she sounded as if she agreed. By then, however, I'd made up my mind I was right. After all, the musicians who were putting me down were playing things I'd known about ten years before. I was only trying to be better, and they didn't like me because I was trying things that were different from what they were used to."

Coleman finally met a few young musicians who were intrigued by his message. Don Cherry, a trumpet player from Oklahoma, had grown up in Los Angeles. He had first met Coleman in a music store in Watts, California. "Ornette was buying the thickest reed you can get. He still had long hair and a beard. Although it was about 90 degrees, he had an overcoat on. I was scared of him." After the fright wore off, Cherry became a disciple and is still with Coleman's quartet. Bassist Don Payne had been born in Texas but grew up in California. He too became a fervent convert. It was at Payne's apartment in 1958 that Red Mitchell, an established bassist, heard a composition by Coleman. Mitchell advised Coleman, who needed money badly, to take the tune to Lester Koenig, owner of Contemporary Records, on the chance that Koenig might suggest one of his contract players use it on a date. It was inconceivable to Mitchell or Coleman that Koenig would decide to ask Coleman himself to make an album.

Koenig described his initial interview with Coleman to Jack Tynan, a *Down Beat* reporter, who was the first critic to recognize Coleman's potential: "I took him to the piano and asked him to play the tunes. Ornette said he couldn't *play* the piano. I asked him 'How did you hope to play your tunes for me if you can't play piano?' So he took out his plastic alto and began to play." Koenig was as impressed by the playing as by Coleman's characteristically bold, angular originals. He set up the first of two Contemporary Coleman albums.

At the time he went to see Koenig, Coleman had exhausted nearly all of his emotional, let alone financial resources. "I was going to give up my music and go back to Fort Worth. I wanted to live a normal life again." Not much happened to encourage Coleman after the Contemporary album, but some work did come in, including a stay in San Francisco. More important than the intermittent jobs was the fact that Don Payne brought Percy Heath, bassist with the Modern Jazz Quartet, to hear Coleman. "I jammed with him," Percy remembers. "It sounded strange but it felt very good, and it felt fresh. I don't say I understood it, but it was exciting and that's one quality jazz has to have.

But believe me, those guys were starving then, and musicians were still walking off the stand when Ornette came in."

Heath brought John Lewis, musical director of the Modern Jazz Quartet, to hear Coleman. Lewis was the next major factor in accelerating Coleman's career. A man rarely given to unfettered enthusiasm, Lewis told an interviewer in June, 1960: "I've never heard anything like Ornette Coleman and Don Cherry before. Ornette is, in a sense, an extension of Charlie Parker—the first I've heard. This is the real need . . . to extend the basic ideas of Bird until they're not playing an imitation but actually something new."

Lewis made arrangements for Coleman and Don Cherry to become students at the School of Jazz in Lenox, Massachusetts, for the 1959 semester. The money was put up by Atlantic Records, the home label of the Modern Jazz Quartet.

Lewis is musical director of the school, the only jazz academy staffed by major jazz instrumentalists and writers. The three-week summer course is exhaustingly intensive. There was some dissension among faculty members concerning Coleman's worth. Trombonist-arranger Bob Brookmeyer at first was angered by what he regarded as Coleman's gratuitous formlessness. Brookmeyer is now an admirer. "What can I say? I kept on listening, and now he gives me great pleasure. It was a lesson for me on quick judgments." Other faculty members, led by Lewis, Max Roach and George Russell, were strongly impressed by Coleman from the start.

Coleman and his principal adviser, John Lewis, realized that Coleman now had to base himself in New York if his career were to grow. Coleman took half his advance for his first Atlantic album to transport his men to New York from Los Angeles.

The guerrilla warfare began as soon as Coleman opened at the Five Spot. For every musician such as John Coltrane who asked to meet Coleman during the day so that he could understand his musical tenets more thoroughly, there were ten who were scornful. Significantly, most of the more thoughtful and original jazzmen reserved their opinions. *Time* quoted Dizzy Gillespie as asking rhetorically, "Are they kidding?" Gillespie, however, recalls: "I never said no such thing. I don't claim to know what they're doing. I've been traveling so much myself that I've hardly had a chance to hear them. But I do know Ornette is a serious musician, and he's not jiving."

Charles Mingus, the inflammable bassist-composer-leader, is not fully convinced that Coleman knows where he's going, but he told a *Down Beat* questioner: ". . . The fact remains that his notes and lines are so fresh. . . . I'm not saying that everybody's going to have to play like Coleman. But they're going to have to stop copying Bird. . . . You can't put your finger on what he's doing . . . [but] it gets to you emotionally."

The most lucid description of what Coleman, in fact, is doing has come from critic Martin Williams, Coleman's leading lay interpreter. According to Williams, "What Coleman has done is, like all valid innovations, basically simple, authentic, and inevitable. . . . The basis of it is this: if you put a conventional chord under my note, you limit the number of choices I have for my next note; if you do not, my melody may move freely in a far greater choice of directions. . . . This does not mean that his music is 'a-harmonic' as is the music of a 'country' blues

Ornette Coleman

By Shirley Glaser

singer . . . nor that he invites disorder. He can work through and beyond the furthest intervals of the chords. . . . As several developments in jazz in the last few years have shown, no one really needs to state all those chords that nearly everyone uses, and, as some events have shown, if someone does state them or if a soloist implies them, he may end up with a harassed running up and down scales at those 'advanced' intervals like a rat in a harmonic maze. Someone had to break through the walls that those harmonies have built, and restore melody. . . . Like the important innovators in jazz, Coleman maintains an innate balance among rhythm and harmony and melodic line. In jazz, these are really an identity, and any change in one of them without intrinsic reshuffling of the others inevitably risks failure. Further, he works in terms of developing the specific, implicit resources of jazz, not by wholesale importations from concert music. . . . To say . . . that his solos . . . do not have a relationship to his melodies is quite wrong. As a matter of fact, most jazz solos are not related to their theme melodies, but to the chords with which the themes are harmonized. Coleman and Cherry may relate to the emotion, the pitch, the rhythm, the melody of a theme, without relating to 'chords' or bar divisions. To a listener such relationships can have even more meaning than the usual harmonic ones."

Coleman himself is quite verbal about his work, and the motif of *pitch*, of wanting his horn to sound as much as possible like the human voice, runs through much of what he says. "There are some intervals," he observes, "that carry that *human* quality if you play them in the right pitch. You can reach into the human sound of a voice on your horn if you're actually hearing and trying to express the warmth of a human voice."

Coleman adds that he always writes the melody line first, because several different chords can fit the same melody line. "In fact, I would prefer it if musicians would play my tunes with different changes as they take a new chorus so that there would be all the more variety in the performance. As for rhythm patterns, I would like the rhythm section to be as free as I'm trying to get, but very few players so far—on horns or rhythm instruments—can do this yet."

Coleman is continually stretching the possibilities of each player's freedom to improvise. "If I don't set a pattern at a given moment, whoever has the dominant ear at that moment can take and do a thing that will change the direction. The drums can help determine direction too. Certain phrases I start to play with my drummer, Edward Blackwell, suddenly seem backward to me because he can turn them around on a different beat, thereby increasing the freedom of my playing. Our group does not begin with a preconceived notion as to what kind of effect we will achieve. When we record, sometimes I can hardly believe that what I hear when the tape is played back is the playing of my group. I want the members of my group to play what they hear in the piece for *themselves*."

"Music," Coleman summarizes his credo, "is for our feelings. I think jazz should try to express more kinds of feelings than it has up to now."

Coleman is also lucid in explaining his fondness for the small, white, plastic alto saxophone that has become his hallmark. The plastic alto has served as a target for attacks on Coleman by several writers who lack the ability to criticize the music on its own terms.

"I bought it in Los Angeles in 1954," Coleman recalls. "I needed a new horn badly but I didn't have much money. A man in the music store said he could sell me a new horn—a plastic model—for the price of a used Selmer. I didn't like it at first, but I figured it would be better to have a new horn anyway. Now I won't play any other. They're made in England, and I have to send for them. They're only good for a year the way I play them. The plastic horn is better for me because it responds more completely to the way I blow into it. There's less resistance than from metal. Also, the notes seem to come out detached, almost like you could see them. What I mean is that notes from a metal instrument include the sounds the metal itself makes when it vibrates. The notes from a plastic horn are purer. In addition, the keyboard is made flat, like a flute keyboard, whereas a regular horn is curved. On a flat keyboard, I can dig in more."

The debate meanwhile continues. Reading the varied appraisals and feeling the stares of the resolutely unconverted professionals, Coleman has felt at times in New York as if he were being exhibited on a revolving stand. He has, however, become fond of the city and has decided to make it his base. He is separated from his wife who remains in Los Angeles with their four-year-old son, Denardo. Coleman misses the boy, but is convinced that New York is the city in which he and his music can most freely grow.

"New York," Coleman explains, "is the best city anywhere for jazz. Even when the snow was thick on the ground last winter, there were nights when the Five Spot was so crowded that people couldn't get in. They don't love music that much anywhere else in America."

Ornette's music has shown a marked increase in clarity of conception since he's had a chance to work every night over a long period of time. Coleman feels, however, that the added clarity could have come as effectively through steady practice. "I'm not sure but what I lose more than I gain by working every night. I get so tired I don't have the enthusiasm to write or rehearse during the day. I'd much prefer longer sets three or four nights a week, and the rest of the time off." Coleman reflected the feelings of many jazzmen when he told Whitney Balliett: "Six hours a night, six nights a week. Sometimes I go to the club and I can't understand what I feel. 'Am I Here? How will I make it through tonight?'"

A new dimension to Coleman's musical experience since his arrival in New York has been his studying with Gunther Schuller, the young classical composer who is an active jazz critic and has been exploring in his writing what John Wilson has termed in The New York *Times* a "third stream" of music that organically incorporates elements of both the jazz and classical traditions. Coleman has been taking instruction in notation and other aspects of music with Schuller.

Since observing Coleman at the School of Jazz, Schuller had been convinced of Coleman's violently expressive power: "His musical inspiration operates in a world uncluttered by conventional bar lines, conventional chord changes, and conventional ways of blowing or fingering a saxophone. The main reason he finally asked me for instruction was that he wanted to write longer pieces and notate them so that other musicians could play them the way he wanted them to sound."

Schuller is not afraid that Coleman's immersion in music theory will inhibit his work. "On the contrary, it'll open up new possibilities of expression for him. It's extraordinary, by the way, how much he'd already learned about harmony by himself. His ear is phenomenal. I'm also amazed, the longer I know him, at the degree of inner peace he's attained. He's a remarkably mature, wise person."

Miles Davis, a shrewd, mordant observer of the jazz scene, is skeptical at such talk of Coleman's inner serenity. "Hell," says Davis, "just listen to what he writes and how he plays. If you're talking psychologically, the man is all screwed up inside."

Whether Coleman is indeed as Buddha-like as he appears, he shows no sign of making any concessions to other musicians or to listeners now that success seems imminent. "I'm still trying," he says, "to make my playing as free as I can. Music is a free thing, and any way you can enjoy it, you should. Jazz is growing up. It's not a cutting contest anymore. . . ."

"This is just the beginning of something," bassist Buell Neidlinger prophesizes. "Something wonderful is going to happen with that guy. He's going to shake up jazz a lot more than he already has."

Whether or not Coleman shakes up jazz to any lasting degree remains to be seen. Furthermore, it's not too important. What is important is the assurance to be drawn from his presence on the scene. For jazz, perhaps more than other art forms, is a volatile, changing thing; largely sustained by what happened yesterday and today but still in need for further nourishment. For, obviously, to continue its growth it must be nourished by musicians in search of tomorrow; heretics who, like Ornette, stubbornly blow their horns their own way, in defiance of all tradition. Only with such musicians can jazz go on renewing itself. Without them it will inevitably stagnate.

Happily, throughout its brief history jazz has ever been a fertile spawning ground for heretics and dissidents. A free music, it has always bred free spirits. And today is no exception. For, in addition to Ornette Coleman, jazz is currently blessed with a healthy number of other free-wheeling innovators. Among them, to name but a few, are Donald Byrd, Chick Corea, Gil and Bill Evans, Herbie Hancock, Keith Jarrett, John McLaughlin, Cecil Taylor, McCoy Tyner, Joe Zawinul, and, of course, Miles Davis, Thelonious Monk, and stubborn Charles Mingus ("I play and write *me*, the way I feel, no matter what's supposed to be hip").

Just as always in the past there's been a youngster to come along at the right moment and blow a new note that upsets the status quo, so is there every reason to believe now that this will continue. It is more than likely, in fact, that before Ornette Coleman ever sees his first grey hair he will see from the stand a young musician at the bar shake his head, turn to a colleague, and say, "Man, wouldn't you think he'd get tired of playing that simple stuff all night long?"

As long as the young continue to challenge the old—and when in history haven't they—the future of jazz is assured.

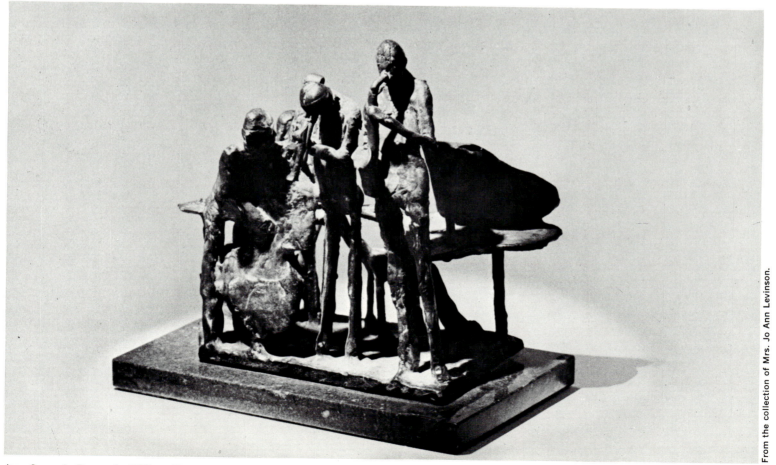

Jazz Group in Bronze by William King.

Discography

John Lissner, who writes about jazz for *The New York Times* and many other publications, compiled the discography that appeared in the original edition of ESQUIRE'S WORLD OF JAZZ. Obviously, many great recordings have been issued since then, so Lissner has been asked to update his original contribution. Like all of us, he remains aware that 100 percent objectivity is an impossibility when assembling a listing of this sort, so don't be surprised if records you feel should have been included have been bypassed for one reason or another, most probably because of lack of space. However, what you will find here are examples of all forms of jazz, ranging from the earliest and most traditional to the latest and most progressive—and, at time of publication at least—all still available.

ALBERT AMMONS, PETE JOHNSON, JIMMY YANCEY

Boogie Woogie Man	French RCA 730 561

Rollicking boogie and barrelhouse from three masters of the form, the selections carefully chosen by producer-collector Jean-Paul Guiter.

LOUIS ARMSTRONG

The Louis Armstrong Story (4 records)	Columbia CL 851–854
The Genius of Louis Armstrong	Columbia G 30416
Great Soloists Featuring Louis Armstrong	Biograph C–5
Louis Armstrong's Greatest Hits	Columbia CS 9438E
July 4, 1900–July 6, 1971	RCA VPM 6044
Rare Items	Decca 79225E

The Columbia four-record **The Louis Armstrong Story**, laying down the basics of jazz improvisation, is the classic Armstrong. Volumes 1 and 2 (the Hot Five and Sevens of 1926–27) finds him tearing loose from the strict New Orleans polyphonic ensembles. Volume 3 (The Hot Five of 1928) features Earl Hines, who transposed Armstrong's trumpet style to the piano, influencing a generation of jazz pianists. Volume 4 covers the late 20's and early 30's, and has brilliant, soaring Armstrong solos set against saccharine big band background (reflecting Satchmo's unyielding admiration for Guy Lombardo). The Columbia **Genius** compresses this era into a two-record set. The Biograph collection is a gem with Armstrong showcased as a featured soloist with various pick-up groups behind blues singer Victoria Spivey, and also as part of the Carroll Dickerson and Luis Russell big bands.

Greatest Hits brings us into the 50's and spotlights *Mack the Knife* plus choice selections from Armstrong LP's of the period. The RCA doubleset is a survey of Louis' recordings for that label; it includes a superb 1933 *St. Louis Blues*, and selections from a joyous 1947 Town Hall concert with Jack Teagarden. **Rare Items** are Swing Era recordings mostly with big bands, and Louis' solos will lift you right out of your chair.

COUNT BASIE

Basie's Best	Decca DXS 7170E
Swinging at the Daisy Chain	British Coral CP 75, 76
Jumpin at the Woodside with J	British Ace of Hearts AH 111
Blues I Love to Sing with	
Jimmy Rushing	British Ace of Hearts AH 119
Basie's Best	Harmony 11247E
Superchief	Columbia G 31124
The Best of Count Basie	Roulette RE 118
April in Paris	Verve 8012
Standing Ovation	Dot 25938

The Decca doubleset, **Basie's Best**, has the cream of recordings by Basie's original band of the 30's. The entire Basie Decca output, which reveals what swing is all about, is spread through the English Coral and Ace of Hearts LP's. This greatest of all swing bands, with a dazzling lineup of soloists including Lester Young, Herschel Evans, and Buck Clayton, played blues and riff themes like the *One O'Clock Jump*, *Swinging the Blues*, and *Jumpin' At The Woodside* with the flexibility and relaxation of a small group. **Basie's Best**, a Harmony budget LP, catches the explosive power of the 1940–42 Basie band. **Superchief** has supercharged broadcast material from the late 30's like *Miss Thing* and *Shout and Feel It*.

Post–World War II Basie orchestras had more of a juggernaut approach to jazz. Crisp solos, hard, biting ensembles and ball-bearing rhythm characterizes the sound of **April in Paris**. Roulette's **The Best of Count Basie** is repackaged material from the late 50's and very early 60's; it includes sharp, trim arrangements by Neil Hefti that show off the band's precision and dynamics. **Standing Ovation** is a splendid Las Vegas nightclub stereo recording of Basie's contemporary band, with powerful, precise performances of Basie classics from three decades.

KENNY BARRON

Sunset to Dawn	Muse 5018

Pianist Barron, one of the many articulate extensions of bop innovator Bud Powell, plays with great imagination, verve and skill on this recording. Contemporary jazz piano at its very best.

CHARLIE BARNET

Charlie Barnet, Vol. 1	RCA LPV 551

Guts and drive were the outstanding qualities of the Charlie Barnet big bands. The leader's highly volatile sound on tenor, alto and soprano sax sparks such swing classics as *Cherokee*, *Redskin Rhumba* and *The Count's Idea*.

SIDNEY BECHET

Bechet of New Orleans	RCA LPV 510

Bechet's brash, voluptuous, often driving soprano saxophone is at its eloquent best in these powerful recordings by his New Orleans Feetwarmers.

BIX BEIDERBECKE

Bix Beiderbecke	Milestone 47019
The Bix Beiderbecke Legend, Vols. 1–2	French RCA 731 037/37
The Bix Beiderbecke Legend, Vol. 3	French RCA 731 131
The Bix Beiderbecke Legend, Vol. 4	French RCA 731 093
The Bix Beiderbecke Story, Vols. 1 & 2	Columbia CL 844 & 845

Beiderbecke's haunting cornet sings fresh and clear after five decades despite the primitive acoustic recording techniques found on the original Gennetts packaged in the the Milestone doubleset, and in spite of ponderous arrangements by the Paul Whiteman and Jean Goldkette bands on the RCA and Columbia collections. The Milestone is a first-rate engineering achievement; every drop has been extracted from the original 1924 Wolverine sides; pitching faults have been corrected; surface noises reduced. Fortunately most of the RCA's and Columbias were electrically recorded, and have a good, clear sound.

BUNNY BERIGAN

Great Dance Bands of the 30s and 40s	RCA LPM 2078

Berigan's big, rich sound—unforgettable and unique—is preserved on the RCA disc on twelve tracks featuring his dance band of the late 30's. His eloquent trumpet swells up massively on *I Can't Get Started*, growls darkly on *Caravan*, tears through *Frankie and Johnny* and *The Prisoners Song*. Each of his solos is a precise lesson in the art of jazz, brilliantly constructed, passionately personal.

CHU BERRY

with Cab Calloway, 1936–41	Epic CSP JEEOO 22007

Available from Columbia Special Products, this is a fine showcase for Berry's swinging tenor saxophone. With a big, brawny sound derived from Coleman Hawkins, Berry is ranked with Hawkins as one of the most expressive voices of the era. Here he's featured with small combos and the Cab Calloway big band as it leaps and swaggers through blockbusters such as *Jive* and *Comin' On with the Come On*. Included are exquisite ballad performances like *Lonely Nights* and *Ghost of a Chance*.

EUBIE BLAKE

The 86 Years of Eubie Blake	Columbia C 2S 847
Eubie Blake Blues and Rags, 1917	Biograph BLP 1011
Eubie Blake, 1921	Biograph BLP 1012

Blake, a mere 86 when this Columbia set was recorded five years ago, is one of the phenomena of jazz. The Columbia double package is an ebullient cornucopia of ragtime, stride piano, barrelhouse and boogie woogie, filled with songs written by Mr. Blake including *I'm Just Wild About Harry* and *Memories of You*. The Biograph material is from early piano rolls. Recorded in stereo under Blake's supervision in 1972, the sprightly lift of the music remains fresh as a breeze.

CLIFFORD BROWN

Clifford Brown and Max Roach at Basin St. East	Trip 5511
The Beginning and the End	Columbia 32284

Brown, one of the most gifted of the neo-bop trumpet players, died in 1956 at the age of 25. Had he lived he might have established himself as one of the titans of the jazz trumpet in a line that includes Armstrong, Eldridge and Gillespie. On *Basin St. East* his fluent, warm-toned lines mesh beautifully with the sound of tenor man Sonny Rollins and pianist Richie Powell as they rework a set of standards. The Columbia LP is taken from a jam session recorded in Philadelphia just hours before Brown was killed in an automobile accident; they contain crackling versions of *Walkin* and *Night in Tunisia*.

DON BYAS

In Paris	Prestige S 7598

Don Byas' opulent, rich-toned tenor sax sound is beautifully captured on sides recorded in Paris in 1946 with pianist Billy Taylor and a group of American ex-patriates and Gallic colleagues.

RAY BRYANT

Alone with the Blues	Prestige P 24040

Bryant, a contemporary jazz pianist of very high caliber, has rarely been able to record the kind of music he plays best. Here he digs in with the blues; the results are striking.

BENNY CARTER

Further Definitions	Impulse S 12

Alto saxist Carter, one of jazz's greatest soloists and most gifted arrangers, has rarely been represented to the best of his abilities on records under his own name. The Impulse collection, recorded about a dozen years ago, finally does him justice. An inspired sax section, including Coleman Hawkins, Charlie Rouse, Phil Woods and Carter, reworks classic Carter arrangements with exciting results.

RAY CHARLES

The Best of Ray Charles	Atlantic S 1543

This is the jazz side of Ray Charles, a marvelous, low-down funky piano player. There are several fine tracks in this collection; *How Long Blues*, included, is one of the great instrumental blues recordings of all time.

CHARLIE CHRISTIAN

with the Benny Goodman Sextet	Columbia CL 652
Solo Flight	Columbia G 30779

Christian died at 23, and his whole recording career lasted two years (1939-41), but in those years he bridged the gap between swing and bop. His most impressive work, with the tightly knit Goodman Sextet, can be heard in a warm-up jam session on CL 652; in addition, the album includes several BG Sextet classics. Alternate takes from many of these same dates, and other Christian-Goodman collectors' pieces appear in the Columbia G doubleset, which also has excerpts from an ad-lib session recorded on acetate discs by a Christian aficionado.

NAT KING COLE

From the Beginning	MCA 2-4020

Before he became a popular singer, Nat Cole was an incisive and swinging jazz pianist with a light, delicate touch. The MCA sides, full of sprightly playing, include such favorites as *Sweet Lorraine* and *Honeysuckle Rose*.

ORNETTE COLEMAN

This is Our Music	Atlantic S 1353
Ornette	Atlantic S 1378
The Best of Ornette Coleman	Atlantic S 1558
Art of Improvisors	Atlantic S 1572

The free-form, fiercely assertive music of Ornette Coleman, while not as controversial as when introduced fifteen years ago, remains full of shocks and surprises. Coleman's plastic alto sax is rooted in the blues, and he has complete mastery of his instrument. This is strong stuff, but fascinating.

JOHN COLTRANE

Plays for Lovers	Prestige S 7426
My Favorite Things	Atlantic S 1361
Ole Coltrane	Atlantic S 1373
Art of John Coltrane	Atlantic S 2313
The Best of Coltrane	Atlantic S 1541
Live at the Village Vanguard	Impulse S 10
Coltrane	Impulse S 21
Expression	Impulse S 9120
Greatest Years, Vol. 3	Impulse ASH 9278
Africa Brass, Vol. 2	Impulse S 9273

Tenor saxophonist John Coltrane's innovations and unique sounds permeate the whole contemporary jazz scene, as well as rock and even "disco-soul." The Prestige **Lovers** is made up of late 50's recordings when he was still part of the Miles Davis group; they are hard-edged but lyric explorations of ballads like *Violet for Your Furs.* The Atlantic **My Favorite Things**, recorded in 1961, features Coltrane on soprano for a mercurial reworking of the title tune's melodic and chordal structure. Coltrane's soprano unleashes another torrent of exotic notes on the eighteen-minute **Ole.** McCoy Tyner's rolling, expansively melodic piano co-stars on *My Favorite Things* and *Ole.* Coltrane's most significant work for Atlantic including *My Favorite Things, Ole, Giant Steps, Equinox* and *Naima* are found in the doubleset **Art of John Coltrane;** *Best* is an abbreviated version of this collection.

In an unceasing search for fullest expression, Coltrane went beyond the "sheets of sound" which dominate the Altantic releases. The Impulse albums reveal a distinct shift in style; a move to an open, more spacious music (indeed, some critics call it "space music"); you can hear him veering in this direction on **Live at the Village Vanguard** and **Coltrane,** with the saxophonist plumbing the harmonic resources of his instrument. **Expression,** a recording made five months before his death in 1967, contains both pastoral and high-tension sounds; one side of the album is devoted to *Offering,* a piece at once visceral and visionary. **Greatest Years, Vol. 3** contains *Offering* and many of Coltrane's most challenging Impulse efforts. **Africa Brass, Vol. 2,** just issued, is a blazing big band date, with rapid-fire work by Coltrane, brilliant Tyner, and breathtaking drumming by Elvin Jones.

EDDIE CONDON

with Bud Freeman (two records)	Atlantic 2–309
The World of Eddie Condon	Columbia KG–31564
Town Hall Concerts, Vol. 2	Chiaroscuro 113

A catalyst and organizer, guitarist Condon was responsible for some of the finest hot jazz ever recorded. The Atlantic doubleset is made up of his splendid Commodore sessions. One record is devoted to raucous, hell-for-leather jazz played by Condon and cohorts Wild Bill Davison, Bobby Hackett, George Wettling, Max Kaminsky and other members of the Condon coterie. The second disc is a reissue of a relaxed, informal date with Bud Freeman, Muggsy Spanier, and Bobby Hackett. Jess Stacy, fresh from his 1938 Carnegie Hall triumph with Benny Goodman, takes two superb solos on *Carnegie Drag* and *Carnegie Blues.* The Columbia two-record collection is a spirited cross section of collector's items made by Condon, and/or his friends and associates. Among the high points: Bud Freeman' *The Eel,* Condon's rousing *Blues My Naughtie*

Sweetie Gave to Me, and Fats Waller and the Melody Makers on *Yellow Dog Blues.* **Town Hall Concerts, Vol. 2** is a roaringly extroverted collection featuring guest artists like Sidney Bechet, Earl Hines, Gene Krupa, James P. Johnson and Cliff Jackson.

CHICK COREA

Piano Improvisations, Vol. 1	ECM 1009

Chick Corea, bucking for top spot in the electronic jazz sweepstakes, recorded this album in 1971 for a small German label. Its supple, delicate music offers strictly intellectual pleasures, especially for those who revel in meditation and reflection and the brilliant play of sound, and rates as one of the most important contemporary solo piano albums.

BOB CROSBY

Greatest Hits	Decca 74856

Bing's younger brother led one of the finest Swing Era bands. They played a zesty, happy music that successfully incorporated the hot, improvised feeling of Dixieland jazz into the big band framework. **Greatest Hits** is just that; it includes the Bob Haggart/Ray Bauduc *Big Noise from Winnetka* and the lusty *South Rampart Street Parade.*

MILES DAVIS

Birth of the Cool	Capitol M 11026
Workin' and Steamin'	Prestige M 24036
Milestones	Columbia CS 9428
Kind of Blue	Columbia CS 8163
Miles Ahead	Columbia CS 8633
Porgy and Bess	Columbia CS 8085
Sketches of Spain	Columbia CS 8271
Greatest Hits	Columbia CS 9808
In a Silent Way	Columbia CS 9875
Bitches Brew	Columbia GP 26
Big Fun	Columbia PG 32866
Basic Miles	Columbia C 32025

Davis, a major voice in jazz, is a constantly evolving, creative musician. **Birth of the Cool** was his first significant recording; here we find his serene horn cushioned by Gil Evans' ethereal ensemble settings. **Workin' and Steamin',** a splendid doubleset, consists of Prestige recordings from the mid and late 50's; they are loose-jointed, free-wheeling sessions made with the now-classic Davis quintet of Miles, John Coltrane, tenor; Red Garland, piano; Paul Chambers, bass; and Philly Joe Jones, drums. **Milestones** is a consistently stimulating album with the same group plus Cannonball Adderley. **Kind of Blue,** using modal scales instead of chord progressions, has the pulsing, hypnotic *All Blues.* On **Miles Ahead, Porgy and Bess** and **Sketches of Spain,** Davis works with a large orchestra again conducted by Gil Evans, and his moody, reflective solos are given depth and dimension by Evans' impressionistic scores. Columbia's **Greatest Hits** is a choice collection of Davis cuts from the significant period, covering roughly 1959–1961.

A new direction in Davis' music begins to take shape on **In A Silent Way,** which incorporates electronic sounds to flesh out long, thematic statements; **Bitches Brew** is a cauldron of high-energy polyrhythms, feverish propulsion, and even more wattage. **Big Fun** consists of excellent outtakes from this period. The two-record set, **Basic Miles,** is a good survey of all Davis' work for the Columbia label.

JOHNNY DODDS

Johnny Dodds	RCA LPV 558

Dodds, one of the most important of all New Orleans clarinetists, had a broad, full tone, strong vibrato and sharp, rhythmic attack. Here he is featured with various groups on sides recorded in the late 20's including such collector's items as *Bucktown Stomp*, *Weary City*, *Blue Piano Stomp*, and *Blue Clarinet Stomp*.

TOMMY DORSEY

The Best of Tommy Dorsey	RCA LSP 3674
This Is Tommy Dorsey, Vol. 2	RCA VPM 6064

TD's powerhouse band had some splendid jazz moments provided by such outstanding sidemen as Bunny Berigan, Buddy Rich, Ziggy Elman, Bud Freeman, Buddy de Franco and Charlie Shavers. These recordings capture Dorsey's band at its best—Berigan's explosive trumpet statements on *Marie* and *Song of India*, Freeman's dancing tenor on *Who*, the high-pitched trumpet duel between Ziggy Elman and Chuck Peterson on *Well Git It!*; Buddy Rich's driving drums on *Hallelujah!*; De Franco's sparkling clarinet on *Opus # 1*.

DUKE ELLINGTON

Flaming Youth	RCA LPV 568
Hot in Harlem	Decca 79247E
Daybreak Express	RCA LPV 506
Ellington Era, Vol. 1	Columbia C 3L–27
The Music of Ellington	Columbia CSP JCL 558
In a Mellotone	RCA LPM 1364
C Jam Blues	French RCA 730 559
Jumpin' Pumpkins	RCA LPV 517
Johnny Come Lately	RCA LPV 541
Pretty Woman	RCA LPV 553
Hi Fi Ellington Uptown	Columbia CSP JCL 830
Piano Reflections	Capitol M 11058
Ellington Indigos	Columbia CS 8053
The Popular Duke Ellington	RCA LSP 3579
Yale Concert	Fantasy 9433
70th Birthday Concert	Solid State 19000
Second Sacred Concert	Fantasy P 24045

Duke Ellington, *the* orchestral master in jazz, and one of its great melodic geniuses, is richly represented on record. **Flaming Youth** and **Hot in Harlem** are from the band's 1920's "jungle period"; **Daybreak Express** contains recordings from the early 30's, and reveals Ellington's band as an increasingly subtle instrument. *The Ellington Era*, a Columbia compilation from 1927 to 1940, is a jazz treasure chest. The Columbia **Music of Ellington** and RCA's magnificent **In a Mellotone** are two of the finest single Ellington collections. **The Music of Ellington**, available from Columbia's Special Products, has peak performances of *Caravan, Mood Indigo, Solitude, I Let a Song Go Out of My Heart, Creole Love Song, Black and Tan Fantasy* and others. **In a Mellotone** (just deleted from the catalog, but still available in most jazz record shops) covers the years 1940–42, considered the highest point in Ellington's career; the sixteen dazzling sides are the very acme of big band jazz (*Cottontail, Mainstem, Warm Valley, All Too Soon*). For those who can't find **In a Mellotone**, **C Jam Blues**, a French RCA pressing, has many of the same selections. **Jumpin' Pumpkins, Johnny Come Lately**, and **Pretty Woman** are splendid RCA Vintage issues with much material from the peak years.

Hi Fi Ellington Uptown, from the early 50's, contains extended, updated versions of Ellington staples, including a hair-raising remake of *The Mooche*. The 1963 **Piano Reflections** is a special treat; moody, delicate Ellington backed only by bass and drums. **Ellington Indigos** and **The Popular Duke Ellington** offer luscious stereo re-recordings of Ellington standards. The **Yale Concert** and **70th Birthday Concert** are vigorous live big band performances recorded in 1968 and 1970. The **Sacred Concert** is a masterful blending of oratory, liturgy and jazz.

BILL EVANS

Tokyo Concert	Fantasy 9457

Recorded in 1973, these are beautifully molded performances by the Evans trio. The pianist lays down delicate, lyric lines supported by the pulsing, probing sound of Eddie Gomez's bass and the dazzling dynamics of drummer Marty Morell.

ELLA FITZGERALD

Ella in Berlin	Verve 64041
Ella at Carnegie Hall, Newport Jazz Festival, '73	Columbia KG 32557

The pure-toned Ella divides her time between pop ballads and jazz. Some of her most forceful swinging is done when she appears before live audiences as on the Verve **Berlin** concert, and the more recent **Carnegie Hall, Newport Jazz Festival, '73**.

ERROLL GARNER

Concert by the Sea	Columbia CS 9821E

A compelling performance by the popular pianist running from strutting, robust swing to quasiimpressionism.

STAN GETZ

Focus	Verve 68412

Getz's distinctive, eloquent tenor sax, originally inspired by Lester Young, has a tour de force on **Focus**, as he solos within the framework of Eddie Sauter's brilliant sketches for strings.

DIZZY GILLESPIE

In the Beginning	Prestige F 24030
Dizzy Gillespie	RCA LPV 530
On the French Riviera	Phillips 60048

In the Beginning and **Dizzy Gillespie** are from the early days of bop, and Diz dazzles with lip-searing technique and blinding speed. On the Prestige doubleset, he and Charlie Parker work out turbulent bop exercises with top drawer jazzmen like Al Haig, Sid Catlett, Cozy Cole, Slam Stewart and Milt Jackson. **On the French Riviera** is an exuberant, live performance from Juan-les-Pins.

BENNY GOODMAN

Carnegie Hall Jazz Concert	Columbia OSL 160 and Columbia CL 814/816
The King of Swing	Columbia OSL 180
The Best of Benny Goodman	RCA LSP 4055E
This is Benny Goodman, Vol. 1	RCA VPM 6040
This is Benny Goodman, Vol. 2	RCA VPM 6063
Small Groups	RCA LPV 521

Put That Swing Back	Swedish Columbia 52964
All Time Greatest Hits	Columbia KG 31547
Great Soloist	Biograph C–1

Goodman's historic **Carnegie Hall Jazz Concert** and **The King of Swing** catch his great 1937–38 band at its peak (The King of Swing consists of broadcast airchecks). Parallel to these recordings are the studio dates of the period found in **Best** and the two **This Is** volumes; there are many high points in these collections including brassy, exuberant, driving jazz such as *Sing, Sing, Sing, Jam Session* and *Bugle Call Rag*; bright, lilting, dancing jazz like *Stompin' at the Savoy* and *Afraid to Dream*. Splendid examples of Goodman's chamber jazz can be found on **Small Groups**. The Swedish Columbia is a collector's bonanza, with vibrant Columbia recordings from the neglected World War II and post–World War II period including *Clarinade, The Dark Town Strutters Ball, Oh Baby* and *Baby Won't You Please Come Home*. The Columbia KG doubleset **Greatest Hits** is a varied survey of Goodman performances, duplicating some of the Carnegie Hall material, but offering gems from the 1940–41 vintage years like *Benny Rides Again, String of Pearls, Clarinet A La King, Why Don't You Do Right?* and the 1945 Quintet masterpiece, *After You've Gone*. The Biograph **Great Soloist** album goes back to Goodman's early days as a young, spirited clarinetist with such orchestras as Ted Lewis.

GRANT GREEN

Grant Green	Muse 5014

Guitarist Green has been a solid rock in contemporary jazz for over ten years. This wonderfully relaxed 1962 date is a tasteful and cohesive jam session where everything works beautifully. The interaction and rapport between Green, tenor saxist Frank Haynes, pianist Bill Gardner, and bassist Ben Tucker lifts it way above a routine blowing trip.

LIONEL HAMPTON

Stompology	RCA LPV 575
The Best of Lionel Hampton, Vol. 1	French RCA 730 640
The Best of Lionel Hampton, Vol. 2	French RCA 730 641
The Best of Lionel Hampton, Vol. 3	French RCA 731 048
The Best of Lionel Hampton, Vol. 4	French RCA 731 053
More Hampton's Stuff	French RCA 731 049
Golden Favorites	Decca 79246

The American RCA **Stompology** and the five French RCA discs present all of the remarkable recordings Hamp made in the Victor studios between 1937 and 1940, drawing on the finest soloists from the Goodman, Basie, Ellington and Calloway bands. The caliber of musicianship is consistently high; the feeling is always mellow and joyous. Some of the finest jazz to come out of the Swing Era. **Golden Favorites** showcases Hamp's roaring big band of the early 40's.

COLEMAN HAWKINS

Body & Soul	RCA LPV 501
Hollywood Stampede	Capitol M 11030
The Hawk Flies	Milestone 2–47015
Coleman Hawkins and the Trumpet Kings	Trip TLP 5515

The late Coleman Hawkins is the patriarch of the jazz tenor saxophone. His big, plush sound reigned supreme until the end of the 30's, when Lester Young's fragile, cool style became an equally important influence. RCA's **Body & Soul** surveys Hawk's music from his early days with Fletcher Henderson on into the 60's—it includes the 1939 *Body & Soul*, note for note, the greatest jazz ballad solo ever recorded. Milestone's **Hawk Flies** documents Hawkins career from the sunset of the Swing Era to the late 50's, his merging of the swing and bop styles, and his attempts to keep up with modern jazz. **Hollywood Stampede** is a splendid collection of sides recorded for Capitol in 1945, and includes such exciting swing/bop fusions as *Stuffy* and *Rifftide*. **Coleman Hawkins and the Trumpet Kings** is from Harry Lima's marvelous 1944 Keystone sessions, full of swinging melody and rich ballad explorations; trumpeter Roy Eldridge never sounded better and pianist Teddy Wilson, one of many stars on the date, is at his lilting best.

WOODY HERMAN

Golden Favorites	Decca 74484E
Greatest Hits	Columbia CS 9291
Jazz Hoot	Columbia C 32530
Thundering Herd	Fantasy F 9452

The late 30's–early 40's "Band That Plays The Blues," a spirited crew that swung with a brassy flare, is heard on the Decca collection which features exuberant Herman classics like *The Woodchoppers Ball, Hot Chestnuts,* and *Woodsheddin' With Woody*. The 1945–46 "First Herd," a young boppish band bursting with excitement and talent (Chubby Jackson, the Candoli brothers, Flip Phillips, Dave Tough, Sonny Berman) and the equally talented Second Herd (Zoot Sims, Al Cohn, Stan Getz) are represented on **Greatest Hits**, an LP that includes many of Herman's finest recordings—*Apple Honey, Caldonia, Northwest Passage, Bijou* and *Four Brothers*. **Jazz Hoot** showcases the explosive fire and drive of the Herman band of the mid-60's, and **Thundering Herd** is Herman's current crew, a dynamic ensemble of young musicians who play today's music with the same élan and authority of previous Herman bands.

FLETCHER HENDERSON

Fletcher Henderson, 1924–41	Biograph C–12
Fletcher Henderson, Vols. 1 & 2	Decca 79227/8 E
Fletcher Henderson, 1927–36	French RCA 730 584

Henderson set the pattern for big band jazz as it developed in the Swing Era. The swing style incubated in the Henderson bands of the 20's and 30's, emerging fully developed by 1931, four years before Benny Goodman took the country by storm. These recordings trace the history of Henderson's orchestras through which passed many important black jazzmen of the 20's and early 30's.

EARL HINES

Grand Terrace Band	RCA LPV 512
Another Monday Date	Prestige P 24043

Hines, a jazz immortal, and one of the most influential of all jazz pianists, led the spirited Grand Terrace Orchestra in the 30's, one of the finest swing/jazz bands. Sixteen Grand Terrace sides are found in the RCA collection, including the immensely popular *Boogie Woogie on the St. Louis Blues*. The Prestige doubleset offers a buoyant Fats Waller tribute and a dazzling set of unaccompanied solos.

JOHNNY HODGES

Things Ain't What They Used to Be	RCA LPV 533

Altoist Hodges, a major Ellington soloist for over forty years, spreads his silken sound over a small group Ellingtonian session which produced masterpieces such as *Squatty Roo, Day Dream, Going Out the Back Way, Passion Flower* and *That's the Blues Old Man.* Extra bonuses on the LP are equally fine combo recordings by Ellington cornetist Rex Stewart.

BILLIE HOLIDAY

Greatest Hits	Columbia C1 2666
Golden Years, Vol. 1	Columbia C 3L–21
Lady Day	Columbia CL 637
The Billie Holiday Story, Vol. 1	Columbia KG 32121
The Billie Holiday Story, Vol. 2	Columbia KG 32124
Strange Fruit	Atlantic 1614
Greatest Hits	Decca 75040E
The Billie Holiday Story	Decca DXS 7171E
The Archetype Billie Holiday	MGM 4948
The Sound of Jazz	Columbia CSP JCL 1096
Original Recordings	Columbia C 32060

The First Lady of Jazz did wonders with the most banal lyrics, the most vapid melody. **Lady Day, Greatest Hits,** and the **Golden Years, Vol. 1,** an impressive boxed set, cover the brash young phase of her life when she sang in ad-lib jam sessions accompanied by Teddy Wilson, Benny Goodman, Lester Young, Ben Webster, Buck Clayton, Bunny Berigan, and countless jazz greats—the flower of the Swing Era. The Columbia **Story,** Vols. 1 and 2, repackages **The Golden Years** into bargain-trial doublesets. **Strange Fruit** includes important Commodore recordings made between 1939 and 1944 with groups led by Frankie Newton and Eddie Heywood. The Decca **Greatest Hits,** with selections like *Good Mornin' Heartache* and *Lover Man,* consists of very commercial recordings, many with string backgrounds, with her voice an increasingly expressive and poignant instrument. **The Archetype Billie Holiday** contains the best of 1950's Verve material recorded for Norman Granz, and though her voice is frayed, she sings with much of the zest and vitality of the old days; swinging accompaniment is by musicians like Oscar Peterson and Charlie Shavers. **The Sound of Jazz,** from Columbia Special Products, contains Holiday's magnificent *Fine and Mellow,* and, ravaged voice and all, it's one of her greatest efforts. There's marvelous support from Lester Young, Ben Webster, Coleman Hawkins, Gerry Mulligan and Roy Eldridge. **Original Recordings,** from Columbia, is the single finest Holiday collection, ranging from blithe and bouyant swing like *Them There Eyes* to one of the last recordings Lady Day ever made, *You've Changed,* where the vocal deterioration seems to add great emotional impact.

HARRY JAMES

Harry James	Harmony KH 32018

Because he once hit commercial heights, Harry James sometimes receives shabby treatment from the jazz world, yet he has been a powerful and imaginative horn man since his days with Benny Goodman. Exuberant, modern, big band jazz is heard on this Harmony budget-priced LP.

KEITH JARRETT

Solo Concerts	ECM 1035–37
Fort Yawuh	Impulse AS 9240

The brilliant young pianist-composer has a stunning showcase in the beautifully boxed ECM set. Stretched out over three records; six sides, Jarrett's mind-boggling solo performance has power, depth and diversity. His orchestrally styled piano moves from pastoral serenity to funky blues roots without missing a beat. **Fort Yawuh** finds Jarrett leading a small combo, but his flowing, lyric and intensely soulful piano is what impresses.

GENE KRUPA

Drummin' Man	Columbia C 2L–29
Gene Krupa and His Orchestra	Columbia CSP JCL 753

Both the boxed two-record set, **Drummin' Man,** and the Columbia Special Projects disc cover the years 1939–45, when Roy Eldridge and Anita O'Day, and later Charlie Ventura sparked many of the outstanding recordings included. Among the choice cuts: the delightful O'Day/Eldridge collaboration, *Let Me Off Uptown,* the Krupa tour de force, *Drum Boogie,* the Gerry Mulligan–arranged *Disc Jockey Jump,* and the driving *Boogie Blues.*

STAN KENTON

Artistry in Rhythm	Creative World ST–1043
Kenton in Stereo	Creative World ST–1004
Cuban Fire	Creative World ST–1008

Capitol Records was so busy with the Beatles and the Beach Boys in the late 60's, that they forgot about jazz and Kenton, who wisely leased all his masters and issued them on his own label, Creative World, along with his new recordings. It is the old Kenton that is still the best jazz—straightforward and less pretentious as on **Artistry in Rhythm** and **Kenton in Stereo. Cuban Fire,** arranged by John Richards, has some electrifying moments.

JIMMIE LUNCEFORD

Lunceford Special	Columbia CS 9515E
Blues in the Night	Decca 79240E

Lunceford led a star-studded orchestra, one of the best Swing Era big bands, and its distinctive, two-beat style gave it a unique, light sound. The Columbia set, has, among others, *Tain't What You Do, Ain't She Sweet,* and *Cheatin' on Me,* immaculately played, infectious swingers. The Decca **Blues in the Night** is early 40's Lunceford and contains, among others, the rocking *Uptown Blues* and his biggest-selling record, *Blues in the Night.*

CHARLES MINGUS

Charles Mingus & Friends	Columbia KG 31614
The Art of Charles Mingus	Atlantic 2–302
At Monterey	Fantasy J 1/2
Best of Charles Mingus	Atlantic S 1555
Better Git It In Your Soul	Columbia G 30628
Mingus Ah Um	Columbia CS 8171
Let My Children Hear My Music	Columbia KC 31039

Bassist Mingus; whose writing and arranging conjures up intense, swirling turmoils of sound, experiences an exciting reunion with such musicians as Charles McPherson, Gene Ammons and Gerry Mulligan on **Mingus & Friends. Art** has more of Mingus' fierce, expressionistic jazz, and **Best** contains the ferocious *Pithecanthropus Erectus* and other 50's classics. The **Monterey** concert, beginning with an Ellington medley, crackles and boils from start to finish. **Let My Children Hear My Music** is a stunning big band concert performance, while the 1959 **Mingus Ah Um** has more of Mingus' Ellington interpretations, plus some sounds considered pretty "far out" even today.

THE MODERN JAZZ QUARTET

European Concert	Atlantic S-2-603

These four talented men (John Lewis, piano; Milt Jackson, vibes; Percy Health, bass; Connie Kay, drums) recently disbanded after a twenty-year run. They were often addicted to overpolite, antiseptic sounds, but when they took the wraps off as on the **European Concert,** there was no modern group more invigorating.

THELONIOUS MONK

Thelonious Monk	Prestige 24006
Pure Monk	Milestone 2-47004
Monk & Trane	Milestone 2-47011
Criss Cross	Columbia CSP JCS 8838
Blue Monk	Columbia CSP JCS 8765
Something in Blue	Black Lion 152

The vitality and originality of Monk's music can be heard in the Prestige, Milestone and Columbia set. **Monk and Trane,** in particular, is an electric pairing of two giant talents. Many thought Monk played out by the end of the 60's, but the Black Lion LP, recorded in London in 1971 with drummer Art Blakey and bassist Al McKibbon, finds him hammering out vigorous, sometimes hilarious jazz that has its dissonant roots in ragtime and stride.

JELLY ROLL MORTON

King of New Orleans Jazz	RCA LPM 1649
Mr. Jelly Lord	RCA LPV 546
Jelly Roll Morton, 1923-24	Milestone M 47018
New Orleans Memories	Atlantic 2-AT 308

The **King of New Orleans Jazz** contains *Dr. Jazz* and many of the Red Hot Pepper sides—delicate, complex musical mosaics—compositions that gently eased Morton's musicians into inspired performances. **Mr. Jelly Lord** has, among other splendid items, the magnificent *Wolverine Blues* (two takes) and *Mr. Jelly Lord.* The Milestone and Atlantic collections are both important doublesets. The Milestone repackages Morton's early Gennett sides, both solo and with small bands, and, while the acoustic recordings muffle the sound, the strength and vitality of the music still comes through; Milestone's engineers have done a superb job, bringing the ancient recording into sharper focus. Another important group of Morton solo recordings originally made for the General label in the late 30's, has now been reissued on the Atlantic doubleset.

GERRY MULLIGAN

Paris Concert	Pacific Jazz 20102
Age of Steam	A&M 3036

Baritone-saxist Mulligan, a cool jazzman who has always played hot, has a formidable showcase for his special sound on the now-classic **Paris Concert** with his quartet's surging *Bernie's Tune* still an aural treat. On **Age of Steam** Mulligan's interweaving front line of baritone, trombone, and alto sax is buttressed by an electric guitar, bass and piano to produce steaming, stomping items like *Pacific 204.*

NEW ORLEANS RHYTHM KINGS

New Orleans Rhythm Kings	Milestone M 47020

Taking King Oliver's Creole Jazz Band as a model, the white NORK created its own buoyant version of black New Orleans jazz. These rollicking versions of *Tiger Rag, Bugle Call Rag,* and *Tin Roof Blues* still come through despite the limited acoustics of these 1924-25 Gennetts.

KING OLIVER

with Louis Armstrong	Milestone M 47017
Papa Joe	Decca 79246 E

The excitement and energy of King Oliver's original Creole Jazz Band, which included Louis Armstrong on first cornet, is dimmed by the crudely recorded acoustic Gennetts repackaged on the Milestone doubleset, which also has some sonically better tracks by Armstrong and the marvelous Red Onion Jazz Babies. Low fi or not, these early recordings are of historical importance. Oliver's Dixie Syncopaters, which succeeded the Creole Jazz Band, was recorded electrically, and their music, on the 1926-28 Decca reissues, speaks to us lustily and vibrantly over the years.

CHARLIE PARKER

Charlie Parker	Spotlight 101-107
Charlie Parker, First Recordings with Jay McShann	Onyx 221
Jazz at Massey Hall	Fantasy 86003
Charlie Parker Memorial	Savoy 12009
The Archetype Charlie Parker	MGM 4949

Altoist Parker, the colossus of modern jazz, is abundantly represented on recordings. The six-record Spotlight series brilliantly displays Parker's swirling, sweeping style as it took jazz by storm on a series of monumental Dial recordings. For serious collectors, this British reissue contains all of the original Dials plus alternate takes. The Onyx issue with Jay McShann's band goes back to 1940 to a very early Bird whose blues-rooted style was still embedded within swing confines. **Jazz at Massey Hall** is taped from a Canadian concert on which Parker and Dizzy Gillespie give electrifying performances. The Savoy set offers some of Parker's most inspired solos (*Parker's Mood, Chasin' the Bird*), and the MGM Archetype album has Verve material including the haunting *Just Friends.*

OSCAR PETERSON

Oscar Peterson Featuring Stephane Grappelli	Prestige P 24041

Peterson can be superb or dull, but when he is at his best, he is among the most exciting of contemporary jazz pianists. This splendid two-record set, recorded in Europe, finds Peterson pulsing, swinging, then shifting gears to play graceful, poignant music. Violinist Grappelli responds to and embellishes Peterson's work, and the rhythm section, with drummer Kenny Clarke and Swedish bassist Niles Pederson, hits high levels of rapport and communication.

BUD POWELL

The Amazing Bud Powell, Vol. 1	Blue Note 81503
The Amazing Bud Powell, Vol. 2	Blue Note 81504

The erratic, often inspired Powell, the Charlie Parker of the piano, is in full command on both these Blue Note LP's. On Vol. 1, along with trumpeter Fats Navarro and saxophonist Sonny Rollins, his vital sense of swing, tremendous technique and long flow of ideas make this a definitive bop collection. Vol. 2 has much of the same spirit plus a number of sensitive ballads.

DJANGO REINHARDT

with the American Jazz Giants	Prestige S 7333

The Belgian gypsy guitarist's best recordings were not with the overrated Hot Club of France, but with visiting American jazz giants as on the Prestige collection. Here Reinhardt gets down to some powerful, driving work stimulated by the presence of Coleman Hawkins on tenor sax, and Benny Carter on alto.

BUDDY RICH

Swinging New Big Band	Pacific Jazz ST 20113

Buddy Rich is one of the few Swing Era jazz giants who has established a rapport with the Rock generation. He has done this by refusing to look back, and instead establishing a classic big band that has come to terms with Rock. The Pacific jazz LP is the first and best album recorded by this band. It showcases the leader's incredible virtuosity and vitality as he leads an ensemble that roars through contemporary arrangements with a crisp, driving swing.

SONNY ROLLINS

Saxophone Colossus	Prestige S 7326
The Cutting Edge	Milestone M 9059

Tenor saxophonist Rollins, one of the major jazz voices, has a highly original, volcanic, often witty style which gets a stunning display on **Saxophone Colossus**. **The Cutting Edge** presents Rollins as of 1974 with a high energy quartet (Masuo, an electric guitarist from Japan, Bob Cranshaw on electric bass, David Lee, drums, Stanley Cowell, piano, and Rufus Harley, bagpipes). Rollins' full, rich ballad sound gets a brilliant workout on *To a Wild Rose* and *A House Is Not a Home*.

ARTIE SHAW

This Is Artie Shaw, Vol. 1	RCA VPM 6039
This Is Artie Shaw, Vol. 2	RCA VPM 6062
Featuring Roy Eldridge	RCA LPV 582

The sounds of Artie Shaw's swing bands have a freshness and vitality that hold up remarkably well after almost three and a half decades. **This Is**, Vol. 1, covers recordings by the wild and wooly swing band of 1938–39; Vol. 2 contains more of this music, plus tracks by Shaw's 1940–42 band that boasted such sidemen as Billy Butterfield, Henry "Red" Allen, and Jack Jenny; there is also some superb chamber jazz by the Gramercy Five. **Featuring Roy Eldridge** focuses on Shaw's powerhouse post–World War II band that included trumpeter Roy Eldridge, guitarist Barney Kessel and pianist Dodo Marmorosa. This fine RCA collection concentrates on Eldridge's steaming work on such numbers as *Little Jazz*.

BESSIE SMITH

Any Woman's Blues	Columbia G 30126
Empress	Columbia G 30818
Empty Bed Blues	Columbia G 30450
Nobody's Blues but Mine	Columbia G 31093
World's Greatest Blues Singer	Columbia G GP–33

Bessie Smith's 160 recordings form the cornerstone of vocal jazz. The queen of the blues with her massive, sweeping voice is heard on the comprehensive Columbia series which spans her entire career. The selections, made in the 20's and early 30's, are treasured by jazz collectors, and Bessie's accompaniment includes such jazz greats as Louis Armstrong, Fletcher Henderson and James P. Johnson, along with her favorite back-up men, cornetist Joe Smith and trombonist Charlie Green. **Empty Bed Blues** is a particularly powerful collection with her majestic, trumpet-like declamations on numbers like *Put It Right Here* sending chills down the spine.

SONNY STITT

The Champ	Muse 5023

One of the finest players in the turbulent Charlie Parker tradition, Stitt is masterful on this album soaring over tunes like *The Champ* and *Midgets*, skimming gracefully over and around melodic contours and chordal changes. Trumpeter Joe Newman complements him to make an excellent front line as they toss out tough, swinging phrases.

ART TATUM

Solo Masterpieces	Pablo 2625 703

For connoisseurs of the jazz piano, Pablo Records has released this thirteen-record box set of unaccompanied piano solos by the virtuoso, Tatum. Originally recorded in 1953 during three three-hour sessions, it is a remarkable showcase for the pianist's fertile imagination and dazzling technique.

CECIL TAYLOR

Solo	Trio PA–7067

Avant-garde pianist Taylor unleashes a powerful maelstrom of notes and the energy and strength of the music demands your attention. Unlike most of Taylor's efforts, this one has some serene points of reference that make it accessible to listeners conditioned to conventional jazz.

FATS WALLER

Ain't Misbehavin'	RCA LPM 1246
African Ripples	RCA LPV 562

Waller sweeps all before him with his irresistible humor, drive, gusto, and strutting, striding piano. **Ain't Misbehavin'** contains Waller's best-known songs including the title tune and *Honeysuckle Rose* and the hilarious and swinging *The Joint Is Jumpin'*. **African Ripples** includes the marvelous *Yacht Club Swing*. Most of the tracks in both albums are by his lively little combo, Fats Waller and His Rhythm, but also included are some fine piano solos.

CHICK WEBB

Chick Webb: King of the Savoy, Vol. 2	Decca DL 79223

One of jazz's finest drummers, Webb led a great Harlem band in the 30's. Many felt the Webb orchestra should have gotten some of the plaudits that went to Goodman, Shaw and the bigger swing names. The Decca collection offers some idea of the band's aggressive, punchy drive, its light, swinging orchestrations mostly by Edgar Sampson, and its splendid soloists, particularly trumpet man Taft Jordan. Ella Fitzgerald appears on several vocal tracks, which helped give the band some commercial success.

BEN WEBSTER

Ben Webster in Europe	Prestige P 24031

Webster, after Coleman Hawkins, is the greatest of all mainstream tenor saxophonists. Never has he been better presented as on this fine doubleset recorded in Copenhagen and Amsterdam where he lived the last ten years of his life. On these memorable sides he works with various European jazz musicians—Dutch, Danish, Swedish, French, and the superb expatriate American pianist, Kenny Drew. Webster plays Monk, Ellington, Horace Silver and originals, and what comes out is swinging and mellow jazz of the highest order.

TEDDY WILSON

Teddy Wilson & His All Stars	Columbia KG 31617

Teddy Wilson's fluent, melodic, graceful piano style was an important ingredient in the success of Benny Goodman's small groups. While working with Goodman, he organized memorable recording sessions in the mid and late 30's, many featuring Billie Holiday along with instrumental giants of the day. Thirty-two of these sides, six with Holiday, turn up on this Columbia doubleset.

LESTER YOUNG

Commodore Years	Atlantic 2–307

Count Basie's tenor saxist, Lester Young, one of the fonts of cool jazz, shares this Atlantic double LP with Chu Berry and Coleman Hawkins. The Young tracks consist of eight recordings made with fellow Basie-ites. Cut under the title, the Kansas City Five, these performances are masterful examples of understated, flowing, gently swinging jazz. Young, on both tenor sax and clarinet, seems to float through each number.

ANTHOLOGIES, COLLECTIONS, COMBINATIONS

A Decade of Jazz, Vol. 2	Blue Note LA 159–02

A good two-record survey of the bop and hard bop recorded on the Blue Note label between 1951 and 1958, A Decade of Jazz includes Bud Powell's *Night in Tunisia*, Monk's original *Criss Cross*, Milt Jackson's *Bags Groove*, Clifford Brown's *Cherokee*, John Coltrane's *Blue Train*, Art Blakey's *Moanin'*, and Horace Silver's *Señor Blues* in addition to some provocative early Miles Davis and Sonny Rollins.

52nd Street, Vol. 1	Onyx 203

An important collection of music by groups which played Swing Street during the twilight of the Swing Era, and the transition years to bop. The Street scene includes four sides by Don Byas and his 1945 quartet, clarinetist Tony Scott with an all-star group that included Dizzy Gillespie, Ben Webster, Trummy Young, and a

young Sarah Vaughan as vocalist; her *All Too Soon* is worth the price of the album.

From Spirituals to Swing	Vanguard 47/48

John Hammond's monumental 1939 concert at Carnegie Hall has been captured with all its excitement in this two-record set. Featured are Count Basie, the Benny Goodman Sextet, Big Bill Broonzy, and a host of swing, spiritual and blues greats.

In the Groove	Readers Digest RD 45–46

This bargain-priced six-record boxed set is a collector's dream. Drawing from RCA's vast Victor and Bluebird files, it offers such swing and jazz rarities as Ziggy Elman's *Zaggin' with Zig*, Charlie Barnet's *No Name Jive*, Benny Goodman's *Roll 'Em* and *Life Goes to a Party*, Lionel Hampton's *Ring Dem Bells*, Tommy Dorsey's *Well Git It!* and *Loose Lid Special*, Fats Waller's *Carolina Shout* and *Lulu's Back in Town*, plus 65 others.

Jazz, Vols. 1 through 11	Folkways 2801–2811

An all-encompassing series that surveys early blues, New Orleans and Chicago jazz, New York in the 20's and early 30's, big bands before 1935, jazz pianists, boogie-woogie and jazz singers. A remarkable cross section of all styles of early jazz, painstakingly collected, well recorded.

The Metronome All Stars	French RCA 731 089

A Swing Era high watermark, these remarkable sessions, produced by Metronome editor George T. Simon, brought together musicians like Count Basie, Buddy Rich, Benny Carter, Charlie Christian, Jack Teagarden, Tommy Dorsey, J. C. Higginbotham, and a score of others. High points: a romping *One O'Clock Jump* and a fiery *Bugle Call Rag*. Also included is a bop date which produced two dazzling sides, *Victory Ball* and *Overtime*, with superb solos by Charlie Parker, Dizzy Gillespie, Buddy de Franco, and Lennie Tristano.

The Original Boogie Woogie Giants	Columbia KC 32708

A fine collection of driving boogie woogie, including the incredible *Boogie Woogie Prayer* by Albert Ammons, Pete Johnson, and Meade Lux Lewis, plus six exhilarating sides with Johnson and Joe Turner, the "Boss of the Blues."

The Smithsonian Collection of Classic Jazz	

Available from Classic Jazz, P.O. Box 14196, Washington, D.C. One of the finest anthologies ever issued, this six-record set with 86 selections, plus a 48-page booklet, is beautifully reproduced, remastered and pressed. Martin Williams, Director of the Smithsonian Jazz program, selected the material from the major recording companies and supplemented them with a few imports and recordings from private sources. The result is a fine cross section of jazz from the 20's through the early 60's. Williams' selections may be weighted in favor of the artists and styles of jazz he prefers (there are six Monk selections as against one Goodman and one Hampton), but if one wants a "crash course" in jazz, look no further.

Index

Credits

79	Charles Peterson	136	Marian McPartland	182	Sy Johnson
80-81	Jay Maisel	139	Marian McPartland	184	Sy Johnson
82	William Claxton and Joachim Berendt, from *Jazzlife*	140-141	Duncan P. Schiedt; Ernest L. Smith Collection	186	Sy Johnson
83	Jay Maisel	143	Top left: Charles Stewart. Others: Robert Parent	187	Sy Johnson
85	Ernest L. Smith Collection			189	Charles Stewart
86	William Claxton and Joachim Berendt, from *Jazzlife*	146-147	William Claxton and Joachim Berendt, from *Jazzlife*	190	Irwin Dermer
91-95	Robert Parent	150-152	Art Kane	191	Irwin Dermer
97	Robert Parent	154-155	Ernest L. Smith Collection (from Paramount)	192	Don Schlitten
99	Robert Parent			193	Irwin Dermer
101	Art Kane	158	Left: Charles Stewart	196-197	Ernest L. Smith Collection (from Columbia Pictures)
102	Charles Stewart	158-159	Stephen Colhoun		
105	Duncan P. Schiedt	161	Charles Stewart		
107	Art Kane	168-169	Art Kane		
108	Charles Stewart	170	Charles Stewart		
110-111	Chadwick Hall	171	Top: William Claxton and Joachim Berendt, from *Jazzlife* Bottom: Charles Stewart		
116-117	Charles Stewart				
119	Charles Stewart				
124	Charles Stewart	172	Duncan P. Schiedt		
135	Mary Lou Williams; photo Roger Prigent	175-176	Charles Stewart		
		181	Sy Johnson		

Photographs of Original Art

22, 36, 43, 77, 88-89, 178, 199, 201, 209—THECLA

41, 54, 61, 121, 157—Jerry Darvin

94 Jeffrey Morton
167 John D. Schiff